CURA ANIMARUM

CURA ANIMARUM

A Theological-Ethical Assessment of the Use
of Social Robots in the Healthcare System

by
IOAN C. VERES
Foreword by C. Ben Mitchell

WIPF & STOCK · Eugene, Oregon

CURA ANIMARUM
A Theological-Ethical Assessment of the Use of Social Robots in the Healthcare System

Copyright © 2025 Ioan C. Veres. All rights reserved. Except for brief quotations in critical publications or reviews, no part of this book may be reproduced in any manner without prior written permission from the publisher. Write: Permissions, Wipf and Stock Publishers, 199 W. 8th Ave., Suite 3, Eugene, OR 97401.

Wipf & Stock
An Imprint of Wipf and Stock Publishers
199 W. 8th Ave., Suite 3
Eugene, OR 97401

www.wipfandstock.com

PAPERBACK ISBN: 979-8-3852-3903-0
HARDCOVER ISBN: 979-8-3852-3904-7
EBOOK ISBN: 979-8-3852-3905-4

VERSION NUMBER 040225

I give thanks to God for the gift of his Son, Jesus Christ, and for the Holy Spirit. I am grateful for his grace and mercy for me, a sinner.

I am grateful to my beautiful wife, Anna, without whose love, support, and encouragement, this dissertation would never have come to fruition.

I am thankful to our amazing children, Nathanael, Miriam, and Lydia, for sacrificing their time away from me during the many hours involved in this work.

I am indebted to my doctoral advisers, Dr. C. Ben Mitchell, for his mentorship, encouragement, friendship, and support of this dissertation, and Dr. Alan Branch, for his constructive comments and suggestions.

I would like to express my sincere gratitude to Gabriel and Melania Bodea for their generous support, which has been instrumental in making the publication of this book possible.

Contents

Foreword by C. Ben Mitchell | ix
Abstract | xiii

CHAPTER ONE
A Theological and Technological Foundation for the Development of Carebot Technology | 1
   Introduction | 1
   A Primer on Carebot Technology | 5
   An Overview of Neighbor-Love | 15
   A Paradigm for the Physician-Patient Care Relationship | 26
   Conclusion | 29

CHAPTER TWO
State of the Question | 32
   Introduction | 32
   Current Studies about AI Care Robotic Technologies | 33
   Conclusion | 43

CHAPTER THREE
Wisdom of the Past | 45
   Introduction | 45
   A Theological Anthropology of a Patient | 46
   An Ecclesiological History of Medical Care | 93
   Concluding Theological Considerations | 109

CHAPTER FOUR
The Neighbor-Love Ethical Framework as a Tool for Navigating the Ethics of Social Robots | 114
   Introduction | 114
   Evaluating Conventional Medical Ethical Models | 115
   Practical Neighbor-Love Ethics | 138

    Conclusion | 164

CHAPTER FIVE
Looking to the Future | 166
    Introduction | 166
    Summary | 166
    Limitations of the Research and Suggestions for Future Work | 170
    Conclusion | 173

Bibliography | 175

Foreword

IN MARCH 2025, MICROSOFT co-founder and billionaire Bill Gates told "The Tonight Show" host, Jimmy Fallon, that over the next decade developments in Artificial Intelligence will replace the need for many human beings, including those in education and healthcare.[1]

While that may sound like science fiction, Artificial Intelligence robots are already a present reality in the healthcare setting. Paro, Moxi, TUG, and Pepper will soon be joined by a phalanx of robots in hospitals and nursing homes around the world. With the so-called silver tsunami—the massive expansion of the number of aging boomers—healthcare systems are going to be stretched to their limits, maybe beyond them. Like other forms of artificial intelligence, carebots seem to be an answer. But are they?

Keeping the patient in view as a whole person is already a challenge for contemporary medicine. Patients are often objectified by their body parts, disease, or location. "That's the ovarian cancer in Room 323," remarks the attending physician to the medical students during rounds. No, that's Crystal, the 42-year-old mother of three children, who is hoping against hope to see her eldest son graduate from college, her daughter get married, and her youngest child start middle school. And that's her husband, Raymond, who is sleeping in that uncomfortable position in a torturous hospital chair.

In his recent volume, *The Finest Traditions of My Calling*, psychiatrist Abraham Nussbaum, MD, observes that "For more than a century, the transformation for physicians like me has been about knowing the body, not the person, of the people we meet as patients."[2] Seeing patients as persons

---

1. Tom Huddleston Jr., "Bill Gates: Within 10 years, AI will replace many doctors and teachers—humans won't be needed 'for most things'," CNBC (26 March 2025). https://www.msn.com/en-my/money/markets/bill-gates-within-10-years-ai-will-replace-many-doctors-and-teachers-humans-won-t-be-needed-for-most-things/ar-AA1BHrHv?ocid=BingNewsVerp

2. Abraham Nussbaum, *The Finest Traditions of My Calling: One Physician's Search for the Renewal of Medicine* (Yale University Press, 2017).

is challenging. Seeing them through the lens of technologies like Artificial Intelligence robots compounds the challenges.

The designation "carebot" is an oxymoron. One thing we know about AI robots is that they do not and cannot care. At least not in the sense of care we mean when we speak of human care and caring. They are non-sentient and non-sapient entities. They can neither be Good Samaritans nor exercise neighbor love, two of the goods health care is covenanted to offer to humanity. At best, they are tools, but like all tools they are not value neutral. We shape our tools and then our tools shape us, as media theorist Marshall McLuhan stated so perceptively. Perhaps in some cases, we shape our tools and they mis-shape us.

I agree with the authors of *Antiqua et Nova* that, "if AI is used not to enhance but to replace the relationship between patients and healthcare providers—leaving patients to interact with machines rather than a human being—it would reduce a crucially important human relational structure to a centralized, impersonal, and unequal framework. Instead of encouraging solidarity with the sick and suffering, such applications of AI would risk worsening the loneliness that often accompanies illness, especially in the context of a culture where 'persons are no longer seen as a paramount value to be care for and respected.' This misuse of AI would not align with respect for the dignity of the human person and solidarity with the suffering."[3]

The global experience with carebots is not encouraging. In Japan, for instance, robots are often seen as a solution to a number of problems. A visit to a local Asian restaurant may prove that point. Increasingly, robots are used to serve meals and return used dishes to the kitchen. In an important study reported in *MIT Technology Review*, James Wright with the Alan Turing Institute, reported evidence showing that, among other problems, robots end up creating more work for caregivers not less.[4]

These are not the only problems. Trust is already at risk when physicians spend more time with their iPads or other digital devices during an office visit than they do actually examining the patient. And, because AI robots are mindless and emotionless, they can't read facial expressions, voice inflection, and other clues about how a patient is experiencing illness and dis-ease.

---

3. Dicastery for the Doctrine of the Faith and Dicastery for Culture and Education, *Antiqua et Nova: Note on the Relationship Between Artificial Intelligence and Human Intelligence*, 14 January 2025. Sec V.71-76. https://www.vatican.va/roman_curia/congregations/cfaith/documents/rc_ddf_doc_20250128_antiqua-et-nova_en.html

4. James Wright, "Inside Japan's long experiment in automating elder care" *MIT Technology Review* (January 9, 2023) https://www.technologyreview.com/2023/01/09/1065135/japan-automating-eldercare-robots/

In the interest of informed consent and patient autonomy, some are suggesting that patients should be educated about the benefits and liabilities of AI tools—including carebots—and be able to opt-out before the implementation of AI in their diagnosis and treatment. Otherwise, patients will lose trust in their physicians and the entire healthcare system. Trust is difficult to earn and very easy to lose.

As Medical College of Wisconsin bioethicists Fabrice Jotterand and Clara Bosco have written, "Keeping the 'human in the loop' is a quintessential dimension to clinical practice."[5] Medical AI may be useful in some ways to augment a physician's toolkit, but it cannot replace the person-to-person choreography of care—the treatment tango—that is at the heart of the physician-patient relationship.

Ioan Veres is at the cutting edge of thinking theologically about the use of carebots. In this volume he provides us with a helpful introduction to carebot technology, a framework for thinking about patients as persons, and insight into the helpful ways robots may be used in the hospital setting. At the same time, he warns that without thoughtful reflection and appropriate application, the use of robots in direct patient clinical care may violate the first principle of medical ethics, *primum non nocere* (first, do no harm).

C. Ben Mitchell, PhD

---

5. Fabrice Jotterand and Clara Bosco, "Keeping the 'Human in the Loop' in the *Age of Artificial Intelligence*," *Science and Engineering Ethics*, Volume 26, pp. 2455–2460, (2020).

Abstract

"Is it ethical to use carebots in direct human care in healthcare settings?" This dissertation contends that, according to the neighbor-love ethical standpoint, AI social robots may be beneficial technologies in specific areas of healthcare but may also erode, corrupt, or even violate other aspects of healthcare, particularly in direct patient care.

To demonstrate this thesis, the work develops its argument based on a theology of covenant care compellingly illustrated in the biblical capstone model of neighbor-love, the good Samaritan parable. Additionally, it proposes theological and ethical criteria that can inform the use of AI robots in healthcare settings.

CHAPTER ONE

A Theological and Technological Foundation for the Development of Carebot Technology

Introduction

CAREBOTS[1] ARE A LESSER-KNOWN technology with uncertain but seemingly powerful potential which have been portrayed in social culture as threats to human primacy in healthcare for decades.[2] Robots in healthcare represent one of the most intriguing and morally challenging applications of new technologies by their use in healthcare scenarios.[3] In recent years, advancements in robotics and AI to support and assist humans in various

---

1. Carebots are also known as social robots, assistive robots, and artificial intelligence robot systems (AiRs). In this dissertation, I will use them interchangeably.

2. Kate Keener Mays, "Humanizing Robots? The Influence of Appearance and Status on Social Perceptions of Robots" (PhD diss., Boston University, 2021), vi.

3. Aimee van Wynsberghe, "Designing Robots for Care: Care Centered Value-Sensitive Design," *Science & Engineering Ethics* 19, no. 2 (2013): 408.

environments, such as churches[4], schools,[5] homes, and workplaces have increased exponentially.

The motivation to develop intelligent assistive robots in numerous settings varies. The existing shortage of caregivers in hospitals and the widespread burnout among caregivers represent a challenge for the healthcare system. Moreover, the needs of an aging population and vulnerable people are growing. Worldwide, 21.1 percent of the population will be above 60 by 2050.[6] Shannon Vallor, professor of ethics and artificial intelligence at the Edinburgh Futures Institute, also mentions that the economic demands upon individuals, private or public institutions to reduce the costs of care, and social pressures to provide increased quality of care, are factors which have contributed to the expansion of AiRs (Artificial Intelligence Robotic Systems).[7]

Technological improvements related to human-robot collaboration and the science of AI reported by the media and academic literature promise to solve the "care crisis" of present times.[8] Klaus Schwab, the founder and executive chairman of the World Economic Forum, introduced to the broader public the term "Fourth Industrial Revolution,"[9] or what the German government called in 2011 "Industry 4.0," to describe the new approaches to manufacturing and technological developments.[10] The term "Fourth Industrial Revolution" describes changes in producing goods and

---

4. For a helpful theological discussion about the potential current use of AiRs in churches, see Cory Andrew Labrecque, "To Tend or to Subdue? Technology, Artificial Intelligence, and the Catholic Ecotheological Tradition," *Religions* 13, no. 7 (2022): 1, and André Ungerer, "Homo Disruptus and the Future Church," *HTS Theological Studies* 75, no. 4 (2019): 8.

5. For a useful investigation concerning student and faculty interaction with chatbot technologies, see David. A. Wood et al., "The ChatGPT Artificial Intelligence Chatbot: How Well Does It Answer Accounting Assessment Questions?," *Issues in Accounting Education* 38, no. 4 (2023): 95–96, and Matthew Grimes et al., "From Scarcity to Abundance: Scholars and Scholarship in an Age of Generative Artificial Intelligence," *Academy of Management Journal* 66, no. 6 (2023): 1619.

6. Maria Kyrarini et al., "A Survey of Robots in Healthcare," *Technologies* 9, no. 8 (2021): 1.

7. Shannon Vallor, "Carebots and Caregivers: Sustaining the Ethical Ideal of Care in the Twenty-First Century," *Philosophy & Technology* 24, no. 3 (2011): 252.

8. Núria Vallès-Peris, Oriol Barat-Auleda, and Miquel Domènech, "Robots in Healthcare? What Patients Say," *International Journal of Environmental Research and Public Health* 18, no. 18 (2021): 2.

9. Klaus Schwab, *The Fourth Industrial Revolution* (New York: Crown Publishing, 2016).

10. Daniel Topf, "'Useless Class' or Uniquely Human? The Challenge of Artificial Intelligence," *Journal of Interdisciplinary Studies* 32, no. 1–2 (2020): 17.

services using new technological innovations. This new industrial revolution combines automation technology with cyber technology, dominated by increased data volume, connectivity, analysis, business intelligence, new forms of human-machine interaction, robotics, autonomous vehicles, virtual reality, and cyber-physical systems.[11]

The introduction of carebots ("bots") may have the capacity to force a restructuring of the healthcare system. For instance, the roles of nurses and doctors will change since bots can perform specific tasks previously performed by human medical staff. The result is that the distribution of responsibilities will also change. Moreover, certain professions, such as janitors and couriers, may no longer exist because their repetitive tasks can be delegated to carebots. Medical staff education must add the necessary skills for working with bots. Scholars Van Wynsberghe and Li also mention that the expertise of healthcare staff may be called into question as specific bots could be considered more prepared than humans. In addition, the financial aspect requires analysis since the purchase and maintenance of robots will change the money flow in the healthcare system.[12]

Given the complexity of carebots' presence in the healthcare system, the present work proposes some answers to several general and particular questions related to the topic. The central research question of this work is this: "Is it ethical to use carebots in direct human care in healthcare settings?" The impact of carebot technology in healthcare, such as humanoid robots, AI avatars, and chatbots, raises many other ethical questions: "Is carebot technology something to be celebrated, managed, or feared?" "Can carebots be a genuine social counterpart, such as taking on the role of a human friend?"[13] "Will the medical profession, considered traditionally and exclusively human, change[14] or become obsolete?" "Has the church addressed the care of neighbors in the past? "What is the Bible's view about care?"[15] "If the church and the Bible have addressed issues related to caring for neighbors, what can modern medicine learn from that?" Researcher

---

11. Michail Chalaris, "In the Fourth Industrial Revolution Era, Security, Safety, and Health," *Journal of Engineering, Science and Technology Review* 16, no. 2 (2023): 183.

12. Aimee van Wynsberghe and Shuhong Li, "A Paradigm Shift for Robot Ethics: From HRI to Human-Robot-System Interaction (HRSI)," *Medicolegal & Bioethics* 9 (2019): 15.

13. Georg Gasser, "The Dawn of Social Robots: Anthropological and Ethical Issues," *Minds and Machines* 31, no. 3 (2021): 330.

14. Wynsberghe and Li, "A Paradigm Shift for Robot Ethics," 11.

15. Ayanna Howard and Jason Borenstein, "The Ugly Truth About Ourselves and Our Robots Creations: The Problem of Bias and Social Inequity," *Science & Engineering Ethics* 24, no. 5 (2018): 1522.

Jacob Shatzer also mentions some helpful sub-questions vital in the more prominent arguments, such as "How does care for the poor matter?" "What is the influence of technology on community life?"[16]

Given the theological and ethical implications of utilizing carebots in the healthcare system, this dissertation contends that, from a neighbor-love ethical standpoint, AiRs may be beneficial technologies in specific areas of healthcare but may also erode, corrupt, or even violate other aspects of healthcare, particularly in direct patient care. A biblical understanding of God's fatherly love, as reflected in neighbor-love, offers a distinct perspective on human relationships and medical care. God's love and its relationship to human love and love toward one's neighbor[17] may provide a much-needed standpoint in healthcare. Key insights from a biblically informed morality have the potential to help make AI technologies compatible with human morality and move these technologies toward a morally good end. A theological anthropology emphasizing the dimension of relationships can contribute to and promote the mutual flourishing of humans and artificial intelligence.[18]

This dissertation seeks to explore carebot technologies in light of the neighbor-love ethical system in the healthcare context utilizing a holistic human care approach. This work also evaluates the potential moral and social ramifications of employing carebots in healthcare from a distinctly biblically informed moral theology. Several methods are employed to reach the aims of this work. The primary method is to provide a theology of care grounded in biblical and historical theology. Based on a rich biblical and systematic theology regarding medicine and care, the second method examines seemingly non-overlapping interdisciplinary perspectives, such as those of computer science and engineering, theology, philosophy, and ethics,[19] that contribute to developing AI technologies in healthcare.

The methodology of this dissertation proposes holistic human care as a paradigm with which to approach the use of carebot technology in a healthcare context. Holistic human care sees "the wholeness of persons as involving interaction among all their significant and interdependent

---

16. Jacob Shatzer, "Theology and Technology: Mapping the Questions," *Ethics & Medicine: An International Journal of Bioethics* 31, no. 2 (2015): 99.

17. Veli-Matti Karkkainen, "'The Christian as Christ to Our Neighbour': On Luther's Theology of Love," *International Journal of Systematic Theology* 6, no. 2 (2004): 102.

18. Mark Graves, "Theological Foundations for Moral Artificial Intelligence," *Journal of Moral Theology* 11 (2022): 211.

19. Graves, "Theological Foundations," 185.

relationships with persons, groups, and institutions."[20] This approach also includes the mind, body, relationships with others, and God[21] to heal brokenness and cultivate flourishing in all life dimensions and the systems that affect a troubled person's life.[22]

This dissertation attempts to develop a neighbor-love ethical framework based on the biblical account of a theology of care regarding carebot technologies and their implications for the relationship between the caregiver and care receiver.

The plan for this dissertation includes five chapters. The first chapter introduces the theology and ethics of care and carebot technology, including an overview of AI robotic technologies. It seeks to provide some working definitions of terms employed in the study and to trace AI's history. The second chapter examines the current literature on the topic. The section examines primary and secondary literature about an evangelical assessment of AI, healthcare, and robotics. Chapter three provides an explicit biblical theological engagement with carebot technologies by mapping some of the critical theological and ecclesiological resources available for such an engagement. The fourth chapter evaluates the neighbor-love theology of care compared to significant ethical systems, such as virtue ethics, utilitarianism, care ethics, and deontological ethics. Moreover, the chapter lays out the neighbor-love grid through which carebots can be evaluated. Chapter five concludes the dissertation by looking to the future. In addition to summarizing the key findings, it suggests future work related to AI and robots in healthcare settings.

A Primer on Carebot Technology

Before turning to the theology of neighbor care, this section offers definitions of terminology and concepts to help ground the discussion. Additionally, this part provides a selective history of AI robots that led to the development of carebots.

---

20. Howard Clinebell, *Basic Types of Pastoral Care & Counseling* (Nashville: Abingdon Press, 1984), 10.

21. Thomas Yohannan, "Holistic Pastoral Care Ministry in Dhading District: An Evaluation of the Holistic Pastoral Care Practice in the Village Churches in Dhading District of Nepal" (DMin diss., Asbury Theological Seminary, 2022), 10.

22. Gert Breed, "Living as a Diakonos of Christ and Pastoral Care to the Narcissistically Entitled Person," *In Die Skriflig* 55, no. 1 (2021): 3.

Defining terms

To discuss the ethics of carebot technology, it is first necessary to define the terms included in the research about carebots, such as artificial intelligence, robots, intelligent robots, and healthcare intelligent robots. By understanding the definitions of these terms, we can better understand the potential benefits and risks of carebot technology and develop ethical guidelines for its use.

Artificial intelligence (AI) is the ability of a computer or machine to perform tasks that are typically associated with human intelligence, such as learning and problem-solving. Robots are machines capable of executing actions automatically without human intervention. Intelligent robots are machines that can "learn" and adapt to their environment. Healthcare intelligent robots are machines specifically designed to be used in healthcare settings. Here are some examples of intelligent healthcare robots: patient monitoring robots, rehabilitation robots, medication-dispensing robots, and mental health robots.

First, artificial intelligence may be defined as a system's ability to interpret external data correctly, learn from such data, and use that learning to achieve specific goals and tasks through flexible adaptation.[23] In other words, AI is the ability of a digital or robotic system programmed to "think" and mimic human actions and to carry out several works that are difficult or even impossible to carry out by humans.[24]

Second, robots may be defined as physical assistants that manipulate the physical world using effectors such as legs, wheels, joints, and sensors.[25] Computer scientist Robin Murphy helpfully mentions that "robot" derives from the Czech word "robota," loosely translated as a menial laborer. Consequently, the term was strictly meant to refer to servants who would help people in any labor.[26] Historically, robots were treated as either tools or joint cognitive systems. The view of robots as tools perceives robotic technology as a device that can perform specific functions but cannot adapt to changes in its world. Secondly, the robot agent category refers to a physically present

---

23. Michael Haenlein and Andreas Kaplan, "A Brief History of Artificial Intelligence: On the Past, Present, and Future of Artificial Intelligence," *California Management Review* 61, no. 4 (2019): 5.

24. Kumar Punith et al., "Artificial Intelligence in Healthcare: A Brief Review," *Suranaree Journal of Science & Technology* 29, no. 2 (2022): 1.

25. Stuart Russell and Peter Norvig, *Artificial Intelligence: A Modern Approach*, 4th ed. (London: Pearson, 2021), 932.

26. Russell and Norvig, *Artificial Intelligence*, 4.

robot with goals that can adapt to new situations. The most intriguing use of robots is in joint cognitive systems, in which robots are part of a human-machine team. Machines do not possess an independent agenda, but robots are considered helpers and intelligent enough to be team members.[27]

Third, the field of intelligence is a vital aspect of the advances of intelligent robots. There are vast differences of opinion as to precisely what intelligence is.[28] In *The Frames of Mind*, psychologist Howard Gardner developed a theory of multiple intelligences. Gardner defines intelligence not as one decisive theory of the range of human intelligence but as dividing it into nine different intelligences. These nine intelligences include logical-mathematical intelligence, linguistic intelligence, interpersonal intelligence, intrapersonal intelligence, musical intelligence, visual-spatial intelligence, bodily-kinesthetic intelligence, naturalist intelligence, and existential intelligence. He claims that humans are not born with all the types of intelligences they can possibly have, but all people possess a form of single general and relatively autonomous intelligence.[29]

There is, however, a consensus that general intelligence exists. As Gardner puts it, general intelligence may be "the ability to solve problems, or to create products, that are valued within one or more cultural settings."[30] Other scholars attempt to define general intelligence using substitutes. Professors Oliver Wilhelm and Randall Engle provide an extensive list of adjectives that describe intelligent activities including abstract, agile, analytic, aware, brainy, clever, complex, detail-oriented, flawless, imaginative, insightful, intellectual, introspective, meticulous, philosophical, questioning, reasonable, sophisticated, and visionary.[31]

What type of "intelligence" does AI display? With the advent of machine learning algorithms, the initial rule-based algorithms of computer technology changed drastically. New systems allow AI scientists to shift from creating algorithms for desired outcomes to creating learning algorithms. As a result of learning algorithms, AI systems can now plan and study the environment somewhat like humans do to succeed in their tasks. AI has the potential to identify patterns and create algorithms that can determine the

---

27. Murphy, *Introduction to AI Robotics*, 20–21.

28. Phillip. W. Bowen, *Emotional Intelligence: Does It Really Matter?* (Wilmington: Vernon Press, 2019), 132.

29. Howard Gardner, *Frames of Mind: The Theory of Multiple Intelligences* (New York: Basic Books, 2011), XII.

30. Gardner, *Frames of Mind*, XXIX.

31. Oliver Wilhelm and Randall W. Engle. "Intelligence: A Diva and a Workhorse," in *Handbook of Understanding and Measuring Intelligence*, eds. Oliver Wilhelm and Randall W. Engle (London: Sage Publications, 2005), 2.

appropriate actions or outcomes based on those patterns.[32] The cognitive nature appears to offer a merely unidimensional conceptualization of AI.[33]

According to the vast theories of intelligence that humans are capable of, the information understood by intelligent robots is limited to a very narrow understanding of intelligence compared to the complexity of human intelligence. The current state of AI in robotic technologies is narrow because the application of machine thinking is to perform a single, limited activity, such as navigating to perform errands and making appropriate decisions in changeable, variable contexts, as in the case of busy hospital corridors. Even though such an activity can be considered flexible, accurate, and consistent, AI's current capabilities cannot be comparable to human intelligence intricacy.[34]

Finally, "healthcare" is defined under a culture of care framework. According to this school of thought, healthcare is not a product or a mere service. On the contrary, healthcare "is intensely personal, often consumed at the most vulnerable times of our lives, and highly dependent upon the values, desires, and beliefs of both those treating and those being treated."[35] Healthcare driven by a culture of care encourages health professionals to serve their patients by knowing about religious traditions and attempting to understand patients' cultural and spiritual contexts.[36] The relationship between care receiver and caregiver is vital to the care system. The trust between the care receiver and caregiver is understood to be one of the fundamental goals of medical care as well as healthcare law and public policy. Trust is also deemed to be essential to a therapeutic and practical course of treatment.[37]

---

32. Jacob Shatzer, "Fake and Future 'Humans': Artificial Intelligence, Transhumanism, and the Question of the Person," *Southwestern Journal of Theology* 63, no. 2 (2021): 132.

33. J.P. Das, "A Better Look at Intelligence," *Current Directions in Psychological Science* 11, no. 1 (2002): 28.

34. Christopher Manning, "Artificial Intelligence Definitions" (Stanford University: Human-Centered Artificial Intelligence, 2020), 1.

35. Ron Paulus, "Introduction," in *Health Care System Transformation for Nursing and Health Care Leaders,* eds. Anne Boykin, Savina Schoenhofer, and Kathleen Valentine, (New York: Springer, 2014), XVII.

36. Warren Kinghorn, "Why Health Care Needs Religion and Vice Versa: Religion Education and Theological Formation for Pre-Health Undergraduates," *Perspectives In Religious Studies* 48, no. 2 (2021): 163.

37. Robin C. Feldman, Ehrik Aldana, and Kara Stein, "Artificial Intelligence in the Health Care Space: How We Can Trust What We Cannot Know," *Stanford Law & Policy Review* 30, no. 2 (2019): 404.

But health from a theological perspective encompasses more than life expectancy and the avoidance of death.[38] Health includes the ability of the body to function normally in the context of a fallen world.[39] I will argue in chapter three that in addition to the somatic restoration that attempts to allow the body to function normally in a world affected by sin, a theological perspective adds another level of health—the quest for wholeness that is ultimately accomplished in life after death, in the new resurrected body, through faith in Jesus Christ. In other words, health as wholeness includes the well-being of the body and mind, personal and social relationships, and a right relationship with God.[40]

To sum up, even though there is no universal agreement on what a carebot may be defined as,[41] AI carebots or computerized caregivers that draw on AI programs[42] may be described as independent machines capable of performing intelligent tasks projected to contribute to the cure of care receivers. Carebots do so by being equipped explicitly with social-communicative functions to respond to care receivers as social and communicative beings. In theory, carebots "should ideally recognize the social needs of humans with the associated feelings and thoughts and respond appropriately according to their respective roles."[43]

From Robots to Carebots: A Selective History

The concept of using computers or, for that matter, robots to simulate intelligent behavior and critical thinking was first described by Alan Turing in 1950. The "Turing Test" to measure the intelligence of machines was considered a milestone in AI research. The test included a human judge who had to decide, based on two written conversations, which of the conversational partners was the human and which was the computer program. Turing argued that a machine could be regarded as intelligent if it could mislead

38. Robert M. Kaplan, *More than Medicine: The Broken Promise of American Health* (Cambridge: Harvard University Press, 2019), 60.

39. Nigel Cameron, *The New Medicine: Life and Death After Hippocrates* (Wheaton: Crossway Books, 1991), 174.

40. Neil Messer, *Flourishing: Health, Disease, and Bioethics in Theological Perspective* (Grand Rapids: Wm. B. Eerdmans, 2013), 112.

41. Filippo Santoni de Sio and Aimee van Wynsberghe, "When Should We Use Care Robots? The Nature-of-Activities Approach," *Science & Engineering Ethics* 22, no. 6 (2016): 1748.

42. Amitai Etzioni and Oren Etzioni, "The Ethics of Robotic Caregivers," *Interaction Studies* 18, no. 2 (2017): 177.

43. Gasser, "Dawn of Social Robots," 329.

the human judge to believe it was a human.⁴⁴ John McCarthy was the first to coin the term "artificial intelligence" in 1956 at the Dartmouth Summer Research Project workshop.⁴⁵ The AI revolution predicted in the following years, such as Marvin Minsky's announcement in 1967 that "the problems of creating artificial intelligence will be substantially solved," did not materialize. As a consequence, the AI winter began.⁴⁶

As researcher Luciano Floridi observes, AI has had several winters. An AI winter refers to hype cycles, entertained by certain emotions, such as hope and fear.⁴⁷ Professor Jacob Shatzer argues that the history of AI records two main reasons for the stagnation of AI systems. First, creating algorithms is complicated; some algorithms needed to be more precise for people to develop at that point in history. Second, due to computing power, speed, and storage limitations, people reached the outer limit of their ability to write complex instructions.⁴⁸ During this AI winter, much of the research funding for AI disappeared. In the 1970s, the best AI programs could only deal with simple versions of the problems they aimed to solve.⁴⁹ Despite the general lack of interest during the 1970s, some programs that continued to be helpful in general AI development were developed.

In this vein, the General Problem Solver (GPS) was a computer program designed with general problem-solving capabilities by mimicking human problem-solving protocols. The kind of problem-solving capabilities were limited according to human standards. For instance, a typical problem that GPS could resolve was the hypothetical situation in which there are three missionaries and three cannibals who want to cross a river. The only way to cross the river is by a small boat with a capacity of two people, all six of whom know how to row. If, at any time, there are more cannibals than missionaries on either side of the river, those missionaries will be eaten by the cannibals. GPS could answer a simple question, such as "How can all six get across the river without any missionaries being eaten?"⁵⁰ Another

---

44. Adrienn Ujhelyi, Flora Almosdi, and Alexandra Fodor, "Would You Pass the Turing Test? Influencing Factors of the Turing Decision," *Psihologijske Teme/ Psychological Topics* 31, no. 1 (2022): 186.

45. Teresa Heffernan, "The Dangers of Mystifying Artificial Intelligence and Robotics," *Toronto Journal of Theology* 36, no. 1 (2020): 93.

46. Christoph Adami, "A Brief History of Artificial Intelligence Research," *Artificial Life* 27, no. 2 (2021): 133.

47. Luciano Floridi, "AI and Its New Winter: From Myths to Realities," *Philosophy & Technology* 33 (2020): 1.

48. Shatzer, "Fake and Future 'Humans,'" 131.

49. Kevin Warwick, *Artificial Intelligence: The Basics* (London: Routledge, 2012), 4.

50. George W. Ernst and Allen Newell, "Some Issues of Representation in a General

example was ELIZA, a computer program successfully developed during this time, capable of processing natural language.[51]

The 1980s presented a significant improvement in AI. Researcher Kevin Warwick summarizes three factors that led to a revival in AI. First, the period saw the development of "expert systems," designed to deal with particular knowledge domains. Thus, the systems were used practically in industry. Second, the philosophical discussions of the 1970s regarding whether or not a machine could think as a human continued somewhat independently of the practical industrial AI work. Third, the development of robotics had a considerable influence on AI. During that time, a new paradigm developed: an intelligent computer must have a body to behave like a human. The resulting advent of cybernetics and its influence on AI geared the development of AI from a practical perspective.[52]

In the late 1980s, AI research adopted a more scientific approach, incorporating machine learning rather than hand-coding and experimental results rather than philosophical claims. During this time, a series of programs were developed relevant to real-world applications rather than toy examples, such as UC Irvine's repository for machine learning data sets and the LibriSpeech corpus for speech recognition.[53] In 1988, a significant improvement occurred between AI and other fields, including Judea Pearl's *Probabilistic Reasoning in Intelligent Systems*, which led to the development of Bayesian networks. The Bayesian learning method uses observations to update a prior distribution over hypotheses.[54]

A remarkable development in the history of AI was the creation of the World Wide Web, which facilitated the creation of large data sets, a phenomenon known as Big Data. Big Data represents the interconnection of technology, people, and data.[55] The data includes trillions of words of text, billions of images, billions of hours of videos, vast amounts of genomic data, clickstream, social network data, etc. Big Data and machine learning helped AI to expand enormously.[56]

Problem Solver" (Conference Paper, Spring Joint Computer Conference, Atlantic City, New Jersey, April 18–20, 1967).

51. Rose Angelique Dizon, "A New Way of Healing: Regulating Healthcare AI," *Ateneo Law Journal* 64, no. 3 (2020): 1139.

52. Warwick, *Artificial Intelligence*, 6.

53. Russell and Norvig, *Artificial Intelligence*, 43.

54. Russell and Norvig, *Artificial Intelligence*, 43.

55. Roman Rakowski, Petr Polak, and Petra Kowalikova, "Ethical Aspects of the Impact of AI: The Status of Humans in the Era of Artificial Intelligence," *Society* 58, no. 3 (2021): 196.

56. Russell and Norvig, *Artificial Intelligence*, 45.

Another critical technological milestone was the advent of wireless, argues Warwick. Wireless technology as a form of communication for computers follows the widespread introduction and use of the internet. Before wireless technology, computer networks existed alone. However, computers were enabled to create networked systems after the creation of wireless technology.[57]

During the 1990s, AI reached several other significant milestones. For instance, in 1997, Deep Blue became the first chess-playing computer to beat a human world chess champion at his own game. In 2002, Kevin Warwick was the first to link the human nervous system to a computer to form a new combined form of AI. In the 2005 Defense Advanced Research Projects Agency (DARPA) Grand Challenge, a robot drove autonomously for 131 miles on an unrehearsed desert trail. The Blue Brain Project team announced in 2009 that they had simulated parts of a rat's brain.[58] In 2011, IBM Research introduced IBM Watson to the general public, an open-domain question-answering system that evolved into IBM Watson Health, a physician clinical decision support system.[59]

The current use of AI impacts the functioning of society at the level of all social subsystems. Robots and computer programming advancements can process millions of tasks per second.[60] AI ranks Google's pages; Booking.com knows the user's preferred holiday destination; Amazon knows what products the user chooses, etc. AI technologies are also among the top investment priorities in the world. According to a Gartner report for 2019–2021, 10 percent of new vehicles have autonomous driving capabilities, compared to less than 1 percent in 2018–2020. The Boston Consulting Group and MIT Sloan Management Review, published in 2017, stated that 72 percent of respondents from various spectrums of society, including technology, media, and the telecommunications industry, expect AI to impact product offerings significantly in the next five years.

AI technologies offer beneficial new solutions to diagnose diseases. AI also impacts the decision-making part of the health process by presenting high rates of diagnostic efficiency, reducing the incidence of errors, improving outcomes, and reducing the time of disease discovery.[61] AI-driven

---

57. Warwick, *Artificial Intelligence*, 9.
58. Warwick, *Artificial Intelligence*, 7.
59. Dizon, "New Way of Healing," 1142.
60. Wolfgang Amann and Agata Stachowich-Stanusch, "Should We Be Afraid of Artificial Intelligence?" in *Artificial Intelligence and Its Impact on Business*, eds. Wolfgang Amann and Agata Stachowich-Stanusch, Contemporary Perspectives in Corporate Social Performance and Policy (Charlotte: Information Age Publishing, 2020), 4.
61. Yousif Saleh Ibrahim et al., "Perception of the Impact of Artificial Intelligence in

machine learning is used in clinical trials, drug development, and Internet of Things (IoT) devices, such as smartwatches, smartphones, and tablets. For instance, in clinical trials, a startup called Deep 6 AI found and validated fifty-eight eligible matches in less than ten minutes by using AI to mine medical records, a task that would take a few months using a traditional method. Further, Big Data and AI may contribute to developing new drugs and treatments by reducing production costs and creating more effective precision treatments for individuals.[62]

The impact of robots in the health area is indisputable. The medical application of robots is extensive, including surgery, rehabilitation therapy, prosthetics and orthotics, medical imaging, monitoring, and therapeutic assistance. For instance, in 2013, the U.S. Food and Drug Administration approved a robot with a video screen that can be sent to a patient's bedside to communicate with their doctor remotely. Furthermore, over 80 hospitals use Pyxis HelpMate SP robots that can navigate autonomously from floor to floor to deliver meals, medical records, supplies, etc. Robots, such as the da Vinci robot surgical system and similar telerobots, are also used in medical procedures, which enable surgeons to conduct minimally invasive surgery with greater agility and to perform delicate procedures that would be very difficult without robotic help.[63]

When robots incorporate AI in the healthcare context, technologies such as carebots are utilized as therapeutic tools to improve an individual's well-being while ill. However, the presence of carebots in the healthcare system impacts the caregiver, care receiver, and the entire health system.[64] A carebot is sometimes seen as poised between health institutions and tech companies. As van Wynsberghe and Li argue, a carebot is neither entirely part of the healthcare system nor entirely part of the tech company. At times, however, a carebot may be part of either. For instance, a carebot is developed by a tech company, yet when used in a health institution, it belongs to the healthcare structure until there is a malfunction and the tech company must repair it. As a result, it is of paramount importance "to raise

---

the Decision-Making Processes of Public Healthcare Professionals," *Journal of Environmental & Public Health* 2022 (2022): 2.

62. Weixiang Chen, "An Overview," in *Transforming Healthcare with Big Data and AI*, eds. Alex Liu, Atefeh Farzindar, and Mingbo Gong, New Methods in the Era of Big Data and AI (Charlotte: Information Age Publishing, 2020), 9–13.

63. Kenneth Kernaghan, "The Rights and Wrongs of Robotics: Ethics and Robots in Public Organizations: Ethics and Robots in Public Organizations," *Canadian Public Administration* 57, no. 4
(2014): 496.

64. Wynsberghe and Li, "Paradigm Shift for Robot Ethics," 12.

awareness of policymakers, caregivers, and patients whose traditional moral codes governing the healthcare system may be in jeopardy when interacting with a bot."[65]

Powered by AI, robots in caring will likely take on more social space. These areas may include care work for children, the elderly, and the sick. They could also become teachers, work colleagues, friends, and even sexual partners.[66]

A particular use of carebots is caring for elderly residents in eldercare facilities. Currently, there are some generally recognized categories of assistive robots for eldercare: assistive rehabilitation robots (ARRs) and socially assistive robots (SARs), such as alternative animal-assisted interventions (A-SARs).[67] ARRs are designed to support older adults by promoting physical activity and supporting those with mild cognitive impairment. ARRs can guide physical exercise sessions and encourage people to perform daily exercises. ARRs can also help memory training by providing daily reminders about taking essential medications and when to perform these tasks.[68]

SARs are created to provide companionship by reducing stress levels. They also seek to increase the activity of older people and enhance their well-being by walking, navigating, and entertaining them.[69] A-SARs, a subcategory of SARs, are pet-like robots called companion robots that serve as friends for independent-living older individuals.[70] Some recent examples of A-SARs are AIBO, a touch-sensitive and interactive pet introduced by Sony as a toy for older adults. Similarly, Paro, a robotic companion shaped like a baby seal, assists older adults. The artificial baby seal responds to petting and may produce effects similar to those of real therapy animals.[71] CuDDler is a small robotic bear developed by the Robotic Senses Research Institute to reduce stress and anxiety by touching interactions. The structure was fabricated in-house using a 3D printer and was initially designed as a toy

---

65. Wynsberghe and Li, "Paradigm Shift for Robot Ethics," 13.

66. Paul Formosa, "Robot Autonomy vs. Human Autonomy: Social Robots, Artificial Intelligence (AI), and the Nature of Autonomy," *Minds and Machines* 31, no. 4 (2021): 596.

67. Ellie Wakabayashi, "A Biomedical Ethical Analysis of Using Socially Assistive Robots with an Animal-Like Form with Elderly Individuals in Institutionalized Care" (McGill University, 2021), 23.

68. Richard Sather Iii et al., "Assistive Robots Designed for Elderly Care and Caregivers," *International Journal of Robotics and Control* 3, no. 1 (2021): 8.

69. Iii et al., "Assistive Robots Designed for Elderly Care and Caregivers," 4.

70. Iii et al., "Assistive Robots Designed for Elderly Care and Caregivers," 8.

71. Gasser, "Dawn of Social Robots," 330.

based on the shape of a polar bear.⁷² JustoCat, also called Hasbro's Joy for All Cat, is a cat-like A-SAR used in nursing homes and hospitals in Sweden to improve the lives of people with dementia. JustoCat has realistic-looking fur and facial expressions. The robotic cat responds to petting by meowing and changing its facial expressions.⁷³ Their aim is restricted to fulfilling specific psychological needs such as interaction and communication.⁷⁴ It is worth mentioning here that studies show that patients suffering from moderate to severe forms of dementia working with animal-shaped robots experienced a decreased quality of life, increased hallucinations and irritability, and increased disinhibition. Thus, A-SARs must be carefully assessed on a case-by-case basis to determine their potential effectiveness.⁷⁵

An Overview of Neighbor-Love

As shown in the selective historical development of carebot technologies, the various fields, such as synthetic biology, information technology, and computational neuroscience, that contribute to the AI robots in healthcare promise countless rewards but pose specific challenges. How will caregivers and care receivers, specifically theologically formed Christian caregivers and care receivers, navigate the promises and perils of the biotech and info-tech⁷⁶ scientific progress and practice the love of God given within the medicine arena?⁷⁷ This section shows that a possible answer can be found in the classic formula of *Cura Animarum* (The Care of Souls).

Cura Animarum is a phrase that encompasses the Christian understanding of care. Presbyterian minister Eugene H. Peterson ably observes that the word *cura* combines the English words cure and care. Peterson maintains that "cure is nurturing a person towards health; care is being a

72. Yeow Kee Tan et al., "Evaluation of the Pet Robot CuDDler Using Godspeed Questionnaire," in *Inclusive Society: Health and Wellbeing in the Community, and Care at Home*, ed. Jit Biswas et al., vol. 7910, *Lecture Notes in Computer Science* (Berlin: Springer, 2013), 103.

73. Jill A Dosso et al., "User Perspectives on Emotionally Aligned Social Robots for Older Adults and Persons Living with Dementia," *Journal of Rehabilitation and Assistive Technologies Engineering* 9 (2022): 3. https://www.doi.org/10.1177/20556683221108364.

74. Wakabayashi, "Biomedical Ethical Analysis of Using Socially Assistive Robots," 24.

75. Sather, et al., "Assistive Robots Designed for Elderly Care and Caregivers," 8.

76. Wendell Wallach, "From Robots to Techno Sapiens: Ethics, Law and Public Policy in the Development of Robotics and Neurotechnologies," *Law, Innovation and Technology* 3, no. 2 (2011): 185.

77. Margaret E. Mohrmann, *Medicine as Ministry* (Cleveland: The Pilgrim Press, 1995), 10.

compassionate companion towards a person in need. The cure requires that we know what we are doing. Care requires that we be involved in what we are doing."[78] Care may be defined as responding to a person in need and relating the immediate problem to the larger story of life. Developing a theological neighbor-love framework for a Christian understanding of care as connecting present needs (cure) and eternal needs (care) is a multifaceted and complex endeavor. Nevertheless, a theological framing of care incorporates three necessary elements in establishing a compelling theological and ethical context for carebot technology,[79] such as a view of divinity, a view of man, and a view of salvation.

A View of Divinity: A Loving Heavenly Father in Christ

Peterson observes that humans, redeemed or not, do not know how to care because of their fallen condition. "We begin with realizing our poverty: We do not know how to care," maintains Peterson.[80] As a result, a Christian must look beyond himself to somewhere else to learn how to care appropriately. A Christian theology of care begins with understanding the Trinitarian God: Father, Son, and Spirit. As Trinity, God must be understood as a "triune society of love," as stated by Karl Barth, cited by the Anglican theologian Graham O'Brien.[81] The very nature of God is expressed in community among the three persons of the Godhead. God exists in a fellowship of love shared among himself and creation.[82]

A Christian theology of care entails the view of God as a caring God involved in creation. A God who is present in creation and yet transcendent lies at the very heart, not only of theology, but of every person's life. The world is God's world, fallen as it is. God is involved in the affairs of this world. Seminary professor Eugene Klug argues that both fatalism and determinism, secularism's favorite alternatives to reality, are unacceptable to the Christian. The fundamental scriptural truth is that there is no τύχη (fortune), but there is only God's providential concurrence in all things.[83] The

---

78. Eugene H. Peterson, "Teach Us to Care, and Not to Care," *Crux* 28, no. 4 (1992): 2.

79. R. Michael Casto and Steven A. Harsh, "Laying the Groundwork for a Christian Theology for Interprofessional Care," *Journal of Interprofessional Care* 12, no. 4 (1998): 390.

80. Peterson, "Teach Us to Care, and Not to Care," 4.

81. Graham O'Brien, "A Theology of Care: Connecting the Present and the Eternal," *Churchman* 134, no. 2 (2020): 145.

82. O'Brien, "Theology of Care," 146.

83. Eugene Klug, "The Caring God," *Springfielder* 37, no. 4 (1974): 224.

Bible proves God's intentional and personal presence in the world. Starting with creation and the garden of Eden, the escape of the Jews from Egypt and Babylon, and the teachings of Christ, the Scripture attests to a highly involved God in creation. Further, the teachings of Jesus Christ present an extraordinarily personal God who is so intimately involved in people's lives that he knows what they need even before they ask (Matt 7:11; 6:32).[84]

A theology of care also suggests that God holistically sees human beings with all of the complexities of the human condition. One of the most valuable ways to describe the relationship of God to his people is to compare him to a father who maintains a caring relationship with his children, as ethicist Frits de Lange argues.[85] Scripture describes God's relationship to his people as adoption. Apostle Paul frequently uses the word υἱοθεσία (adoption) (Rom 8:15, 23; 9:4; Eph 1:5). According to Paul, the adoption of Christians is derived from that of Jesus, who is God's Son in a unique sense. Adoption of Christians is possible through the work of Jesus Christ, and by Christians' identification with him, they are adopted as God's children.[86]

A revealing biblical text about God's adoption is Gal 4:4–7, in which the paterfamilias (the male head or father of a family or household) chooses to adopt those not part of the family. The adoption analogy emphasizes that God, in his Son, makes the gift of the Spirit available to all those who believe. All who believe are submerged into Christ, and the adoption becomes a reality by sending the Holy Spirit to the Jew and the gentile. All people were slaves to various στοιχεῖα (the elemental things of the world), but in Christ, everyone can receive adoption into God's redeemed family.[87] Transformed from slaves to sons and daughters, believers have been given freedom and the power to use it responsibly. The soteriological significance of Christ's sonship with the Father is that believers can call God Ἀββᾶ ὁ Πατήρ (Abba, the Father) as heirs of the Father through Christ.[88] Because we are adopted by God and heirs of his kingdom, it appears safe to argue that the only

---

84. Haydn J. McLean, "Thinking Out Loud: Pondering the Providence of God," *The Journal of Pastoral Care and Counseling* 62, no. 3 (2008): 304.

85. Frits de Lange, "The Heidelberg Catechism: Elements for a Theology of Care," *Acta Theologica* 20 (2014): 162.

86. Roy E. Ciampa, "Adoption," *New Dictionary of Biblical Theology*, ed. T. Desmond Alexander and Brian S. Rosner (Downers Grove: InterVarsity Press, 2000), 377.

87. David. A. DeSilva, *The Letter to the Galatians*, The New International Commentary of the New Testament (Grand Rapids: Wm. B. Eerdmans, 2018), 909.

88. Frederick Fyvie Bruce, *The Epistle to the Galatians*, The New International Greek Testament Commentary (Grand Rapids: Wm. B. Eerdmans, 1982), 497.

presupposed responsible way of acting for the Christian caregiver towards the needs of another human being is by caring.[89]

In addressing God as Father, Christians express their belief that God is the person offering them all the essentials as the one who has created them.[90] God, as loving Father, is a reminder of the character of God who is generous and whose divinity is most adequately understood as inherently empowering rather than oppressive.[91] Additionally, God the Father was active and affected by Jesus' ministry and passion. The Father is actively present in Jesus' suffering without abandoning his Son on the cross in absolute terms but instead was left in helpless condition before his enemies as the Father drained the cup of wrath at Golgotha.[92] God understands suffering and walks with his children amid a fallen world because of the cross.

In the Father-son relationship, God has an intimate, personal relationship with his adopted sons and daughters in Christ. God is the almighty creator and the loving Father of his redeemed.[93] According to a Christian view of the Father-son relationship, God is understood as an intimate and good Father, such as in the case of a healthy human parent-child relationship. The human parent-child relationship creates a bond that includes "the desire for individuals to be near to their attachments, their return to them as safe havens, their view of them as secure bases of operation for venturing out into the world, and absence of or separation from their attachment creates anxiety and even distress."[94]

The powerful biblical metaphor of Father-son love also emphasizes that God's fatherhood implies divine chastisement. In a biblical context, God's purpose for discipline is "to teach, test, and to stimulate obedience or remembrance; to provide assurance, acceptance, or hope; to employ temporal chastisement to cleanse and restore."[95] The biblical paternal relationship between God and his people is by its very nature forgiving, corrective,

---

89. Joachim Ostermann, "Fraternity as Natural Being," *Religions* 13, no. 9 (2022): 1.

90. Rainer Stahl, "The Sixth Supplication of the Lord's Prayer: God, The Father, Does For US the Good," *Religion. Church. Society.* 9 (2020): 90.

91. Ian A. McFarland, "God, the Father Almighty: A Theological Excursus," *International Journal of Systematic Theology* 18, no. 3 (2016): 266.

92. Terry Root, "Apathy or Passion? The New Testament View of God the Father at the Cross," *The Evangelical Quarterly* 88, no. 1 (2016): 12.

93. de Lange, "The Heidelberg Catechism: Elements for a Theology of Care," 162.

94. Tim L. Anderson, "God Our Father as a Script of Intimacy for Those Suffering Shame," *Journal of Spiritual Formation and Care* 9, no. 2 (2016): 250.

95. Eric J. Bargerhuff, "Divine Discipline in Ecclesial Expression: An Analysis of God's 'Fatherly' Love as Embodied in the Church" (PhD diss., Chicago, Trinity Evangelical Divinity School, 2005), 129–30.

instructive, and intimate. God's paternal discipline encourages his children to learn, mature, grow, and correct when they fall into self-destructive disobedience.[96] The adoption into the family of God, and God as the Father of his children, not only represents a permanent legal standing but also results in intimate peace, security, and privilege that only children can enjoy,[97] even when they do not entirely understand the nature of God's caring actions for them. In a biblically informed view of Fatherly care, the caregiver and care receiver can live in a healed, loved way. Even though the reason for his suffering might not be apparent to the Christian care receiver, he can rest assured that the wound is more than a wound:

> It is access to the outside, to God, and to others. The Christians standing at the intersection where all this carnage is going on, are the ones who know that this wound is more than a wound, it is access. The wound must not be bandaged over as fast as possible; it is there to be a listening post, a chance to exit the small confines of a self-defined world and enter the spaciousness of a God-defined world.[98]

For the caregiver, the wound, as seen by Peterson, is an opportunity to help people listen to God's words, allowing them to respond adequately. The caregiver's responsibility is to care and help the one in need of health, get in touch with God and his neighbor, and offer love and grace.[99] Without using these difficult situations to teach people to pray and to know God's fatherly love more intimately, the caregiver provides only a cure without the care needed in holistic care. The primary role of a caregiver is to partner with Christ in building a relationship with the care receiver. Specifically, the primary role of the Christian caregiver is to partner with Christ to help restore people's relationship with God so that in Christ, they can be restored as children of God in the fullest sense. In so doing, the medical procedures performed by a Christian caregiver represent more than a helping hand; they represent a caregiver's faith in God and their community.[100]

In conclusion, a Christian's view of God informs the care and love for his neighbor. God cares for creation and loves his people. God's love is a fatherly love. As a result, a Christian understanding of neighbor-care

---

96. Bargerhuff, "Divine Discipline in Ecclesial Expression" 139.

97. Anderson, "God Our Father as a Script of Intimacy for Those Suffering Shame," 258.

98. Peterson, "Teach Us to Care, and Not to Care," 5.

99. Peterson, "Teach Us to Care, and Not to Care," 5.

100. O'Brien, "Theology of Care," 152.

mirrors God's fatherly love as image-bearers through an intentional relation between caregiver and care receiver, characterized by love.

A View of Man: A Caring Being

The Christian view of humanity is that humans are God's most incredible creation, his masterwork, the only beings made in his image and likeness (Gen 1:26–27). The speech of God begets the man and the woman to display God to the created world. Man is not a cosmic accident, nor an evolved product of other creatures, but is made by God.[101]

A theological understanding of humanity is that humans are caring creatures because they are made in the image and likeness of God. God is a caring person. Consequently, God cannot be uncaring towards his creation. As a result, among other things, being human means caring and resembling God's care. That is to say, a lack of care in the relationship with one's neighbor means acting nothing less than inhumanely. Since God is love in Christ, Christians are to show care to everyone, not only as image-bearers of God but as redeemed people. Additionally, the character of Jesus' ethics is caring. Based on the parables of the sheep and the goats, the rich man and Lazarus, and the parable of the good Samaritan, those who care for people in poverty, hunger, thirst, or sickness are caring, metaphorically speaking, for Jesus. Christ expects that human relationships are to express care. The right way to materialize a relationship is to care.[102] In doing so, the love of God through Christ's work can be shown in action to the person in need. God's love for his redeemed is similar to a compassionate companion who empathizes and walks with the person in need. Therefore, a Christian's caregiving means companionship that meets the needs of the whole person—physically, emotionally, and spiritually.[103]

Furthermore, the act of care seems to be theologically located in the love for one's neighbor. In the dialogue with the Pharisee lawyer, as recorded in Matt 22:34–40 based on Lev 19:18 and Deut 6:5, Jesus stresses that the greatest commandment in the Scripture is the love of God and neighbor. The principle is that if one truly loves God, one will love his image-bearers.

---

101. Owen Strachan, *Reenchanting Humanity: A Theology of Mankind* (Fearn, Ross-shire: Mentor, 2019), 15.

102. Nan-Jou Chen, "A Reflection on the Bioethical Dilemmas from the Perspective of a Human Being as a Relational Being and The Ethics of Caring: The Case of Genetic Screening," *Theologies and Cultures* 3, no. 1 (2006): 58.

103. O'Brien, "Theology of Care," 147.

When one loves human beings, one expresses love to his creator.[104] To put it differently, the love of God is first and above all else, and the love of neighbor exists within and flows out from the love of God.[105] According to the Lord Jesus, love for neighbor is part of the essence of Old Testament doctrine.[106] The Gospel of Matthew assumes that fallen humans cannot love their neighbors as themselves if they have not submitted to the obligation to love God first. For Matthew, the instinctive love for oneself is a prerequisite of human nature in relationship with others.[107] Jesus' praxis of love is anchored in a covenantal framework and its laws. Love is the central focus of the human-divine covenant and the human-human relationship.[108] Jesus' understanding of the double love commandment seems to be the climatic statement of the *Streitgesprächen* (discussions), in which Christ is the clear victor.[109]

According to a Christian view of care, the focus of care is a tangible expression of God's love for care receivers, first and foremost, as human beings. Those needing care are more than just a manifestation of an illness looking for medical service. Care receivers experiencing pain, fear, or suffering, and needing response from fellow human beings, possess dignity and value derived from God.[110] Physician Edmund Pellegrino maintains that healthcare is "the provision of assistance to persons in need of care, cure, prevention, or help related to trauma, illness, disease, disability, or dysfunction by other persons knowledgeable and skillful in providing such assistance. The central feature of healthcare is the personal relationship between a health professional and a person seeking help."[111] Pellegrino supports the idea that the receivers of care are persons. Health or amelioration

---

104. David. L. Turner, *Matthew*, Baker Exegetical Commentary on the New Testament (Grand Rapids: Baker Academic, 2008), 833.

105. Helen Creticos Theodoropoulos, "Love of God and Love of Neighbor in the Mystical Theology of St. Bernard of Clairvaux and St. Symeon the New Theologian" (PhD diss., The University of Chicago, Chicago, 1995), 107.

106. Charles L. Quarles, *Matthew*, Exegetical Guide to the Greek New Testament (Nashville: B&H, 2017), 585.

107. Turner, *Matthew*, 837.

108. Werner G. Jeanrond, *A Theology of Love* (New York: T&T Clark, 2010), 33–34.

109. Francois P. Viljoen, "The Double Love Commandment," *In Die Skriflig* 49, no. 1 (2015): 4.

110. Susanne Salmela, "The Human Being in Need of Nursing Care: Patient, Customer or Fellow Human Being?" *International Journal of Caring Sciences* 10, no. 3 (2017): 1163.

111. Edmund D. Pellegrino, "The Commodification of Medical and Health Care: The Moral Consequences of a Paradigm Shift from a Professional to a Market Ethics," *Journal of Medicine and Philosophy* 24, no. 3 (1999): 247.

of disease may be the end of medicine, but health itself is not a commodity. A commodity is a transaction that can be traded and consumed. In contrast, the medical relationship must be highly personal to be compelling and unique as a human activity.[112]

Caring is also a community endeavor based on a biblical worldview of care. Pellegrino argues that healthcare is both an individual and a social good. Society benefits when healthy members flourish.[113] More than that, the church, as Christ's body, is a caring community. When there is suffering in the body, there is an opportunity for Christians to show the care of Christ experientially. Scripture reinforces the proposition that care lies at the heart of the Christian idea of community (1 John 4:10; Phil 2:4, 5–7;1 Thess 2:7; Col 3:12–14; etc.). Practical theologian Robert Banks argues that the New Testament church established new patterns of caring in the ancient world. The church's motive of care no longer insisted on reciprocity or desire for acknowledgment as the motor behind social aid. Another pattern of care shows that God's redemptive care was unobtrusively given to all. The community explicitly helped those who had the least to offer. Every aspect of a person's physical or material life concerns the ecclesial community.[114]

These new approaches resulted later in creating hospitals, orphanages, etc. The care for the sick contrasted pagans and Christians in antiquity. Pagan cults saw the care of the sick as a private matter, while Christians saw it as a communal concern. Christians were able to generate a community of belonging, while the pagan society was more accustomed to leaving the sick and their families to themselves, often resulting in abandonment.[115] The first-century community of Christ understood that humans are fragile beings and that suffering is part of believers' lives on earth as they await bodily resurrection and glorification. The body was regarded as God's good creation, and one would experience future resurrection.[116] Caring for a person involves, at times, nothing but the presence of loved ones. The ministry of presence is a ministry of caring by the church community. Professionals in the healthcare community are trained to do rather than to be. Christian care includes the "to be" with the care receiver without directly doing something for the person. The simple presence at the bedside of a dying believer without "doing" might sound foreign to the training and experience of many

112. Pellegrino, "Commodification of Medical and Health Care," 248.

113. Pellegrino, "Commodification of Medical and Health Care," 262.

114. Robert Banks, "The Early Church as a Caring Community," *Evangelical Review of Theology* 7, no. 2 (1983): 92.

115. Jeremiah Mutie, "Care for the Sick in Early Christianity: Lessons for the Current Covid-19 Stricken Church," *Vox Patrum* 78 (2021): 81.

116. Mutie, "Care for the Sick in Early Christianity," 66–67.

caregivers. On the other hand, for the Christian community, the physical presence of the sick is an illustration of God's timeless and limitless care.[117]

In conclusion, a Christian view of care proposes a radical perspective grounded in a conception of neighbor-love. The radical perspective is that the caregiver should care for the patient by loving him as himself. As understood in a care framework, the system of neighbor-love recognizes that a patient's humanity is more than a mere manifestation of disease. Neighborly love improves the therapeutic relationship by helping the care receiver feel understood, respected, and encouraged to face and overcome difficulties.[118]

A View of Salvation: Toward a Salvation-Driven Care

The nature of salvation is central to a Christian theological framework for neighbor care. Besides a view of God and man, it is necessary to develop a view of the cross included in the metanarrative of care due to its impact on the individual's immediate and future life. Jesus' death and resurrection frame the final deliverance from bodily and spiritual affliction, a promise in the gospel of Christ.[119]

The ultimate act of caring of God for humanity is in the person and the finished work of Jesus Christ on the cross. The birth, death, and resurrection of Jesus represent the most vivid and concrete expression proclaiming that God deeply cares for fallen humanity.[120] The person and work of Jesus Christ is the picture and goal of the gospel. The good news of Jesus Christ is that the eternal Son of God, the second person of the Trinity, became truly and fully human. Through his sufferings and death at the cross and his resurrection, he accomplished what humanity could not do for itself, that is, salvation from sin and its consequences, including sickness and, ultimately, death.[121] There was no suffering, illness, or death before the fall. As a consequence of Adam's disobedience, sin entered the world, as did the

---

117. Casto and Harsh, "Laying the Groundwork for a Christian Theology for Interprofessional Care," 395.

118. Bengt Karlsson et al., "To See Each Other More Like Human Beings . . . From Both Sides: Patients and Therapists Going to a Study Course Together," *International Practice Development* 3, no. 1 (2013): 2.

119. Bruce T. Morrill, "Christ the Healer: A Critical Investigation of Liturgical, Pastoral, and Biblical Sources," *Worship* 79, no. 6 (2005): 483.

120. Casto and Harsh, "Laying the Groundwork for a Christian Theology for Interprofessional Care," 394.

121. Oren R. Martin, "How Do the Old and New Testaments Progress, Integrate, and Climax in Christ?" in *40 Questions about Biblical Theology*, 40 Questions (Grand Rapids: Kregel Academic, 2020), loc. 825, Kindle.

curse of sin in the form of human disfigurement, illness, disease, and death of both humanity and creation. Medicine was needed to attempt to restore something that was lost in the garden of Eden through healing.

Medicine may be defined from a theological perspective as "a relational, healing covenant that images and participates in the covenantal healing relationship between God and his people as an outworking of the covenant of redemption."[122] Caring is a central bond between caregivers and care receivers that binds professional health personnel to those they serve.[123] In other words, caring is more than a cure because care ultimately illustrates and expresses God's salvation for humanity as provided in Christ. Caring foreshadows a central dimension of God's relationship with his people, including the eschatological resurrection from the dead of believers.

The biblical couplet of Christ, both the healer and the healed, the great physician and the suffering patient, is particularly relevant. Christ healed persons in body and soul as part of his earthly ministry.[124] The New Testament often sees Christ as the caregiver or healer. The healing ministry of Jesus was a demonstration announcing that the kingdom of God had broken into human history.[125] For instance, Matt 8:17 cites Isa 53:4, in which Matthew views the healings and exorcisms performed by Jesus as evidence for the presence of God's reign in anticipation of the future glorious kingdom. Christ's healing is more than just physical healing for the care receiver because, in the Matthean perspective, healings are only temporary tokens of the ultimate eschatological results of Jesus' redemption.[126] According to Mark 2:17, Christ calls himself a ἰατροῦ of spiritually sick. The Son of God can save the sick from their spiritual death just as physicians work among the sick to bring healing. In the Markan context, the dualism of wellness/sickness becomes a metaphor for the forgiveness of sin.[127] Luke 7:11–17 records Jesus' compassion for a widow in Nain whose son has died. Scholar John Nolland opines that the Lukan text hints that the funeral procession at

---

122. Kimbell Kornu, "The Beauty of Healing: Covenant, Eschatology, and Jonathan Edwards' Theological Aesthetics Toward a Theology of Medicine," *Christian Bioethics* 20, no. 1 (2014): 50.

123. Casto and Harsh, "Laying the Groundwork for a Christian Theology for Interprofessional Care," 394.

124. Kornu, "The Beauty of Healing: Covenant, Eschatology, and Jonathan Edwards' Theological Aesthetics Toward a Theology of Medicine," 52.

125. Harold Ellis Dollar, "A Cross-Cultural Theology of Healing" (PhD diss., Fuller Theological Seminary, 1980), 112.

126. Turner, *Matthew*, 395.

127. Robert H Stein, *Mark*, Baker Exegetical Commentary on the New Testament (Grand Rapids: Baker Academic, 2008), 248.

the gates of Nain was providentially ordered. Jesus appears to be likened to the Old Testament prophet Elijah, who also met a widow at a city gate and later restored her son to life.[128] Christ cared for the widow in Nain in the same way God cared for the widow in the times of Elijah. The Lukan language subtly underlies Christ's care and concern for the widow in the detail that he gave the young man to his mother.[129] The raising from the dead of a widow's son is an example of Christ's care for the needs of a widow. More broadly understood, the pericope attests to Christ's authority over death, mirroring the eschatological resurrection of the dead by Christ's power.

Not only is Christ the caregiver, but he is the care receiver. According to Matt 25:31–45, in the account of the judgment of the goats, Christ identifies with the least of his brothers and sisters, including the sick. Jesus mentions several acts of ministry, such as ministering to the hungry, thirsty, and strangers. Ministering to one of those is tantamount to helping Jesus himself.[130] Furthermore, not only does Christ identify with those in need, but Christ also became a sick and needy patient. According to Isa 53:10, it was God's will to crush the servant and to make him suffer or ill.[131] God made Christ sick, among other trials, to be offered as an atoning sacrifice for the sins of his people. Christ became a sacrificial offering so that through his wounds, sinners are healed (Isa 53:5). Christ suffered not only with his people but also with those who accepted his atoning sacrifice. The servant did not deserve any welts of his own, but he offered healing in return to those who could not procure spiritual health for themselves.[132] The very means by which Christ brings about healing is through his suffering as a dying care receiver. As a patient, Christ fulfills Christ's role as a healer in the darkest moment of humiliation at the cross.[133]

In conclusion, the act of care seen through the lenses of the cross assumes that people can experience, in part, the restoration of health that finally belongs to life after death. Because of what Christ has already achieved, Christians can experience something about the eschaton.[134] As scholar

---

128. John Nolland, *Luke 1:1–9:30*, Word Biblical Commentary (Grand Rapids: Zondervan, 2000), 893.

129. Leon Morris, *Luke*, Tyndale New Testament Commentaries (Downers Grove: IVP Academic, 2008), 271.

130. Turner, *Matthew*, 939.

131. Gary V. Smith, *Isaiah 40–66*, The New American Commentary (Nashville: B & H Publishing, 2009), 758.

132. John N. Oswalt, *The Book of Isaiah. Chapters 40–66*, The New International Commentary on the Old Testament (Grand Rapids: Wm. B. Eerdmans, 1998), 517.

133. Kornu, "Beauty of Healing," 10.

134. John Goldingay, "Theology and Healing," *Churchman* 92, no. 1 (1978): 30.

Kimbell Kornu notes, "Humanity lives in the eschatological already-not-yet dialectic of Christ's redemptive restoration."[135] According to a salvation-driven view of care, any healing that occurs prefigures the complete healing of Christ that will take place at the end of this age.

A Paradigm for the Physician-Patient Care Relationship

The nature of the caregiver-care-receiver relationship is central to medical care.[136] The doctor-patient relationship provides a rich and challenging discussion.[137] In the context of a vast body of literature on competing medicine models, this dissertation approaches the discussion of care relationships based on the writings of Farr Curlin and Christopher Tollefsen, *The Way of Medicine*. The argument is that the doctor-patient relationship is oriented to the good of the patient's health, motivated by a vocational commitment, and characterized by solidarity and trust.

In *The Way of Medicine*, Curlin and Tollefsen convincingly argue that contemporary medical practice has lost its clarity about the end of medicine or what the end of medicine should be. For the authors, medicine exchanged its once-recognized purpose for something amorphous, subjective, and shadowy.[138] Curlin and Tollefsen explore the caregiver-care-receiver relationship by considering two medical models.

First, the provider of services model (PSM) refers to a set of technical skills to be put to work to satisfy patient-client preferences. Healthcare workers merely provide services undertaken for patient well-being, understood to fulfill the patient's wishes. PSM is dominated by a consumerist understanding that has resulted in consequentialism, contractarianism, and principlism. According to the authors, "If the law permits an intervention, is technologically possible, and is autonomously desired by the patient,

---

135. Kornu, "Beauty of Healing," 52.

136. James J. Delaney, "The Doctor-Patient Relationship: Does Christianity Make a Difference?" *Christian Bioethics* 27, no. 1 (2021): 1.

137. For a broader discussion about the main models of the physician-patient relationship such as the paternalistic, the informative, the interpretative, and the deliberative models, see Ezekiel J. Emanuel and Linda L. Emanuel, "Four Models of the Physician-Patient Relationship," *The Journal of the American Medical Association* 267, no. 16 (1992): 21–26.

138. Farr A. Curlin and Christopher Tollefsen, *The Way of Medicine: Ethics and the Healing Profession*, Notre Dame Studies in Medical Ethics and Bioethics (Notre Dame: University of Notre Dame Press, 2021), 1.

medical practitioners should provide the intervention."[139] In this model, the physician approaches the status of functionary who serves not the human flourishing of the patient but the patient's raw desires.[140]

Curlin and Tollefsen mention three consequences of the provider-of-service model. Professional authority is eroded because the physician's expertise is merely technical. Thus, medical practitioners are subject to the power exercised by lobbyists and political advocacy groups. Second, the authors maintain that by declining professional authority, the pretense of moral seriousness is a charade, and its attempts at professionalism are a façade. Finally, the physician's claims of conscience in the medical profession come to be viewed as minimal and in competition with the profession's norms.[141]

The second model of medicine is *The Way of Medicine*. Curlin and Tollefsen maintain that *The Way of Medicine* is an alternative vision for medicine to the PSM. The Way provides physicians with a path out of the PSM. It offers physicians the resources necessary to resist the forces pushing medical practitioners to think of their relationship as merely an economic exchange. Curlin and Tollefsen articulate the Way as the internal morality of medicine,134 subject to a two-step process.

The authors uphold that medicine is a paradigmatic practice elevated to a profession. According to the Way, health or genuine human good is an objective of medical practice. A good physician orients his skills around the good of health. That is to say, the physician and the medical profession should not pursue what is unrelated to health as an objective reality. As a result, the Way protects the physicians who refuse to act in ways that would intentionally damage or destroy the good of health.

Medical care is more than a career; "It is a profession whose members make life-shaping commitments to care for particularly vulnerable persons."[142] The Way also justifies the physician who allows the patient to occupy a privileged position in his life as an objective of his concern and care. Furthermore, the medical doctor pursues patients' health while remaining mindful that health is not the only good.[143]

---

139. Curlin and Tollefsen, *Way of Medicine*, 2.

140. Christopher Tollefsen and Farr A. Curlin, "Solidarity, Trust, and Christian Faith in the Doctor-Patient Relationship," *Christian Bioethics* 27, no. 1 (2021): 15.

141. Curlin and Tollefsen, *Way of Medicine*, 3.

142. Tollefsen and Curlin, "Solidarity, Trust, and Christian Faith in the Doctor-Patient Relationship," 16.

143. Tollefsen and Curlin, "Solidarity, Trust, and Christian Faith in the Doctor-Patient Relationship," 16.

Secondly, Curlin and Tollefsen argue that medicine depends on and is accountable to the requirements of natural law and practical reason. Practical reason is conducive to human flourishing because it guides people into rational actions for their benefit. Natural law affirms the principle that health should be valued and pursued because health is instrumentally excellent and suitable for its own sake.[144] Human health is objective in the sense of being knowable, in fact, and genuinely good. The authors clarify what health is according to the Way. They argue that health, in its primary meaning, is not that of parts but of wholes. To determine the well-being of an organism, its current health must be compared to the state that precedes it metaphysically and temporally. Moreover, health is associated with activities. Health is not only concerned with the workings of the organism as a whole. Still, health also manifests in the living body's characteristic activities that are performed according to its species-specific form of life.[145] The practice of medicine does not allow the damage or destruction of an instance of an essential good for the sake of some other good. In other words, the Way is committed to doing no intentional harm.[146]

Solidarity and trust are two virtues that support the commitment to holistically serving the patient's health, assert Curlin and Tollefsen. The authors define solidarity as a firm and enduring commitment to the good of other persons. Solidarity is also not one-sided, but patients will the doctor's good in the way that patients can—the patient considers the physician to be a good doctor. From the patient's perspective, solidarity treats the doctor as a person, not simply as a functionary. Curlin and Tollefsen rightly affirm that failure of solidarity ruptures the community of the doctor-patient relationship.[147]

Physicians can also fail in solidarity with their patients. Caregivers can fail to show the much-needed solidarity in their relationship with their care receivers when they are more concerned with medicine and health without being concerned for their patients as persons. Health is seen as the goal; thus, patients represent opportunities to achieve health. Patients can also be treated as objects at the mercy of scientific investigation and technical control.[148] By lacking solidarity, physicians can see themselves as mere "me-

---

144. Tollefsen and Curlin, "Solidarity, Trust, and Christian Faith in the Doctor-Patient Relationship," 17.
145. Curlin and Tollefsen, *Way of Medicine*, 30.
146. Curlin and Tollefsen, *Way of Medicine*, 39.
147. Curlin and Tollefsen, *Way of Medicine*, 60.
148. Curlin and Tollefsen, *Way of Medicine*, 61.

chanics" of the body, thereby ignoring the totality of the human being.[149] Additionally, physicians can fail in solidarity when they deny the possibility of knowing the patient's real, objective good. This failure reduces the patient's health to a subjective well-being. Curlin and Tollefsen contend that the doctor-patient relationship is a community that makes it the physician's business to care about everything that matters to the patient. The hallmarks of the type of solidarity that focuses holistically on the patient as a person are numerous and include listening, communication, honesty, patience, silence, respect, and humility. The authors argue that by showing solidarity, caregivers respect the patient's authority and enable the patient to make decisions.[150]

The caregiver-care-receiver relationship entails the virtue of trust. Trust presupposes having faith or confidence that a person will act in ways governed by genuine concern. That is to say, trust and reliance are different. Reliance, such as relying on a car, does not require a personal relationship.[151] Trust is a matter that regards persons.

To summarize, the paradigm of the caregiver-care-receiver relationship, as revealed in *The Way*, is beneficial not only because it challenges the PSM model but also because it promotes the main trajectories of caring relationships, such as being oriented holistically to the patient, avoiding harm, and showing solidarity and trust—virtues critical especially to healing human relationships. In chapter three, Curlin and Tollefsen's view is further developed into a more biblical perspective under the theological covenant of care.

Conclusion

Chapter one endeavored to provide a theological and technical foundation that structures the theological and ethical assessing framework for using carebots in a healthcare setting.

The first section provided a primer on carebot technology. By defining the most critical terms, such as AI, robots, intelligent robots, and carebots, the chapter aimed to clarify the meaning of the terms and what is meant when the taxonomy of AI, robotics, and healthcare and carebots is used in

---

149. Mark W. Bigney, "Neither Mechanic nor High Priest" (Master of Arts, McGill University, 2006), 19.

150. Tollefsen and Curlin, "Solidarity, Trust, and Christian Faith in the Doctor-Patient Relationship," 22.

151. Tollefsen and Curlin, "Solidarity, Trust, and Christian Faith in the Doctor-Patient Relationship," 23.

this work. Furthermore, the chapter provided a selective history of the technological progress from robots to carebots to show how carebot technology is currently used and its impact on therapeutic procedures.

The second section attempted to offer a neighborly love theological framework of care within three categories of thought, including the view of God, man, and salvation. According to a theological view of care, the view of God determines the care relationship between a caregiver and care receiver. It was argued that since humanity is made in the image of a God who cares, to be human means to care. God holistically meets the needs of his people, and thus, humans must holistically approach the act of care. The caring relationship between God and people is arguably best described through the metaphor of a fatherly love toward his son. God offers security and peace, while his children adopted in Christ can enjoy the love and contentment of God as Father. The act of care is located in the second biblical commandment of importance, namely the love of neighbor. As emphasized by the Lord Jesus, the first commandment is the love of God, followed by a love of people. The implication is that care receivers must be treated and respected as human beings, not mere symptom manifestations. The role of the communion of believers is instrumental in holistic care by showing their presence and support for the sick and dying. The category of salvation underlined that God's ultimate act of care is found in the person and the finished work of Christ on the cross. Christ, in the atoning sacrifice, offers forgiveness and spiritual healing for the believers. As a result, the act of care is more than just a therapeutic endeavor; it prefigures the fullness of healing of both body and soul in the life after death.

The third section described Curlin and Tollefsen's understanding of the relationship between caregivers and care receivers as the Way. For Curlin and Tollefsen, health is an objective reality and concerns the entire organism. Medicine is also accountable to the requirements of the natural law, which is oriented to human flourishing and is genuinely good. Solidarity and trust are two mutual characteristics that describe the relationship between care professionals and care receivers.

Based on a *Cura Animarum* view of care, carebot technology appears to assist in the cure more than care, as discussed earlier in the complete sense of *cura*. Carebots may present certain benefits in indirect care such as efficient diagnosis and treatment. Carebots contribute to the relationship between caregiver and care receiver only in terms of trust in the clinical procedures as an intelligent instrument, an auxiliary tool, or an additional possibility for more efficient therapeutic care. On the other hand, based on a theological understanding of care, carebots cannot offer holistic care by themselves in a manner equivalent to that provided by a human being.

Finally, the act of care should mirror the fatherly love of God and the eschatological salvation in Christ because it allows the church to practice the love of neighbor.

CHAPTER TWO

State of the Question

Introduction

This chapter explores the current question about using AI robotic technologies in healthcare from a distinct evangelical theology perspective. It aims to reveal a gap in the literature on care robots by showing the need for theological evangelical resources that can contribute to robot ethics. This chapter claims that there is a rich literature available that covers the spectrum of AI, healthcare, and robotics from a scientific perspective. On the other hand, the chapter asserts that, despite the massive volume of literature on robots and robotics, the evangelical literature about roboethics is still in its infancy. This part of the dissertation aims to highlight the existing gap in the evangelical literature and to show how a theological evangelical framework could contribute to the conversation. Another goal of the chapter is to summarize current debates and identify questions for future research that a biblical view about roboethics could answer.

This chapter comprises two sections that examine the current literature from scientific, philosophical, and theological perspectives. The first section explores writings about AI care robotic technologies. The second section examines current literature about the dialogue between theology and philosophy and AI medical robotics. Each section ends with an evaluation that points out the strengths and weaknesses of the literature.

Current Studies about AI Care Robotic Technologies

The scientific literature about AI technology and computer engineering is well-documented. Even though the history of AI research covers a few decades, it can be observed that the enthusiasm and research have increased considerably since 2010. For instance, AI papers increased twenty-fold between 2010 and 2019 to about twenty thousand yearly. Machine learning, computer vision, and natural language processing were the most popular categories of study. Course enrollment increased five-fold in the U.S. and sixteen-fold internationally from their 2010 levels. Moreover, attendance at the NeurIPS conference has risen 800 percent since 2012 to 13,500 attendees. AI startups increased twenty-fold to over eight hundred in the US. China appears to publish more papers on AI per year than the US and about as many as Europe. Error rates for object detection improved from 28 percent in 2010 to 2 percent in 2017, exceeding human performance. The amount of computing power used in top AI applications doubles every 3.4 months. Finally, by 2019, AI systems met and exceeded human-level performance in chess, Go, ImageNet object detection, speech recognition in a limited domain, skin cancer detection, prostate cancer detection, protein folding, and diabetic retinopathy diagnosis.[1]

One of the most comprehensive manuals about AI is *Artificial Intelligence: A Modern Approach* by Stuart Russell and Peter Norvig. The authors explore the breadth of the expanding field of AI from a current perspective (2021). Their endeavor encompasses logic, mathematical formulas, pseudocode algorithms, history, ethics, and learning, to name a few. This work is appealing because the only prerequisite for reading this book is knowledge of some basic computer science concepts, and it avoids excessive formality while retaining precision.[2]

Artificial Intelligence: The Basics by Kevin Warwick is a valuable introduction to the fast-developing world of AI. Besides the technicalities of AI, Warwick helpfully offers an overview of the philosophy of AI and classical AI. Equally advantageous is his discussion about the meaning and nature of intelligence.[3]

The compendium of essays found in *Artificial Intelligence (ICAI 18)* is a profitable resource for researchers and scholars looking for the latest

---

1. Christopher Tollefsen and Farr A. Curlin, "Solidarity, Trust, and Christian Faith in the Doctor-Patient Relationship," *Christian Bioethics* 27, no. 1 (2021): 22.

2. Stuart Russell and Peter Norvig, *Artificial Intelligence: A Modern Approach*, 4th ed. (London: Pearson, 2021), 8.

3. Kevin Warwick, *Artificial Intelligence: The Basics* (London: Routledge, 2012), 1.

research results. This more technical-oriented book focuses on computer science, engineering, and applied computing. Some of the topics related to medicine are "Designing convolutional neural network architecture using genetic algorithms" and "Adaptive radius immune algorithm for multimodal function optimization in dynamic environments."[4]

Artificial Intelligence: Approaches, Tools, and Applications, edited by Brent Gordon, offers a broad perspective on the application of AI to various industries, including the medical field. For instance, some of the essays discuss the "Application of artificial intelligence in the upstream oil and gas industry," "AI applications to metal stamping die design," "Passive system reliability of the nuclear power plants using fuzzy set theory in artificial intelligence," and "Emergent tools in AI."[5]

A handy textbook on the science of designing intelligent agents is *Artificial Intelligence: Foundations of Computational Agents* by David Poole and Alan Mackworth. The authors spend considerable time discussing the nature of the reasoning and evaluating a multiagent framework system.[6]

Roboethics: A Navigating Overview by engineer Spyros Tzafestas provides an overview of the fundamental concepts, principles, and problems in robot ethics. Consequently, the book describes the core elements of ethics, such as ethics branches and theories. The work also explores the world of robots, including medical, assistive, socialized, war, and mental roboethics.[7] *Systems, Cybernetics, Control, and Automation: Ontological, Epistemological, Societal, and Ethical Issues,* by the same author, engages from a philosophical point of view cybernetics and automation. Tzafestas also discusses the ethical and societal issues related to the use of AI robots.[8]

Medical doctor Timothy Craig Allen argues in the journal article *Regulating Artificial Intelligence for a Successful Pathology Future* that AI regulation is strongly suggested in healthcare technologies. He points out that AI medical malpractice may increase liability by raising the standard of care by introducing additional measures that a physician may choose not

---

4. Hamid R. Arabnia et al., eds., *Artificial Intelligence (ICAI' 18)*, The 2018 WorldComp International Conference Proceedings (Las Vegas: CSREA Press, 2018).

5. Brent M. Gordon, ed., *Artificial Intelligence: Approaches, Tools, and Applications*, Scientific Revolutions (New York: Nova Science Publishers, 2011).

6. David L Poole and Alan K Mackworth, *Artificial Intelligence: Foundations of Computational Agents* (Cambridge: Cambridge University Press, 2010).

7. Spyros G. Tzafestas, *Roboethics: A Navigating Overview*, vol. 79, Intelligent Systems, Control and Automation: Science and Engineering (Cham: Springer International, 2016), 1.

8. Spyros G Tzafestas, *Systems, Cybernetics, Control, and Automation: Ontological, Epistemological, Societal, and Ethical Issues*, River Publishers Series in Automation, Control and Robotics (Gistrup: River Publishers, 2017).

to use. Allen also fruitfully discusses in this article the future developments of AI in medical care by highlighting that human doctors might be entirely unnecessary to diagnose or suggest a treatment.[9]

Philosopher Kyle Bogosian argues in his article *Implementation of Moral Uncertainty in Intelligent Machines* that there is an apparent disagreement between engineers and philosophers in determining a reasoning framework. He intriguingly maintains that the proper response to competing approaches regarding moral philosophy is to design machines to be fundamentally uncertain about morality.[10]

Engineer and theologian Michael S. Burdett, in his article *Artificial Intelligence and Robotics: Contributions from Science and Religion Forum* based on the work of Martin Buber, Gabriel Marcel, and Martin Heidegger, reasons that some kind of "you" speaking for artifacts is needed to combat the reduction of the world to pure utility. He also argues that there should be some limitations to the "I-you" relation to artifacts to preserve some genuine relationships with other people.[11]

Bioethicist Wendell Wallach forcibly argues in his article "From Robots to Techno Sapiens: Ethics, Law and Public Policy in the Development of Robotics and Neurotechnologies" that governmental authorities need to develop evaluative methodologies given the challenges posed by the emerging technologies. The risks associated with robotics and neurotechnologies are existential risks, ethical and legal concerns, combinatorial risks, and societal impacts.[12]

Scientist Edoardo Datteri suggests in the paper "Predicting the Long-Term Effects of Human-Robot Interaction: A Reflection on Responsibility in Medical Robotics" that despite the ethical novelty introduced by medical robotics, prospective responsibility is related to robotics engineering. Datteri vigilantly classifies possible harmful events in anomalous robotic behaviors that roboticists can address. The second category of harm, which is more ethically complex, involves actions involving no anomalous robot behavior. The author also points out the tremendous assistance AI robots

---

9. Timothy Craig Allen, "Regulating Artificial Intelligence for a Successful Pathology Future," *Archives of Pathology & Laboratory Medicine* 143, no. 10 (2019).

10. Kyle Bogosian, "Implementation of Moral Uncertainty in Intelligent Machines," *Minds and Machines* 27, no. 4 (2017).

11. Michael S. Burdett, "Artificial Intelligence and Robotics: Contributions from the Science and Religion Forum," *Zygon* 55, no. 2 (2020).

12. Wendell Wallach, "From Robots to Techno Sapiens: Ethics, Law and Public Policy in the Development of Robotics and Neurotechnologies," *Law, Innovation and Technology* 3, no. 2 (2011).

can give healthcare. Nevertheless, some responsibility problems must be evaluated by ethicists, theologians, and scientists.[13]

A helpful article about machine learning is "A Data-Driven Approach to Predicting Diabetes and Cardiovascular Disease with Machine Learning." This work makes a compelling case that machine learning can build models that can predict future developments; it can improve diagnostic accuracy, augment diagnoses, and improve outcomes, and it is the most cost-efficient. The most significant improvement is that machine learning advances the efficiency of the healthcare system.[14]

"When AIs Outperform Doctors: Confronting the Challenges of a Tort-Induced Over-Reliance on Machine Learning" is a vital resource discussing the legal implications of machine learning in AI robotic technologies. The authors believe that there will be a day when diagnostics generated by ML will have better success than those generated by human doctors. As a result, the existing medical malpractice law will require improvements to a new standard of care represented by ML-generated medical diagnostics.[15]

Philosopher Nel Noddings argues in *Caring: A Relational Approach to Ethics and Moral Education* for an intriguing moral approach to therapy from a feminist perspective. Noddings proposes that a motherhood language that focuses on relationships, needs, care, response, and connection rather than principles, justice, rights, and hierarchy is a viable approach to medical ethics. For Noddings, the ethics of care puts limited faith in principles by going deeper behind the principle and by maintaining and enhancing caring relations.[16]

In *Building Moral Robots: Ethical Pitfalls and Challenges*, ethicist John Stewart Gordon maintains that building a moral machine from a theoretical standpoint is possible, but the builders need suitable ethical expertise. Furthermore, Gordon adds to the discussion that it might be helpful to use a pluralistic ethical method for a machine to solve moral problems instead of relying solely on a particular moral approach.[17]

13. Edoardo Datteri, "Predicting the Long-Term Effects of Human-Robot Interaction: A Reflection on Responsibility in Medical Robotics," *Science and Engineering Ethics* 19, no. 1 (2013).

14. An Dinh et al., "A Data-Driven Approach to Predicting Diabetes and Cardiovascular Disease with Machine Learning," *BMC Medical Informatics and Decision Making* 19, no. 1 (2019).

15. Michael A. Froomkin, Ian Kerr, and Joelle Pineau, "When AIs Outperform Doctors: Confronting the Challenges of a Tort-Induced Over-Reliance on Machine Learning," *Arizona Law Review* 61, no. 1 (2019).

16. Nel Noddings, *Caring: A Relational Approach to Ethics & Moral Education*, 2nd ed. (Berkeley: University of California Press, 2013).

17. John-Stewart Gordon, "Building Moral Robots: Ethical Pitfalls and Challenges,"

In the *Landscape of Machine Implemented Ethics,* computer scientist Vivek Nallur indicates there needs to be a consensus on which ethical theory best suits AI technologies in medicine. Another valuable concern pointed out by Nallur is a viable alternative to insert some ethical standard in an autonomous machine is the training of the human software developer. By training the human developer, Nallur considers it possible to consciously or subconsciously insert ethical standards into the machine.[18]

The leading textbook with an enormous impact on bioethics is the *Principles of Biomedical Ethics* by Tom Beauchamp and James Childress. Beauchamp's and Childress's bioethics principles, including autonomy, nonmaleficence, beneficence, and justice, are prominent ethical theories in medicine. The four principles are intended to synthesize a vast area of moral principles into a basic rule of bioethics.[19] Despite the immense value of Beauchamp's and Childress's work, it has been criticized. Ethicist Matthew Shea argues in "Principlism's Balancing Act: Why the Principles of Biomedical Ethics Need a Theory of the Good" that a significant problem with principlism is that it lacks a theory of the good. As a result, principlism cannot be an adequate ethical framework until it develops a theory of the good that will offer a satisfactory solution to the problems of specification and balancing.[20]

In *Demystifying AI in Healthcare: Historical Perspectives and Current Considerations,* the authors argue that it is unlikely that AI machines will replace clinicians. On the contrary, they believe that AI has the potential to make healthcare more succinct and personalized by augmenting some processes. However, to have AI used in healthcare, the authors contend that training both emerging and experienced clinicians and clinician acceptance and change management will be needed.[21]

Science and Engineering Ethics 26, no. 1 (2020).

18. Vivek Nallur, "Landscape of Machine Implemented Ethics," *Science and Engineering Ethics* 26, no. 5 (n.d.).

19. Tom L. Beauchamp and James F. Childress, *Principles of Biomedical Ethics,* 8th ed. (New York: Oxford University Press, 2019).

20. Matthew Shea, "Principlism's Balancing Act: Why the Principles of Biomedical Ethics Need a Theory of the Good," *The Journal of Medicine and Philosophy: A Forum for Bioethics and Philosophy of Medicine* 45 (2020): 441.

21. Daniel Quest et al., "Demystifying AI in Healthcare: Historical Perspectives and Current Considerations," *Physician Leadership Journal* 8, no. 1 (2021).

An Assessment of Current Literature on AI Care Robots

The current literature, from a scientific perspective, is vast. The works cover topics from the most elemental parts of AI technologies, such as hardware and software, to the difficulties posed by the endeavor to insert values and ethics into program computer systems.

What appears to be a recurrent theme is that the future of AI and all its implications is simply unpredictable. There is a trackable history of AI technologies and robotics. AI robots are also used in many areas, from the medical spectrum to war robots. However, considering the emerging technologies within AI, such as machine learning and artificial neural networks, it appears safe to argue that the future course of AI could be more precise.

Furthermore, most literature highlights both positive and negative implications of AI technologies. The current works do not appear to emphasize an exciting AI-dominated future, nor do they resort to fear and panic. Given the history of AI with its so-called "winters," it could be argued that current literature has reached a level of maturity, especially in managing the emotional side involved in developing emerging technologies. The negative implications of AI technologies seem to be similar in most studies. They vary from data and privacy violations to algorithmic biases that could be integrated into systems.

In addition, an overwhelming amount of literature stresses the need to develop some AI policies. To maximize the benefits of AI, such as cost and time effectiveness, there is a growing interest in developing strategies to minimize the risks inherent to such a system. From an ethical perspective, there are recurring morally problematic issues, including bias, privacy, and security.

Also, the current literature is uncertain about the irreplaceability of human doctors in the context of emerging AI technologies. Considering that there are areas where AI outperforms clinicians, scholarly resources cannot give a definite response regarding the future of AI in healthcare and the role of human doctors.

Within the body of AI research, there is a significant disagreement regarding the ethical systems that should be implemented in machines. Some scholars favor top-down approaches, while others prefer bottom-up methods to be embedded in AI systems. However, what appears to be a somewhat unifying idea is that scientists are open to developing a pluralist ethical approach to emerging intelligent technologies.

Current Studies on the Dialogue Between Theology and AI Care Robotic Technologies

The evangelical theological engagement with AI care robots is limited. This engagement has been explored in very few studies. *The Way of Medicine: Ethics and the Healing Profession* by physician Farr Curlin and philosopher Christopher Tollefsen adds much to the conversation between philosophical theology and medicine. They argue against the highly compartmentalized view of medicine that separates the personal from the professional so that personal values will not interfere with professional obligation. Curlin and Tollefsen propose a traditional vision of medicine that is different from the mainstream healthcare model, where medicine is merely a provider of services. The authors argue for the Way of Medicine model, where medicine is a profession and health is an objective natural norm for any organism in its totality.[22]

Bioethicist Edmund Pellegrino and Professor David Thomasma maintain in *For the Patient's Good: The Restoration of Beneficence in Health Care* that neither the paternalistic view of medicine nor the principle of patient autonomy works. Helpfully, they propose and elaborate on the beneficence model, which has a covenantal relationship between physician and patient at its center.[23] *The Christian Virtues in Medical Practice* is another helpful resource by the same two authors. In this work, Pellegrino and Thomasma emphasize the kind of person a Christian physician should be. Based on the works of Thomas Aquinas and the Bible, they employ a conjunction of natural and revealed ethics from virtue-based ethics.[24]

In *Vulnerability and Care: Christian Reflections on the Philosophy of Medicine,* theologian Andrew Sloane proposes a philosophical-theological framework that intriguingly claims that medicine has nothing to do with health or alleviating suffering. For Sloane, medicine is an expression of care for vulnerable human beings. Medicine aims to care for vulnerable people, demonstrate solidarity with them, and enable patients to return to a reasonable level of functioning in relationships.[25] Similarly, Sloane expounds on

---

22. Farr A. Curlin and Christopher Tollefsen, *The Way of Medicine: Ethics and the Healing Profession*, Notre Dame Studies in Medical Ethics and Bioethics (Notre Dame: University of Notre Dame Press, 2021).

23. Edmund D. Pellegrino and David C. Thomasma, *For the Patient's Good: The Restoration of Beneficence in Health Care* (New York: Oxford University Press, 1988).

24. Edmund D. Pellegrino and David C. Thomasma, *The Christian Virtues in Medical Practice*, ed. David G. Miller (Washington: Georgetown University Press, 1996).

25. Andrew Sloane, *Vulnerability and Care: Christian Reflections on the Philosophy of Medicine*, vol. 4, T & T Clark Religion and the University Series (London: Bloomsbury T & T Clark, 2016), 4–5.

his ethical framework in an article, "Love in a Time of Ebola: Reflections on Theology of Medicine in Resource-Challenged Environments." The author maintains that medicine is about care. The goal of medicine in a resource-challenged context is to care for a patient so that his inherent worth as a member of the human community is affirmed and that he can function well in the community.[26]

Another work contributing to the discussion is "The Beauty of Healing: Covenant, Eschatology, and Jonathan Edwards' Theological Aesthetics Toward a Theology of Medicine" by ethicist Kimbell Kornu. The author intriguingly proposes a biblical ethical framework through the lens of Edwardsian beauty with Christ as an archetypal physician and patient for a covenantal, eschatological medicine theology. According to Kornu, bodily or spiritual healing is a gift of God. It creates images and participates in the eschatological already-not-yet dialectic of Christ's redemptive restoration.[27]

The Anticipatory Corpse: Medicine, Power, and the Care of the Dying by philosopher Jeffrey Bishop also argues for a caring principle for the patient, as informed by philosopher Michel Foucault's genealogy of medicine and power. This resource provokes thought and argument since it goes against the mainstream message of contemporary medicine that functions to preserve life. Bishop stimulatingly claims that death is at the center of medicine. For him, death informs a philosophy of medicine, as seen in the practices surrounding the dying.[28]

Hostility to Hospitality: Spirituality and Professional Socialization Within Medicine makes the case that medicine should integrate religion and spirituality to deliver a holistic healthcare service. Sociologist Michael Balboni and radiation oncologist Tracy Balboni contend that American medicine is spiritually sick because the healthcare system separates the scientific element from the spiritual care of patients. The authors make the case that clinicians should provide deep human care to the sick in a medical system dominated by impersonal and mechanical factors.[29]

---

26. Andrew Sloane, "Love in a Time of Ebola: Reflections on Theology of Medicine in Resource-Challenged Environments," *Christian Journal for Global Health* 3, no. 1 (2016): 77.

27. Kimbell Kornu, "The Beauty of Healing: Covenant, Eschatology, and Jonathan Edwards' Theological Aesthetics Toward a Theology of Medicine," *Christian Bioethics* 20, no. 1 (2014): 52.

28. Jeffrey P. Bishop, *The Anticipatory Corpse: Medicine, Power, and the Care of the Dying* (Notre Dame: Notre Dame Press, 2011), 8.

29. Michael J. Balboni and Tracy A. Balboni, *Hostility to Hospitality: Spirituality and Professional Socialization within Medicine* (New York: Oxford University Press, 2019), 6.

Against Balboni's perspective, Professor Christine Davis argues in a journal article, "Hospitality Happens: Dialogic Ethics of Care," that medical care is in and of itself an inherent manifestation of spirituality. For Davis, spirituality is found in caring acts, regardless of the amount of religiosity or theological jargon in medical care. Thus, the author argues that the seeming gap between medicine and faith, between the sacred and the secular, is one of definition, not practice.[30]

Sociologist Raymond De Vries in *Making Medicine Care* also responds to Balboni's thesis. For De Vries, Balboni's dividing gap in medicine, the religion-medicine gap, obscures the relationship between the two institutions. De Vries argues that Balboni does not understand how the spirituality of immanence interacts with religion and how faith operates in medicine and medical science.[31]

Biologist James Bradley suggests in *Re-Creation Nature: Science, Technology, and Human Values in the Twenty-First Century* that modern biotechnologies can determine the future of human nature itself. His discussion about robots and robot ethics is constructive. Bradley adds to the debate concerning robot ethics, emphasizing the relationship between humans and robots. He argues that humans should focus on the relationships with AI, not on mechanics, for the moral use of robotics in healthcare.[32]

In his PhD dissertation, "An Evangelical Critical Assessment of AI-Driven Robotic Persons and the Risks of Dehumanization," Joshua K. Smith claims that evangelical scholarship lags behind in addressing the current trends in robotics and AI. The evangelical assessment of personhood in the field of AI robots is compulsory to address the forthcoming anthropological crisis, as none currently exists, believes Smith. The author makes the case that "the closer potential AI-driven robots come in proximity to the identity of humans, the further the image of God in humans is distorted."[33]

Computer scientist Derek Schuurman believes that AI technologies are inevitable and invites evangelical academics to join the conversation about theology and AI technologies. In his article "Artificial Intelligence: Discerning a Christian Response," he makes the case that based on a Christian worldview, an evangelical philosopher should navigate the world of AI

---

30. Christine S. Davis, "Hospitality Happens: Dialogic Ethics of Care," *Society* 56, no. 2 (2019): 131–32.

31. Raymond De Vries, "Making Medicine Care," *Society* 56, no. 2 (2019): 135.

32. James T. Bradley, *Re-Creation Nature: Science, Technology, and Human Values in the Twenty-First Century* (Tuscaloosa: The University of Alabama Press, 2019).

33. Joshua K. Smith, "An Evangelical Critical Assessment of AI Driven Robotic Persons and the Risks of Dehumanization" (PhD diss. Midwestern Baptist Theological Seminary, 2020), 1.

by discussing ontological issues. For Schuurman, the natural progression of the discussion should start by clarifying the ontological elements, such as the difference between humans and machines, and then move on to epistemology. As a result, a Christian philosopher can be equipped to wrestle with the ethical issues that arise in AI technologies.[34]

The Ethics & Religious Liberty Commission (ERLC) produced a statement in 2019 titled "Artificial Intelligence: An Evangelical Statement of Principles." Intended to help Southern Baptist believers significantly, the document clarifies that AI technologies will allow people to achieve unprecedented possibilities. On the other hand, the documents acknowledge the potential risks AI poses if used without wisdom and care.[35] According to this statement, AI is not morally neutral, and only the Lord Jesus can fulfill humanity's ultimate needs. Regarding the use of AI in medicine, the document maintains that medical technologies are expressions of God's common grace through and for people. Intriguingly, the ERLC position favors using some basic principles of medical ethics, such as beneficence, non-maleficence, autonomy, and justice, "which are all consistent with the biblical principle of loving our neighbor." The ERLC statement observes that utilitarian applications regarding healthcare distribution should not override the dignity of human life. Moreover, the statement forcibly rejects the consequentialist ethical system "that understands medical applications of AI as a means of improving, changing, or completing human beings."

An Assessment of the Dialogue Between Theology and AI Care Robotic Technologies

The dialogue between theology, philosophy, and medicine includes a rich conversation that has developed over time. According to the current literature, there is a significant discussion between secular-informed moralities and faith-based literature, especially from writers in the Catholic church. Nevertheless, the evangelical works that evaluate AI systems (and to a lesser extent those concerning AI care robots in healthcare), though limited, do offer well-thought-out critical evaluation to the conversation. For instance, the ERLC statement about the general AI, which is biblically informed,

---

34. Derek C Schuurman, "Artificial Intelligence: Discerning a Christian Response," *Perspectives on Science and Christian Faith* 71, no. 2 (2019): 79.

35. "Artificial Intelligence: An Evangelical Statement of Principles" (ERLC, 2019), https://www.erlc.com/resource-library/statements/artificial-intelligence-an-evangelical-statement-of-principles/.

emerged only in 2019. While useful in the conversation, the ERLC document arguably joined the debate relatively late.

The theological and philosophical works do not agree on the definition of medicine or its goals. A definition of medical care covers a broad spectrum of areas, from preserving health to preventing disease and from relief of suffering to care for the ill. Some philosophers prefer to approach medicine from a strictly somatic perspective. In contrast, others envision a more holistic method of health that includes both the body and the spiritual component of a human being.

Furthermore, the approach differs between the more traditional health methodologies and the latest ones. One observation is that the ethical theories that dominated medical care in the last couple of decades, such as Beauchamp's and Childress's principles of bioethics, appear to be challenged by some moral theories of care. If the focus was more on the scientific/mechanical model of health in the past, the last developments arguably tend to emphasize a relationship-care approach to health.

Conclusion

This chapter describes and analyzes the state of the question about AI care robots in healthcare. It also argues that rich literature covers the spectrum of AI, healthcare, and robotics from a scientific and philosophical perspective. This section also highlights that the evangelical literature about roboethics needs to develop.

Overall, the studies on the scientific aspect of AI envisage a future where intelligent machines will become part and parcel of life. The future involves a digital era that implies substantial societal changes. However, there needs to be more consideration in the current literature about the future role of humans in congruence with intelligent autonomous agents. This dissertation highlights what is more concrete in the scientific literature, specifically related to the future of AI and human doctors. This work favors a position that encourages a relationship between human doctors and AI assistants that contributes to patient-human doctor care instead of a purely AI-based healthcare service.

The current literature proves a prolific discussion between theology, philosophy, and medicine. However, given the disagreements concerning even the elemental understanding of medicine, there appears to be a need in the academic literature to help clarify it. This work develops a much-needed view of medicine and its goals, which are faithful to a biblical account concerning AI care robots in healthcare. More than that, spirituality in medicine is another category of thinking that could be improved. Spirituality, which is involved in a theology of care, offers an alternative to a mechanistic view of medicine. Furthermore, there appears to be a need from a distinct evangelical theological framework to engage more deeply in how AI will affect societies and people's lives, especially concerning the critical role that AI robots play in medical care.

CHAPTER THREE

Wisdom of the Past

Introduction

THIS CENTRAL CHAPTER OF the dissertation builds upon the examination of a theological, ecclesiological, and historical perspective of care. The rich care tradition in Scripture and the early church provides a paradigmatic epistemic framework for the neighbor-love ethical system. The articulation of this framework both allows for an in-depth discussion of care issues and represents an invaluable resource to inform ethical guidelines about current usages of AiRs technologies in a healthcare context developed in the next chapter. The main argument of this section makes the case that based on a theological-ecclesiological-historical view of care, carebot technologies must only be used in ways consistent with a biblically informed vision of medicine and with how the early church sought care and healing for a sound moral assessment.[1] Rather than creating a novel version of ethical care, the main objective of a biblical and ecclesiological understanding of medicine is to care for the sick and dying aided by the possibility of curing.

This chapter also attempts to answer a simple yet profound question: "What does it mean to turn to Scripture as a moral resource (and for that matter, to the early church's practice of medical care) for carebot technologies?" More specifically, the chapter tries to answer questions such as "Do

---

1. See Kevin Vanhoozer and Owen Strachan, "Introduction: Pastors, Theologians, and Other Public Figures," in *The Pastor as Public Theologian: Reclaiming a Lost Vision* (Grand Rapids: Baker Academic, 2015), 26.

AiRs have the capacity to serve the biblical purposes and methods of care?" and "How has the church addressed the care of neighbors in the past?"

The section is divided into three parts to answer these questions and to provide evidence for the chapter's main argument. The first part deals with the theological anthropology of a patient under four primary categories: (1) patients as sick people, (2) health and flourishing in a fallen world, (3) flourishing within the boundaries of a fallen condition, and (4) flourishing and life after death. The second part focuses on the church practice of medical care. This section synthesizes the development of the care of the sick in the classical world and the Christian age. The final part of the chapter provides some theological considerations that integrate Scripture and church practice about carebot technologies in direct patient care.

A Theological Anthropology of a Patient

Before discussing a theological perspective of medical care as informed by a theological anthropology of a patient, an answer to two basic questions needs to be in place. The two fundamental questions are "What is medicine?" and "What is medicine for?" As discussed in chapter one, Curlin and Tollefsen criticize the modern view of medicine as a provider of services model (PSM) that considers medical care to comprise a set of technical skills to be put to work to satisfy patients' preferences.[2] The PSM's perspective of medicine results in health professionals merely providing services that satisfy the patient's wishes. The physician's judgment and claim to conscience are regarded as in competition with the profession's norms. A physician's conscience in performing the act of care is only considered as an intrusion of private concerns "into transactions that should be governed by physicians' professional commitment to providing legally permitted services to patients who request those services."[3]

Medicine is also seen as a profession that aims for patients' health. According to Curlin and Tollefsen, medicine is a paradigmatic practice elevated to a profession because of its social importance. Medical care is concentrated around the good of health by avoiding entanglement with goods or socially constructed norms other than health. The good of health is objective rather than abstract and focused on the patient's concrete needs.

---

2. Farr A. Curlin and Christopher Tollefsen, *The Way of Medicine: Ethics and the Healing Profession*, Notre Dame Studies in Medical Ethics and Bioethics (Notre Dame: University of Notre Dame Press, 2021), 2.

3. Curlin and Tollefsen, *Way of Medicine*, 3.

The patient's needs are central to the medical profession and care.[4] Based on Curlin and Tollefsen's view of medicine, health is the end of medicine. Even though later in the chapter, there will be a more extended discussion about health and flourishing, it is sufficient here to mention that health is the end of medicine, as it is supported by the evidence of authority developed for thousands of years. In addition, the proposal is sustained by diverse moral communities that health is the intrinsic purpose of medical care. Preserving health and alleviating suffering is central to Judaism, Christianity, Islam, and those not considered religious.[5]

Margaret Mohrmann's understanding of medicine appears helpful in developing Curlin and Tollefsen's instrumental definition theologically. Mohrmann's perspective enriches the concept of medicine as a profession and a ministry. The Christian theological tenets provide an ethical framework focusing on the patient's needs. Medicine as a ministry is a service to those who suffer that draws its workers from within and beyond the ranks of medical professionals. Not only that, but Mohrmann also maintains that the profession of a Christian health worker is an instrument where God's love can be applied to people.[6] Accordingly, Pellegrino and Thomasma argue that medicine can be distorted when considered only as a career. However, medicine can be perfected when regarded as a vocation or commitment. For the Christian health worker, medicine is a vocation when God's call for believers transmutes any occupation in service for others.[7]

Ethicist William May uses similar terms to describe the relationship between caregiver and care receiver, such as "covenant." But the rich theological term "covenant" suggests an even more inclusive understanding of views of medicine than Curlin and Tollefsen, as well as Mohrmann. For May, covenantal medicine is more than a transactional exchange. Covenant in medicine refers to the internal nature of the parties involved, not merely the external nature of contractual terms. Covenants also presuppose a graceful, growing edge that springs from ontological change and builds relationships.[8] A vital element of a covenant is its location in the transcendent.

---

4. Curlin and Tollefsen, *Way of Medicine*, 4.

5. Curlin and Tollefsen, *Way of Medicine*, 20.

6. Margaret E. Mohrmann, *Medicine as Ministry* (Cleveland: The Pilgrim Press, 1995), 10.

7. Edmund D. Pellegrino and David C. Thomasma, *Helping and Healing: Religious Commitment and Health Care* (Washington, D.C.: Georgetown University Press, 1997), 95.

8. William F. May, *The Physician's Covenant: Images of the Healer in Medical Ethics*, 2nd ed. (Louisville: Westminster John Knox Press, 2000), 128.

Transcendence lays out the larger horizon in which human service occurs and the standards to measure that service, argues May.⁹

What does applied covenantal ethics look like in relationships with colleagues and patients? The practical results of the PSM versus covenantal model of care are cogent. According to May, professional self-regulation and discipline are part of the long tradition of medicine dating back to Hippocrates that distinguished between codal duties to patients and covenantal obligations to the physician's teacher. The physician's indebtedness to the teacher or professional colleagues in the modern world implies a sense of gravity in medical care. The depth of commitment to the medical profession and the patients "includes the codal duty to become technically proficient; it includes the obligation to meet the minimal terms of contract, but it also requires much more. This more intense obligation, moreover, may finally help not only patients but also troubled colleagues."¹⁰

May also sees covenantal ethics as owing a double fidelity, both to medical knowledge and to the sufferer who benefits from the healer's professional virtue. The fidelity of the medical practitioner requires disinterested discernment, judgment, and action for the patient's well-being. Professional medical ethics should avoid interested fidelity to the patients, as in the cases of overtreatment and undertreatment. Additionally, May maintains that fidelity to patients is not only transactional but transformational. The transformational side of covenant care responds not only to the patient's self-perceived wants but to the deeper needs that concern the roots of the medical problem, such as the case of insomnia. In dealing with deep issues that may cause physical suffering, the physician needs to be truth-telling with prudence and discretion. Even though the medical practitioner cannot cure some physical problems, such as cancer, she can help keep the patient whole, even in extreme situations. May concludes that physicians should dispense "pellets of the truth" about a patient's condition, but "such pellets, unsupported by faithful care and by care that takes the form of sensitive teaching, can be lethal and anything but respectful to the patients."¹¹

Covenants, in the biblical sense, describe relationships between persons, not between providers and clients; this is the opposite of the PSM. For Ben Mitchell, covenantal medicine, rooted in the ancient covenants between God and his people, is based on unequal relationships where physicians

---

9. May, *Physician's Covenant*, 139.
10. May, *Physician's Covenant*, 142–48.
11. May, *Physician's Covenant*, 148–54.

offer clinical art and skill "over against patient's disease." Not only that, but covenants are relational, where patients are cared for as persons.[12]

To sum up, it appears safe to suggest that a theological understanding of medicine is that medical care is a covenantal ministry aiming at a patient's health. By shifting from a covenantal view of medicine to a contractual paradigm, medical care exacerbates the lack of trust that may exist between a patient and a health provider. Contracts emphasize the need for terms, whereas covenants emphasize the loving, deep, and enduring relationship that goes beyond specific actions and terms. Another possible consequence of moving from a covenantal to a contractual system is the misplaced priority in medical care. For care providers, pursuing wealth may become more of a priority than caring for the patient and putting their interests, needs, and well-being first.

According to covenantal medical care, patients are sick people who desire to be healthy and flourish. Medical covenant also sees illness and disease as real, not ultimate, with the hope of bodily resurrection in the Eschaton. The development of this argument follows.

Patients as sick people

Covenant medical ministry relates to patients as sick people. Medical technical terminology includes an extensive vocabulary for describing body parts, treatments, and bodily functions and often needs some explanations of words that seem straightforward. One such term is the word "patient." Anyone who seeks medical attention inside the hospital is called a patient. A patient is someone who suffers or awaits. Seeing patients as sick people encourages picturing a natural person needing help. To take a step further in a theological understanding of the sufferer is to see her in the light of the second person of the Godhead, Jesus Christ, who is the perfect human being and the exact representation of God.

A General Understanding of The Image of God

According to a Christian perspective, one of the foundational understandings of human beings is that people are created in the image of God. Being made in the image of God bestows dignity and honor on every person,

---

12. C. Ben Mitchell, "Medicine: Contract or Covenant. (Editorial)," *Ethics and Medicine* 36, no. 1 (2020): 5–6.

regardless of social, mental, or physical status.[13] To be created in the צֶלֶם (image) and תְּמוּנָה (likeness) of God sets the foundation for human identity and relationships, including the caregiver-care-receiver relationship. The terms "image" and "likeness" employ a Hebrew form of speech in which parallelism is used to clarify how a phrase is used in its present context. Genesis 1:26–27 teaches that to be created in God's image is equivalent to God's likeness. Being made in the image and likeness of God means resembling God's character.[14] However, according to scholar Victor Hamilton, the term "likeness" is somewhat less critical than "image" based on its omission in the following verse. A possible reason is that even though man is created in the image of God, a person is not the exact image of God.[15]

In discussions of theological anthropology, the issue of the image of God has been problematic. The entire teaching concerning the image rests on a small number of biblical texts, such as Gen 1:26–27; 5:1–2; 9:6, and Jas 3:9. Professor John Hammett helpfully summarizes the three primary ways in which the image of God in humans has been understood in recent history. Hammett explains that (1) John Collins understands the image to be a resemblance, symbolic and relational; (2) J. Wentzel van Huysteen and Millard Erickson suggest that image can be seen in substantive, functional, and relational terms; (3) Marc Cortez also provides a structural, functional, and relational valence to the image.[16] In what follows, the section briefly documents some defining aspects of human nature, emphasizing the central consensus of the interpretation of the image of God, such as relational capacity.

Humans as Relational Beings

Being created in God's image means having dominion and being fruitful. In addition, human beings created in God's likeness appears to suggest that human relationships are part of the created order. Human relationships are not accidents of history but resemble the nature of God who created them. The three persons of the Trinity are in a relationship with each other. Since human relationships are part of creation and based on God's nature, they are

---

13. Judith Allen Shelly, Arlene B. Miller, and Kimberley H. Fenstermacher, *Called to Care: A Christian Vision for Nursing*, 3rd ed. (Downers Grove: InterVarsity Press, 2021), 58.

14. Nathan Jastram, "The Image of God and Marriage," *Logia* 30, no. 3 (2021): 41.

15. Victor P. Hamilton, *The Book of Genesis Chapters 1–17*, The New International Commentary of the Old Testament (Grand Rapids: Wm. B. Eerdmans, 1990), 324.

16. John S. Hammett, "A Whole Bible Approach to Interpreting Creation in God's Image.," *Southwestern Journal of Theology* 63, no. 2 (2021): 29.

a distinct part of what it means to be human.[17] To be made in the image of God includes a particular type of relationship that refers both to God and other people. People are made with the capacity to have a relationship with God. A relationship with God should lead to the right relationships with other humans and the creation itself.[18]

According to Gen 2:18, God created humans to live in a community. People were made to live in a relationship with each other. A primary example of the most basic unit of relationships is the family. The concept of family is God's idea and is regarded highly throughout Scripture. What is remarkable in the Bible's perspective about family is that God's people were called to care for those people who did not have families.[19] Deuteronomy 10:17–22 presents some of the desires of the God of Israel to his people. Verses 17–18, in particular, point to a powerful assertion of God's character that illustrates the Lord's commitment to justice as essential fairness. God is committed to equity in judicial resolution, regardless of a person's economic, social, or racial status. Specifically, God appears to be determined to defend the justice of the orphans and widows who were outside the supportive social network of the community and who were susceptible to being victimized and reduced to poverty.[20] Shelly et al. also argue that the New Testament expands the concept of family to include the whole believing community characterized by love and relatedness.[21] John 13:34–35 makes the case that the people of the new covenant will demarcate themselves from the rest of the world by loving one another. Christian love for one another is grounded in the work of God and is an expression of the nature of God himself.[22]

Furthermore, Scripture is clear that loving relationships go beyond the family and Christian community. The image of God in people determines that Christians love their neighbors, even the enemy. According to Luke 10:25–37, the Lord Jesus deliberately chose an outsider and a hated man to indicate that being a neighbor is not a matter of nationality or race. The

---

17. Jastram, "Image of God and Marriage," 41.

18. Hammett, "Whole Bible Approach to Interpreting Creation in God's Image.," 36.

19. Shelly, Miller, and Fenstermacher, *Called to Care: A Christian Vision for Nursing*, 63.

20. Bill T. Arnold, *The Book of Deuteronomy Chapters 1–11*, The New International Commentary of the Old Testament (Grand Rapids: Wm. B. Eerdmans Publishing, 2022), 1423.

21. Shelly, Miller, and Fenstermacher, *Called to Care: A Christian Vision for Nursing*, 63.

22. Edward W. Klink III, *John*, Zondervan Exegetical Commentary on the New Testament (Grand Rapids: Zondervan, 2016), 1194.

Lukan text illustrates that the love of one's neighbor should transcend all natural or human boundaries such as race, ethnicity, religion, and economic or educational status.[23] Based on a relational understanding of the image of God in people, care cannot be adequately discussed if people are seen only as isolated individuals. As Shelly et al. maintain, care is applied well when sick persons are viewed in the context of families, communities, and cultures.[24]

Finally, every human life is precious and valuable because God has made them sacred. Humans are created in the image of God, but that does not mean that they are sacred beings. The lives of human beings are not inherently sacred because only God is holy. However, as physician Margaret Mohrmann puts it, any human being possesses derived sacredness from God's holiness.[25]

Humans as Multidimensional Beings

Fundamental to the understanding of human beings made in the image of God is that both man and woman are embodied souls who have received the breath of God. A human being is made of body and soul, according to Gen 2:7. Adam is created according to the will and design of God and becomes a living being (שְׁפֶן הָיָח). This implies that God's creative work results from the soul and body.[26] Human beings are different from animals because they are embodied souls. As an embodied soul in the image of God, man receives the ruling authority to act as God's vice-regent to name the animals.[27]

The multidimensionality of human beings is expressed through different words in Scripture. Concerning the physical part of a person, the Bible uses a broad conceptual spectrum of terms. The word שְׁפֶן (soul) refers to a person as a living creature, but it also implies the inner self, such as thinking, feeling, willing, and desiring.[28] Other words that describe a person in the Old Testament are הָיָוּג (body), רָשָׂב (flesh), מָצֵע (bone), בֵּל (heart), דִי (hand), עוֹרְזָא (arm), לְגֶר (foot), שׁאר (head), זוֹשֵׁל, (tongue) and הָפ (mouth).

23. Robert A. Stein, *Luke*, The New American Commentary (Nashville: B & H Publishing, 1992), 624.

24. Shelly, Miller, and Fenstermacher, *Called to Care: A Christian Vision for Nursing*, 64.

25. Mohrmann, *Medicine as Ministry*, 32.

26. Strachan, *Reenchanting Humanity*, 23.

27. Kenneth Jr. Cherney, "Distinctively Human: An Anthropology of Genesis 1 and 2," *Wisconsin Lutheran Quarterly* 119, 1 (2022): 25.

28. Mangum, Douglas, ed. *A Dictionary of Biblical Languages with Semantic Domains: Hebrew*, s.v. "נֶפֶשׁ." Bellingham, WA: Lexham, 2014.

The New Testament uses similar terms to describe human beings. These words are σῶμα (body), σάρξ (flesh), καρδία (heart), χείρ (hand), κεφαλή (head), γλῶσσα (tongue), στόμα (mouth) and πρόσωπον (face).[29]

Scripture describes the spiritual dimension of a person, including terms such as רוּחַ (spirit). Its basic meaning of רוּחַ is wind, a wind that sweeps over the waters, and a breezy time of the day. The word also means breath and, by extension, vital powers or strength. For instance, a person's spirit sustains her through illness (Prov 18:14), and when taken back, the person returns to dust (Ps 104:29–30). In addition, the spirit can refer to feelings, such as when the queen of Sheba was left breathless when she saw the wisdom and wealth of Solomon (1 Kgs 10:5). The spirit also uses a meaning concerning the will. God stirs the spirits or wills of people to rebuild the temple (Ezra 1:5). Another example is when Caleb had a different spirit from the other spies (Num 14:24).[30] The closest New Testament word for רוּחַ appears to be the term πνεῦμα (spirit). Πνεῦμα can mean the air in movement, such as wind, breathing out of the air, and that which animates or gives life to the body. The word is also understood as a part of human personality, which denotes the immaterial part (2 Cor 7:1 and Col 2:5). In addition, it is a source of insight, feeling, will, and a state of mind (Mark 2:8; Luke 1:47; 1 Cor 16:18; Gal 6:1).[31]

In light of the wide variety of words that the Bible uses to describe human beings, a biblical view of individuals sees them as whole persons, not divided between body and soul (body/soul dualism). From a Christian perspective, medical care should provide physical and mental care, and emotional and spiritual support.[32]

Humans as Moral Beings

Another defining aspect of God's image in human beings is that people are moral beings. As moral beings made in the image of God, people are rational creatures, which makes them morally conditioned to understand and

---

29. Swanson, James A. *Lexham Theological Wordbook*, s.v. "body." Faithlife: 2002.

30. Carl Schultz, *Evangelical Dictionary of Biblical Theology*, ed. Walter A. Elwell (Grand Rapids: Baker Books, 1996).

31. Frederick William Danker, ed. 3rd ed. *A Greek-English Lexicon of the New Testament and Other Early Christian Literature*, s.v. "πνεῦμα. Chicago: University of Chicago Press, 2000. Logos Edition.

32. Sharon Ann Falkenheimer, "Equipping Healthcare Professionals to Care for the Whole Person," *Christian Journal for Global Health* 3, no. 2 (2016): 129.

respond to moral concepts of right and wrong.[33] As moral beings, humans have the capacity to evaluate objects, events, and behaviors as good or bad, correct or wrong,[34] though sin prevents them from doing so in the way God intended (Rom 3:20, 23). Only transformation in Christ gives them true moral capacity and motivation to act ethically.[35]

God set ethical boundaries in the garden of Eden. According to Gen 2:15–17 and 3:1–6, a moral sense is embedded in humans, separating them from the rest of the animals. The serpent challenged the moral boundary defined by God, and the result was that Eve used her ethical decision-making process based on what she perceived to be good. She rationalized that the good she saw outweighed the good God intended, and then she acted on her decision.[36] Eve's eyes were open, a metaphor for knowledge, suggesting that she found a sort of awareness not previously possessed. Adam and Eve realized their nakedness and were burdened with human guilt and embarrassment. They became like God by obtaining wisdom in exchange for death and likewise forfeited their true moral capacity.[37]

According to ethicist John Davis, people know God's moral requirements. God reveals his moral will for humanity through Scripture and the general revelation of nature and conscience.[38] Apostle Paul contends in Rom 1:19–20 that God provided sufficient evidence of himself to hold all who reject that revelation accountable. The beauty and complexity of creation carry with it the responsibility of acknowledging the creator above the natural order. The recipients of God's natural revelation are responsible for not believing. Paul makes it clear that rebellious people are ἀναπολόγητος (without excuse). The term suggests that unbelieving people have been stripped of any defense from a legal standpoint before a holy God.[39] Not only do unbelievers have no excuse, but God calls nations to account for violating fundamental moral principles. For instance, God sent judgment

---

33. Mark Wesley Foreman and Lindsay C. Leonard, *Christianity and Modern Medicine: Foundations for Bioethics* (Grand Rapids: Kregel Academic, 2022), 15.

34. Heather Looy, "Embodied and Embedded Morality: Divinity, Identity, and Disgust," *Zygon* 39, no. 1 (2004): 219.

35. I would like to thank Dr. Jack Painter for this helpful clarification in a private conversation.

36. Shelly et al., *Called to Care*, 70.

37. Kenneth A. Mathews, *Genesis 1–11:26*, The New American Commentary (Nashville: B&H, 1996), 413.

38. John Jefferson Davis, *Evangelical Ethics: Issues Facing the Church Today*, 4th ed. (Phillipsburg: P&R Publishing, 2015), 11.

39. Robert H. Mounce, *Romans: An Exegetical and Theological Exposition of Holy Scripture*, vol. 27, *The New American Commentary* (Nashville: B & H Publishing, 1995), 116.

upon the generation of the flood (Gen 6–7) and Sodom and Gomorrah (Gen 18–19). The prophet Jonah was sent with a message to the people of Nineveh. Prophet Amos denounced the war atrocities of one nation against another (Amos 2:1).[40]

Every person is born with some sense of justice and a need for rules. In the field of medical ethics, it is particularly relevant to know what is good for others. Moral nature makes human beings strive to do good. However, what does it mean to act ethically in the medical context? Christianity provides a compelling answer to medical ethics even though, as Shelly et al. contend, "Being a moral Christian in the real world is difficult. The line between life and death is often blurred. New technology makes old definitions of death obsolete. The twentieth century has compounded the problem with the frantic pace of technological development."[41] Christian ethics, according to Professor Daniel Heimbach, is "to be a matter of divinely revealed moral truth, studied and applied by human minds, under the guidance of the Holy Spirit, relying only on what God reveals by his authority and initiative, and which therefore evaluates but never submits to, depends on, or combines with human philosophy or anything else arising from human reason, feelings, or experiences apart from God."[42]

Making moral judgments as Christians implies the priority of God's Word over human speculation. To assess emerging medical technologies, Christian moral theology looks at "something ancient, fixed, universal, transcendent, and dogmatic" that finds the one unified moral truth in the person and work of Jesus Christ.[43]

An Understanding of the Image of God in the Incarnation: The Perfect Image in Christ

The understanding of beings created in the image of God would be incomplete without including the culmination of that image in the God-man, Jesus Christ. The incarnation is the most significant argument for the derived sanctity of human life. Christ took on human flesh and dwelt among people to redeem fallen humanity through faith in him.[44] The only begotten Son

---

40. Davis, *Evangelical Ethics*, 12.

41. Shelly et al., *Called to Care*, 71.

42. Daniel R. Heimbach, *Fundamental Christian Ethics* (Nashville: B&H Academic, 2022), 29.

43. Heimbach, *Fundamental Christian Ethics*, 33.

44. Daniel Becker, *Personhood: A Pragmatic Guide to Prolife Victory in the 21st Century and the Return to First Principles in Politics* (Alpharetta: TKS Publications,

of God becomes the Son of Adam to remove the fallen humankind from God's curse and condemnation to eternal death that is reserved for unbelievers. First Timothy 3:16 makes clear that Jesus Christ is both the self-revelation of God and the mediator between the Father and humanity. God, who has manifested in the flesh through the person of Jesus Christ, made himself known to the children of Adam to restore the sinful humanity lost in Adam.[45] God's mysterious redemptive work throughout history has at its center the incarnation of Jesus and his work on the cross; thus, the doctrine of Christ is the *sine qua non* of Christian theology and understanding.[46] Several texts in the New Testament speak about Christ as the incarnate image of God.

Christological Texts: 2 Cor 4:4, Col 1:15, Heb 1:3, John 14:19

Two texts speak of Christ as the exact image of God (2 Cor 4:4 and Col 1:15). According to these two texts, Christ is the image of God. At the same time, humans are made in or according to the image.[47] Second Corinthians 4:4 supports the view that those spiritually blinded by Satan are prevented from seeing the glory of Christ, who is the image of God. For Paul, an image was not considered distinct from the object it represented. Christ, as the image of the invisible God who lives in unapproachable light, brings reconciliation to fallen people from the dominion of darkness through his death on the cross.[48] The light comes from the glory of Christ and can be seen by those who are transformed into his image. Specifically, Paul claims that the world's darkness is universal, demonic, and cosmic. However, the minds of those whom the God of this age has blinded can be enlightened by the gospel Paul proclaims.[49] Colossians 1:15 refers to the Son as the εἰκών (image) of the invisible God. Jesus Christ is the visible image of the invisible God in creation. The intent in this verse may be that the apostle Paul wants to identify the Son of God with the first human being (cf. Rom 5:12–21).

2011), loc. 760. Kindle.

45. Randall C. Zachman, "Jesus Christ as the Image of God in Calvin's Theology," *Calvin Theological Journal* 25, no. 1 (1990): 49.

46. Walter L. Liefeld, *1 & 2 Timothy, Titus*, The NIV Application Commentary (Grand Rapids: Zondervan, 1999), 214.

47. Hammett, "Whole Bible Approach to Interpreting Creation in God's Image," 33.

48. David E Garland, *2 Corinthians*, The New American Commentary (Nashville: B & H Publishing, 1999), 370.

49. Paul Barnett, *The Second Epistle to the Corinthians*, The New International Commentary of the New Testament (Grand Rapids: Wm. B. Eerdmans, 1997), 310.

Adam was to rule creation, but a reversal occurred in Adam's relationship with creation because of his sin. However, in Christ, the reversal is reversed. The image of God is fulfilled in Christ, who is the new or second Adam.[50] Jesus bore the image of the earthly, Adam, and the image of the heavenly, God. For Paul, the Lord Jesus was the unique manifestation of God and man, continuously embodying the best of both wherever he was. By using the word εἰκών, Paul stresses that God was present wherever Jesus was.[51]

Two other texts express the same idea of Christ being the image of God but in different terms. Hebrews 1:3 describes Jesus as the exact χαρακτήρ (expression) of God's being. The biblical author describes the unique relationship between the Son and the Father. God the Father intervened in human history with his sovereign word addressed to humankind. However, God's ultimate self-revelation was spoken through one distinguished from others because of his unique relationship with God. Jesus unites in his person the attributes and privileges of the royal Son, the wisdom of God, and the royal priest.[52] The word χαρακτήρ also indicates that the Son bears the perfect imprint of God's being. In Greek usage, χαρακτήρ described an impression placed on an object, such as coins, which came to signify a representation. Based on Hebrews 1, the Son is the true embodiment of God as he is.[53]

John 14:9–10 uses visual terms to explain that one who has seen Jesus Christ has seen the Father. Jesus elaborates on his unique and close relationship with the Father by asserting that no one can or has ever seen the Father. The closeness of this relationship is explained in intimate familial notions. The relationship between the Father and the Son is not mystical but instead of great intimacy, love, and trust.[54] The Johannine Gospel anticipated this relationship in the prologue (John 1:1, 14). The Gospel has depicted the ministry of the three persons of the Trinity in the person of Jesus in the world. The preposition ἐν (in) emphasizes familial language, which speaks unavoidably of the mutuality of the Father and the Son. The two persons of the Trinity, the Father and the Son, are so close that "everything Jesus is, has said, and has done is an expression not only of or about the Father but even

---

50. David H. Johnson, "The Image of God in Colossians," *Didaskalia* 3, no. 2 (1992): 11.

51. Richard R. Melick, *Philippians, Colossians, Philemon*, The New American Commentary (Nashville: B & H Publishing, 1991), 387.

52. William L. Lane, *Hebrews 1–8*, Word Biblical Commentary (Grand Rapids: Zondervan, 1991), 347.

53. David G. Peterson, *Hebrews*, Tyndale New Testament Commentaries (Downers Grove: IVP Academic, 2015), 105.

54. Andreas J. Köstenberger, *A Theology of John's Gospel and Letters*, The Biblical Theology of the New Testament (Grand Rapids: Zondervan, 2009), 596.

by the Father. While we can differentiate the persons of the Father and the Son, the Father and the Son maintain a functional inseparability through the person and work of the Son."[55]

The doctrine of incarnation is vital for a Christian understanding of medical care. Shelly et al. maintain that the only way people can know what God intended for them in creation is to look at Jesus Christ. Only in a relationship with the Son of God can people recognize the truth and become genuine persons.[56]

Renewal Texts: Rom 8:29; 2 Cor 3:18; Col 3:10; and Eph 4:24

The final category of God's image in humans as it relates to the incarnation is found in the renewal or dynamic texts.[57] The image of God is dynamically renewed in people through the mediatorial work of Christ on the cross. The incarnation of Christ is fundamental to a proper understanding of humanity. Jesus Christ is not only the divine Son of God, but he is also a human being and is not ashamed to call believers brothers and sisters (Heb 2:11). More than that, the Bible clarifies that Jesus is truly human and, because he assumed a human nature in organic continuity with those he came to save, makes it possible for Christians to be renewed into his image.[58]

In the first text, Rom 8:29 explicitly states that God's sovereign will foreordained believers to be brought into conformity to the likeness of his Son. Without resemblance to the Father's family, of which the Son is the firstborn, Paul implies that the intention of the Father to redeem a vast family for himself would never be realized.[59] Theologian Douglas Moo maintains that the biblical use of "know" and "foreknow" often refers to God's entering into a relationship with someone. God's plan for the believers began with a relational decision that led to predestination. According to Moo, "The last stage of Christian existence is to be conformed to Christ's glorious body. God enters into a relationship with us so that we may attain that goal."[60]

---

55. Klink, *John*, 1081.

56. Shelly et al., *Called to Care*, 60.

57. Hammett, *Whole Bible Approach to Interpreting Creation in God's Image*, 34.

58. Brandon D. Crowe, *The Lord Jesus Christ: The Biblical Doctrine of the Person and Work of Christ*, We Believe: Studies in Reformed Biblical Doctrine (Bellingham: Lexham Academic, 2023), 118.

59. Mounce, *Romans*, 277.

60. Douglas J. Moo, *Romans*, The NIV Application Commentary (Grand Rapids: Zondervan, 2000), 433.

Furthermore, 2 Cor 3:18, based on Exod 34:35, states that all Christians can, like Moses, approach God's glory with unveiled faces and experience transformation. The glory of God can be seen through the ministry of the Spirit as in a mirror. Even though the mirror meant something "indistinctly" or "in a distorted way," the mirror anticipates the eschatological seeing of God "face to face," argues David Garland. A direct vision of God awaits the end of this age. However, Christ, as God's image, allows believers to see God's glory in Jesus. Christ mirrors God for believers and can be met in the heart of the Christian who turns to the Lord and is transformed into a veritable likeness. Garland also helpfully points out that the fall tarnished the image of God in human beings but not irreparably. The transformation concerns not the physical appearance but rather the moral reformation of persons done by God. The inner being is transformed into the likeness of God, beginning with the mind, so that the Christian is not conformed to the world and its perceptions and values.[61] Also worth mentioning is the fact that according to the apostle Paul, the transformation into God's image in Christ is gradual and progressive, from one stage of glory to yet a higher stage, climaxing in Rom 8:30. The Spirit works the change, transforming believers into the likeness of Christ, the new Adam, until they attain their promised destiny and enjoy the freedom that is their birthright under the terms of the new covenant.[62]

In the third text, the apostle Paul states in Col 3:10, alluding to Gen 1:26–28, that believers have begun to be identified with Christ's resurrection by faith as the new creation in Jesus. Adam marred God's initial image in humanity, foreshadowing a last Adam who would be faithful and genuinely reflect the divine image. God transforms believers even though they are accountable for striving to lay aside sin. Gregory Beale correctly maintains that this verse aligns with the first creation when Adam and Eve did not create themselves but were created by God, who made them in God's image.[63] The Pauline new creation theology views the inner change accomplished by the inner transforming work of God. The Spirit works transformation in distinctive christological terms. Scot McKnight notices that the work of the Spirit transforms each person into the image of God, Christ himself. This christoformity is seen in the moral transformation of the sanctification work of God's Spirit into the depth of truth.[64]

61. Garland, 2 *Corinthians*, 273–74.

62. Ralph P. Martin, 2 *Corinthians*, Word Biblical Commentary (Grand Rapids: Zondervan, 2014), 487.

63. G. K. Beale, *Colossians and Philemon*, Baker Exegetical Commentary on the New Testament (Grand Rapids: Baker Academic, 2019), 602.

64. Scot McKnight, *The Letter to the Colossians*, The New International

Finally, the transformational language of "putting off" and "putting on" occurs in Eph 4:24. For apostle Paul, it is of utmost urgency to lay aside the old being, which is in a state of ever-deepening corruption, and move to ongoing renewal and a new creation. The object of continual renewal is the human spirit, the controlling center of the human being. The apostle uses the creation language of Gen 1, where the image marred in Eden is being recreated in Christ. The endeavor for a new creation is a work of God already accomplished on the cross. The Ephesians text adds to the discussion of the significant role of the incarnation, an ethical dimension concerning righteousness and holiness. The hendiadys emphasizes that righteousness and holiness have their source in truth, the truth found in Jesus Christ.[65]

The renewal texts appear to provide the capstone interpretation of the image of God in humanity. Apostle Paul contends that something in the spiritual dimension of the human being can be renewed in conversion, something into which believers are increasingly transformed. John Hammett convincingly concludes that the image's meaning is "something dynamic, capable of suffering damage, but also capable of renewal, transformation, and perfection in believers."[66] Christ, God's actual image, serves as humanity's archetype. Humanity is called to reflect the image of God in creation, given Adam's created state of holiness, which suggests that the image of God entails the goal of moral holiness or renewal, a goal to which humanity should aspire.[67]

Health and Flourishing in a Fallen World

Theological anthropology of a patient concerns health and flourishing in a fallen world. This section discusses a theological understanding of health and flourishing by advocating for a metaphysical instrumental view of health aiming at flourishing relational care.

A Theological Understanding of Health

The literature on health and flourishing allows for different interpretations of health and flourishing. The World Health Organization (WHO)

Commentary on the New Testament (Grand Rapids: Wm. B. Eerdmans, 2018), 640.

65. Klyne Snodgrass, *Ephesians*, The NIV Application Commentary (Grand Rapids: Zondervan, 1996), 356.

66. Hammett, "Whole Bible Approach to Interpreting Creation in God's Image," 35.

67. Crowe, *Lord Jesus Christ*, 97.

idealistically defines health as "a state of complete physical, mental, and social well-being and not merely the absence of disease or infirmities."[68] As Messer notes, the WHO definition helps articulate that health is necessary for realizing many human goods and goals. On the other hand, this definition poses problems and drawbacks. Messer observes that the WHO's definition is vague because it understands health with the term well-being, which is even more contested than health. In addition, the WHO perspective tends to make pursuing health a never-ending quest for an unattainable goal. Finally, Messer contends that the WHO's definition tends to medicalize every area of human life. By conceptualizing health as a theory of everything and the meaning of health being stretched too broadly, as is the case of the WHO definition, the result is an inadequate notion of "everything." The WHO explanation suggests a too-wide understanding of the health perspective but also implies a too-narrow view of human flourishing.[69]

Others interpret health in terms of dimensions. For instance, nurse educator Ruth Stoll defines health as including five dimensions. Shelly et al. present Stoll's dimensions of health as comprising (1) wholeness, (2) transformation, (3) relationship, (4) coping and adaption, and (5) human paradox. First, health is perceived as wholeness, meaning the harmonious unity of the person within herself. Second, transformation refers to a dynamic internal process is also involved in health progressively reflected in a person's outward behavior. Furthermore, health concerns include experiencing a loving relationship with God, self, and others. Health is also oriented to reality, allowing a person to adapt to internal and external change. Finally, health is a paradox insofar as it refers to living with sin, redemption, and restoration.[70]

Somewhat differently, health theoretician Christopher Boorse argues in *Health as a Theoretical Concept* that health is normal functioning, where normality is statistical and the functions biological.[71] Despite Boorse's arguably helpful contributions to health theory, such as the connection between health and biological sciences, the biostatistical model faced numerous critiques. Messer maintains that the biostatistical perspective is too narrow because it places health solely in the field of evolutionary biology.

---

68. Neil Messer, *Flourishing: Health, Disease, and Bioethics in Theological Perspective* (Grand Rapids: Wm. B. Eerdmans, 2013), 2.

69. Messer, *Flourishing*, 3–5.

70. Shelly et al., *Called to Care*, 191.

71. Christopher Boorse, "Health as a Theoretical Concept," *Philosophy of Science* 44, no. 4 (1977): 542.

The disease is a loss of function that is part of a species-typical contribution to survival and reproduction.[72]

Another significant interpretation, especially among Christian theoreticians, is health as wholeness or *shalom*. Christian ethicists correctly criticize modern healthcare as being more concerned with biological/organic endeavors and medical means and procedures than with the total welfare of a person.[73] Abigail Evan explains shalom as a social happening that cannot be objectified and set apart but can be found in interpersonal relations.[74] Moreover, shalom incorporates the elements that make a spiritual community focused on God, peace in relationships, prosperity, security, etc.[75]

Defining Health

Despite the difficulties in defining health and well-being, perhaps a better way to define health is based on Karl Barth's version of health, which is the strength of being human. Barth understands health as meaning capability, vigor, and freedom. Health "is a strength for human life. It is the integration of the organs to exercise psycho-physical functions."[76] Barth understands health in dimensions such as capacity, vitality, and freedom to exercise psychical and physical functions. Pursuing health is a desirable objective. According to Barth, to be healthy in body and soul is

> to be man at all: man and not animal or plant, man and not wood or stone, man and not a thing or the exponent of an idea, man in the satisfaction of his instinctive needs, man in the use of his reason, in loyalty to his individuality, in the knowledge of its limitations, man in his determination for work and knowledge, and above all in his relation to God and his fellow-men in the proffered act of freedom.[77]

A vital part of Barth's argumentation is correctly aligned with the biblical view of human beings as ensouled bodies. A sick person does not cease

---

72. Messer, *Flourishing*, 6.

73. Apolos Landa, "Shalom & Eirene: The Full Framework for Health Care," *Christian Journal for Global Health* 1, no. 1 (2014): 57.

74. Abigail Rian Evans, "Health, Healing, and Healers: A Theological and Philosophical Inquiry" (PhD diss., Georgetown University, 1984), 217.

75. Shelly, Miller, and Fenstermacher, *Called to Care: A Christian Vision for Nursing*, 187.

76. Karl Barth, *Church Dogmatics*, ed. Geoffrey W. Bromiley and T. F. Torrance, trans. A. T. Mackay et al., vol. III.4 (New York: T&T Clark International, 2004), 356.

77. Barth, *Church Dogmatics*, III. 4, 354

to be a person. The attempt to heal does not differentiate between soul and body as separate accounts. The person is the soul of his body, a rational soul of his vegetative and animal body. For Barth, the soul and body are in a mutually united relationship.[78] Messer notes that, by resisting splitting off body and soul and giving one or the other greater priority, Barth's perspective of the will to be healthy reflects the Christian notion of health as wholeness. Although Barth understands health as wholeness, it is still one human good among others and should be taken to encompass the totality of human well-being, contends Messer.[79] The good of the body and the soul comprises proper hygiene of the physical and physical life. Proper hygiene and sports are fundamental to preventing diseases.

Furthermore, the role of the medical personnel is to assist the sick by using the possibilities of the creator provided to man. A physician will be better if she is conscious of her limitations. The task of the health professional is to find and apply a new and specific form of science and its application to the individual patient. The relationship between caregiver and care receiver can be built on solid relative confidence that the caregiver has better general information than the patient regarding disease. The result must be, according to Barth, that the care receiver should show confidence in the physician's judgment, advice, direction, and even intervention in her particular case. A helpful warning in the care process is that the patient must remember that the physician is not a priest. A doctor has only "a very limited power even over the health or sickness of his organs, of the psychical and physical functions in which that strength and the will for it must express themselves in conflict against the weakness."[80]

In line with Barth's reasoning, Graham O'Brien proposes that healing is an attempt to restore the image of God affected by illness and disease in a patient. As already stated, the image of God in people comprises the concept embedded in human nature: relationality. People are made to be in communion with God and their neighbors. As a result, *cura* includes a dimension that goes beyond the physical and consists of the notion of restoration for all types of relationships in light of God's purposes for the patient. Physical incapacities may result in violating relationships between human beings and even the internal unity of each person—a lack of health may lead to individualization and conflict.[81]

---

78. Barth, *Church Dogmatics*, III.4:358.
79. Messer, *Flourishing*, 138.
80. Barth, *Church Dogmatics*, III.4:362.
81. Graham O'Brien, "A Theology of Care: Connecting the Present and the Eternal," *Churchman* 134, no. 2 (2020): 150.

In other words, being healthy means functioning as God created people to be. Shelly et al. see health as "reconciliation with God and others, forgiving and accepting forgiveness, loving and being loved, finding meaning and purpose in life leading to a sense of joy and hope, as well as freedom from physical ailments."[82] This definition also avoids claiming an impossible ideal for medical procedures; thus, the healing process is only an attempt to achieve health using technical capabilities. Based on a realistic approach to medical conditions and human suffering, a Christian view of healing accepts that not every physical problem can be fixed. Therefore, the realities of suffering and mortality temper technical enthusiasm by accepting that health practitioners are not God and are not in complete control.[83]

Similarly, Karl Barth sees sickness realistically. However, Barth highlights a particular feature of sickness that is prominent in Scripture:

> Sickness is a forerunner and messenger of death, and indeed of death as the judgment of God and the merited subjection of man to the power of nothingness in virtue of his sin. From this standpoint, sickness, like death itself, is unnatural and disorderly. It is an element in the rebellion of chaos against God's creation. It is an act and declaration of the devil and demons. To be sure, it is no less bound to God and dependent on Him than the creature which He created. Indeed, it is impotent in relation to him in a double way. For like sin and death, it is neither good nor is it willed and created by God at all, but is real, effective, powerful, and menacing only as part of that which He has negated, of His kingdom on the left hand, and therefore with its nullity.[84]

Messer helpfully observes that for Barth, health is a genuine but penultimate good that is important for the sake of the ultimate good.[85] The ultimate good of health is witnessing God's creative goodness, the forerunner and messenger of eternal life. Barth's view of God is intimately connected to his view of health. That is to say that health and becoming healthy is in God's hands, and sickness in its form of weakness, destruction, growing old, and dying is subdued to God, the Lord and victor of sickness and the realm of death.[86] Health as a messenger of eternal life should encourage the virtue

---

82. Shelly et al., *Called to Care*, 185.
83. Shelly et al., *Called to Care*, 192.
84. Barth, *Church Dogmatics*, III.4:365.
85. Messer, *Flourishing*, 139.
86. Barth, *Church Dogmatics*, III.4:373.

of humility in the biomedical sciences and healthcare professions, suggests Messer.[87]

A Theological Understanding of Human Flourishing

A theological understanding of health suggests that health is indispensable to human flourishing. "Health is not good only in order to achieve some purposes; its goodness is what philosophers call basic," argues Curlin and Tollefsen.[88] Health is indeed an objective good for the patient's well-being. More than that, human flourishing includes health for its benefits and health that helps meet human goods, goals, and ends given by God in creation.[89]

Defining Flourishing

A metaphysical teleological approach to health and flourishing may be helpful in an attempt to develop a theologically shaped understanding of human flourishing. Health goes beyond bodily curing (metaphysics), leading to human flourishing (teleology). Human flourishing and well-being arguably are, in essence, a right relationship with God and well-ordered interpersonal and social relationships. Flourishing also regards a "good functioning of body, mind, and emotions, the availability of sufficient resources to sustain bodily needs, the richness of cultural and aesthetic experience, and a positive relationship with the non-human creation."[90] Mohrmann similarly proposes that health is not an absolute good because it could lead to the idolatry of health. Health is always instrumental, a subordinate good because it enables people to be the joyful, whole persons God created and to serve their neighbors the way God called humanity to do.[91]

Messer helpfully contends that Scripture clarifies what it means to flourish as a human being by witnessing to Christ. To live a fully human life, one must be centered on Christ.[92] A biblical account of theological anthropology shows people's perversion and corruption. The truth of the sinfulness of human beings is that "man is a betrayer of himself and a sinner

---

87. Messer, *Flourishing*, 141.
88. Curlin and Tollefsen, *Way of Medicine*, 6.
89. Messer, *Flourishing*, 174.
90. Messer, *Flourishing*, 114.
91. Mohrmann, *Medicine as Ministry*, 16.
92. Messer, *Flourishing*, 135.

against his creaturely existence."[93] Only Christ is a portrayer of what human existence means and, by extension, what flourishing entails because "He is engaged in the fulfillment of it, in the exercise of its functions, in the claiming of its privileges and the carrying out of its obligations."[94]

Given the broad theoretical understanding of flourishing (i.e., as climaxing in Christ and relational terms), a specific question may guide the conversation: "What are some possible norms to govern the physician-patient relationship toward flourishing?" Curlin and Tollefsen believe that the answer must begin with human action being oriented to the basic good, an intrinsic aspect of human flourishing. For them, essential irreducible goods regard life, health, knowledge, friendship, integrity, aesthetic experience, religion, and marriage.[95] In *The Way of Medicine*, Curlin and Tollefsen suggest that the first guiding norm toward flourishing is "in acting and willing, always be[ing] fully open to the goodness of the goods and to the persons for whom those goods are good."[96] The authors argue that one should never damage an instance of an essential good based on emotion or prejudice for the greater good. Another possible norm is that there needs to be fairness in the distribution of benefits and burdens. The physician-patient relationship will not be for the patient's good if the caregiver allows feelings of biases of race and class to shape medical practice unduly.[97]

A Flourishing Care Relationship

The relational nature of human beings is undeniably intrinsic. As imagers of God, people are, in their essential nature, relational. The Trinity is relational at the core. The Father, Son, and Holy Spirit are one God in three persons. The relational nature of the Trinity manifests in love. Mohrmann rightly notes that the Father and the Son eternally give and receive love, and "the love that flows back and forth constantly in this mutual giving and receiving, the love that is this mutuality, is the Holy Spirit of God."[98]

Despite human beings' relational nature, the caregiver-care-receiver relationship may be threatened by two major competing views present in the act of medical care such as (1) absolute patient autonomy and (2)

---

93. Karl Barth, *Church Dogmatics*, ed. Geoffrey W. Bromiley and T. F. Torrance, trans. H. Knight et al., vol. III.2 (New York: T&T Clark International, 2004), 49.

94. Barth, *Church Dogmatics*, III.2:64.

95. Curlin and Tollefsen, *Way of Medicine*, 35.

96. Curlin and Tollefsen, *Way of Medicine*, 38.

97. Curlin and Tollefsen, *Way of Medicine*, 39–40.

98. Mohrmann, *Medicine as Ministry*, 37.

a strong paternalistic model of medicine.[99] According to a paternalistic model, the physician can determine the patient's best interests. The caregiver and her values can force subjective ethics on the sick person. The reason for hierarchical authority rests on the belief that the doctor is the technical expert who always knows what is in the best interest of her care.[100] Pellegrino and Thomasma point out in *The Patient's Good* that the advancements in medical technology challenge the paternal view on several issues. First, physicians may be tempted to believe that the patient's interest is truly in the medical technological solution rather than acknowledging the patient's good values.[101] Cindy Wesley argues that the marriage of paternalism and the "technological imperative" leads to the objectification of the patient. Consequently, "the patient, in the technological age, is often treated as an object of study, even of experiment, rather than as a person with whom the physician is to interact as a peer."[102]

Furthermore, Pellegrino and Thomasma question if it is in the patient's best interest to prolong life through technological instruments more than the average expectancy of the terminally ill. Grounded on the philosophy of medicine related to the quality of life, the authors believe that medical technology solutions may prolong life but could also extend suffering.[103] Thus, while a medically indicated course of treatment may be technologically possible, there is still a potential to harm the patient's good.

The paternal model will likely fail as a useful physician-patient relationship. Curlin and Tollefsen note that the time of paternalism is past. A physician with strong paternalistic inclinations cannot practice for long without cultivating patients' trust and accommodating their concerns. However, the authors also observe that shortly after the paternalistic view was more or less removed, the patient's autonomy became normative. According to the patient autonomy view, the patient chooses, and the physician provides.[104] Within the autonomy framework, healthcare services should provide interventions to maximize the patient's well-being and fulfill the sick's desires, including the goal of dying with dignity.[105] In addition,

---

99. Huang Yeewen, "Contemporary Challenges of the Physician-Patient Relationship," *Theologies and Cultures* 3, no. 1 (2006): 66.

100. Cindy Wesley, "Medical Progress and the Physician-Patient Relationship," *ARC* 22 (1994): 92.

101. Pellegrino and Thomasma, *For the Patient's Good*, 93.

102. Cindy Wesley, "Medical Progress and the Physician-Patient Relationship," *ARC* 22 (1994): 96.

103. Pellegrino and Thomasma, *For the Patient's Good*, 93.

104. Curlin and Tollefsen, *The Way of Medicine*, 52.

105. Farr A. Curlin and Christopher Tollefsen, "Medicine against Suicide: Sustaining

the physician-patient relationship becomes obstructed due to the reduction of the caregiver to a functionary whose job is to provide a service without concern for the practitioner's judgment about morality.[106]

Since neither strong paternalistic nor absolute autonomy models seem to fit within a biblical understanding of flourishing, what is the place of autonomy and authority in the physician-patient relationship, if any? Mohrmann argues that based on a Trinitarian orientation, autonomy in and of itself is a chimera. Suffering persons are not served in solitary independence and isolation but in the context of their relations with other people.[107]

Curlin and Tollefsen again prove helpful for understanding autonomy in their analysis found in *The Way*. Autonomy is morally good only when it is a choice for good without disregarding the foreseeable downstream effects on others. That is, an ethically sound decision in the context of medical care is not a self-destructive choice. A person's freedom to self-governing is fundamental to flourishing only insofar as a patient decides for herself what is best without hindering the physician's discernment and reasonable judgment.

Likewise, the concept of authority based on Curlin and Tollefsen's convincing view includes some necessary categories of thought. First, they argue that the doctor has authority and expertise based on her training and knowledge. However, even an expert will acknowledge some limits in recognizing that the best health solution may not be the best outcome. For instance, medical interventions do not offer only benefits but also burdens in terms of side effects. Even though medically feasible, a doctor's expertise may not be the best course of action in a patient's context. Thus, the doctor's knowledge creates the initial framework for the patient to make choices. In this way, a physician's prudent exercise of authority allows the patient to consult other options for her case.[108]

Some Virtues of a Flourishing Relationship: Trust, Solidarity, and Love

What virtues could be pursued in the physician-patient relationship that leads to the sufferer's good and mutual relational flourishing? First, trust appears to be one of the fundamental elements of a flourishing

---

Solidarity with Those Diminished by Illness and Debility," *Christian Bioethics* 27, no. 3 (2021): 251.

106. Curlin and Tollefsen, *The Way of Medicine*, 69.
107. Mohrmann, *Medicine as Ministry*, 51.
108. Curlin and Tollefsen, *Way of Medicine*, 72–77.

caregiver-care-receiver relationship. Trust entails faith in someone who will act in ways that are governed by genuine concern.[109] The patient's trust in the physician is generated by the conviction that the doctor has a firm vocation to act for health rehabilitation and provide the most appropriate treatment and adequate medical care. Trust is an instrument of therapeutic value and a catalyst between doctors and patients.[110] In other words, without trust, medical care is undermined.

Cojocaru et al. argue that the effects of trust in a relationship are irreplaceable. The level of communication is improved by trust between the caregiver and the sufferer and her family through a better information flow about the health status of the associated therapeutic effort. In addition, at the level of the patient, the patient's family, and physician, trust improves the relationship by bringing greater comfort and openness concerning medical treatments. Finally, trust is translated into the patient's self-esteem at the level of the family and the patient's involvement in the therapeutic process and in improving care management.[111] The sources of trust of care receivers in their physicians rely on the doctor's professional competencies and expertise. The health practitioner's knowledge and technical skills are foundational for a trusting relationship. Then, the doctor's communication competencies are demonstrated in the ability to provide information and specific explanations to the patient in a common language, which is essential. Trust is also encouraged by the doctor's respectful attitude and mindfulness toward cultural variations found in a multicultural society. The physician's accessibility and ability to connect beyond the technical dimension of a professional relationship by showing genuine interest in the patient are significant factors that build trust.[112] Communication is critical since most patients lack the knowledge to evaluate medical treatments accurately. The outcome of communication that builds trust results in better patient compliance, fewer diagnostic tests, less likelihood of litigation and malpractice claims, reduced treatment avoidance among patients, and an overall better clinical outcome.[113]

---

109. Curlin and Tollefsen, *Way of Medicine*, 64.

110. Daniela Cojocaru, Cristina Gavrilovici, and Sorin Cace, "Christian and Secular Dimensions of the Doctor-Patient Relationship," *Journal for the Study of Religions and Ideologies* 12, no. 34 (2013): 38–41.

111. Cojocaru et al., "Christian and Secular Dimensions," 43.

112. Cojocaru et al., "Christian and Secular Dimensions," 49–50.

113. Hyehyun Hong and Jee Hyun Oh, "The Effects of Patient-Centered Communication: Exploring the Mediating Role of Trust in Healthcare Providers," *Health Communication* 35, no. 4 (2020): 504.

Solidarity is a second fundamental element of a flourishing relationship. The literature about solidarity and therapeutic relationships is massive.[114] Solidarity is a firm commitment to the good of other persons that requires concrete relationships in particular communities.[115] Solidarity is essential for quality care. Curlin and Tollefsen stress the reciprocal nature of solidarity in the physician-patient relationship. Generally, the purpose of the physician-patient relationship is to pursue the patient's good. The doctor flourishes when she is not treated as someone who merely performs a job. Being willing to be well cared for means wanting the physician to be a good doctor in all the relevant and necessary ways. Practicing reciprocal solidarity means that the patient's health is important but also the good of the doctor in terms of the physician's flourishing and fulfillment as a person.[116] The caregiver is human and needs human connection, argue Koloroutis and Trout.[117] Thus, solidarity must go both ways for a flourishing relationship.

Solidarity found in a therapeutic care relationship that aims at flourishing ideally conveys compassion, empathy, and an understanding of the meaning and magnitude of the illness to the patient and family. Moreover, solidarity requires authentic connections.[118] Koloroutis and Trout believe that a caring relationship is possible when all participants are regarded as unique persons and partners in the flow of information and explanations to make appropriate decisions. Patients then perceive that they are treated with dignity when caregivers confer about and with them. Further, patients perceive that they are cared for when they are listened to and heard and when health practitioners recognize and respect the magnitude of the illness. Patients also feel safe when caregivers give them support to cope with and find meaning in their illness by knowing that they will not be abandoned.[119]

Love is a third virtue encompassing the entire spectrum of relational flourishing. A loving relationship finds its root in the essential nature of

---

114. See the works of Sidney Marshall Jourard, *The Transparent Self*, Revised (New York: Von Nostrand Reinhold, 1971); Carl R. Rogers, *Client Centered Therapy: Its Current Practice, Implications and Theory*, Reprinted (London: Robinson, 2021); Martin Buber, *I And Thou*, 2nd ed. (New York: Charles Scribner's Sons, 1958); C. Terry Warner, *Bonds That Makes Us Free: Healing Our Relationships, Coming to Ourselves* (Nashville: Shadow Mountain, 2001), and Jean Watson, *Nursing: The Philosophy and Science of Caring*, Revised (Boulder: University Press of Colorado, 2008).

115. Curlin and Tollefsen, *Way of Medicine*, 60.

116. Curlin and Tollefsen, *Way of Medicine*, 60.

117. Mary Koloroutis and Michael Trout, *See Me as a Person: Creating Therapeutic Relationships with Patients and Their Families* (Minneapolis: Creative Health Care Management, 2012), 13.

118. Koloroutis and Trout, *See Me as a Person*, 16.

119. Koloroutis and Trout, *See Me as a Person*, 47.

God, the God in whose image we were created, maintains Mohrmann. Love is reciprocal because during the expenditure process, giving and receiving happens between the parties—love comes from the caregiver and from the one the caregiver is called to heal. The reciprocal love is seen in the double role of the health worker, who must be both the giver and receiver of love and so must be the neighbor.[120] Being created in the image of God, who is relational, means that the relational nature of people is defined by constant mutual giving and receiving.

A question may arise: "How can a patient show reciprocal love to the physician?" Mohrmann speaks of reciprocity provided by the patient as an opportunity to love and serve. The sickness is a medium through which the physician can serve and show neighborly love. The patient presents an unparalleled gift to the caregiver in which the physician can encounter Christ by binding the wounds of the sufferer. The suffering context allows the physician to receive access to the deepest and most feared secrets, access to the hidden life.[121] A sick person can also show reciprocal love to the doctor when she shapes the lives of health workers. Though a patient only indirectly shapes the physician's life, he does teach the nature of his illnesses and the meanings of his sufferings. Not only that, but patients shape the lives and substance of caregivers' lives by giving content, form, and meaning to health workers' life stories.[122]

A physician's love for the sufferer may be described in several categories of thought. The heart of the medical practice, according to Mohrmann, is the physician's silent presence that allows the doctor to show love through a genuine sharing of burdens of knowledge and fear that pass between the healer and sufferer. A genuine sharing of burdens implies that physicians can serve aptly not only because of their technical expertise but also because of their frailties.[123] A genuine relationship and mutual, reciprocal love are possible because physicians are also human beings who may have experienced physical weakness or seen the reality of suffering in neighbors. In other words, a human physician understands by nature the reality of sickness and dying and the magnitude of healing. To become a good physician, one necessary ingredient is to recognize one's foibles, argues physician Daniel Sulmasy. A wounded healer is a good physician when she acknowledges that she is wounded and needs healing.[124]

120. Mohrmann, *Medicine as Ministry*, 41–45.
121. Mohrmann, *Medicine as Ministry*, 46–47.
122. Mohrmann, *Medicine as Ministry*, 48–49.
123. Mohrmann, *Medicine as Ministry*, 65, 110.
124. Daniel P. Sulmasy, *The Healer's Calling: A Spirituality for Physicians and Other*

In the same line of thought, pastoral work may inform the practice of medical love. A pastor may be considered a wounded soul's physician, needing healing found in Christ's cross. How a pastor is present and listens to a parishioner's soul issue is similar to the medical profession. The multifaceted dimensions of the cure of souls begin with the correct diagnosis. A pastor shows loving care when he listens with great attentiveness. Listening and being present in times of need provide immense therapeutic benefits. The pastor must first listen to the soul before he can minister to the soul, argues the Lutheran pastor Harold Senkbeil. Influential physicians of the soul must listen to the sufferers' hearts in their complexities before the pastor can efficiently minister to the people.[125] A pastor loves his people by caring enough for them to listen to their souls before suggesting an intentional treatment.

Ultimately, love is an intrinsic part of any relationship, particularly the clinician-patient relationship. To transform medicine into a science of engineering is the most dehumanizing stance one can take toward patients. Sulmasy concludes, "Conceiving of the patient merely as an object to be scientifically manipulated, essentially no different from a tadpole in a dish, undermines the meaning of healing."[126]

A Biblical Understanding of Health and Flourishing

Turning to Scripture as a moral resource to understand health and flourishing enlarges the already-discussed theological spectrum. What do healing and flourishing mean in biblical terms? To answer this question, this section comprises only the essential biblical teaching in some theological thesis grounded in eclectic scriptural texts. To work on exhaustive critical exegesis or extensive biblical theology of topics related to healing would go beyond the objective of this dissertation. Nevertheless, discussing some primary biblical texts may help to provide a perspective on biblical healing and flourishing.

Health Care Professionals (New York: Paulist Press, 1997), loc. 1200, Kindle.

125. Harold L. Senkbeil, *The Care of Souls: Cultivating a Pastor's Heart* (Bellingham: Lexham Press, 2019), 68–69.

126. Sulmasy, *Healer's Calling*, loc. 1251.

Healing and Flourishing in the Old Testament

Healing in the Bible covers a multitude of meanings. Healing from a biblical perspective does not focus only on the physical body alone but refers to the restoration of health in the total sense. According to biblical accounts, people in the ancient world thought of sickness holistically; thus, healing must be holistic. The source of sickness may be not only in the ill person's body but also in their social environments. Hence, healing may comprise the healing of relationships and one's bodily issues.[127] To the sufferer, healing concerns the alleviation of symptoms but also involves the mind, soul, spirit, community, ethics, and justice. To be healed is to be complete or to have shalom. Even though complete healing is available only in the Eschaton, there are opportunities for genuine flourishing in this age.[128]

The Old Testament acknowledges healing and flourishing as God's work. Humans are part of God's creation. In Ps 139:14, the psalmist states that people are wonderfully made and that creation remains sound despite being affected by sin and death. God the creator continuously works to heal people and creation through the channels of creation, including the body's self-healing properties and healing made possible through human talents, creativity, and imagination.[129] In other words, God the healer may bring healing through humanity's capability to steward creation for good purposes.

Yahweh is the healer of his people. According to the Law, God heals barrenness (Gen 20:17), leprosy (Exod 4:6), and poisonous snake bites (Num 21:4). God's healing of uncurable diseases and curses is strongly connected to the Lord's covenantal blessings.[130] In Exod 23:25–26, God is identified as Israel's healer. God promises blessings for those who abide by his Law. God will give food, health, fertility, and long life to those faithful to the covenant. God, as the source of healing, both spiritual and physical, also provided the health standard for Israel, which was far higher than that of neighboring lands, such as Philistia or Egypt, where plagues were endemic.[131] Ingrained in these verses and Exod 15:26 is the assumption

---

127. J. B. Green, "Healing," in *New Dictionary of Biblical Theology*, ed. Sinclair B. Ferguson and David F. Wright (Downers Grove: InterVarsity Press, 2000), 536.

128. Frederick J. Gaiser, *Healing in the Bible: Theological Insights for Christian Ministry* (Grand Rapids: Baker Academic, 2010), 242.

129. Gaiser, *Healing in the Bible*, 245.

130. Jared Mulvihill, "The Defeat of Disability in the Victory of Christ: An Exegetical Theology of Healing in the Age to Come" (PhD diss., Midwestern Baptist Theological Seminary, 2023), 125.

131. R. Alan Cole, *Exodus*, Tyndale Old Testament Commentaries (Downers

that God may bring healing through natural and supernatural means. The natural means of relief is obeying God's hygiene law, which is conducive to good health. Israel's revealed laws, if obeyed by the people, would minimize sickness in the promised land. The standards of hygiene, good diet, preserving family, and securing the young, the aged, the weak, and the defenseless relieve anxiety and stress. Moreover, God's laws provided a full day of rest, relief from guilt, and protected property rights, benefits generally applicable to a healthy population. Furthermore, the Exodus verses promise that Israel could call God to deliver them whenever a plague or disaster occurs. God supernaturally healed people on many occasions. However, the supernatural aspect of God's promise did not permit willful violation of its natural aspect.[132]

In the Prophets, God heals barrenness (Judg 13:3–25), tumors (1 Sam 6:3), and a withered hand (1 Kgs 13:6), to name a few. Mulvihill helpfully observes that healing episodes in the Law are found in the prophetic literature. Still, they move beyond the Law by revealing healing in direct reference to the keeping of the Law. In the Law, God promises the blessings of healing and curses, but in the Prophets, Yahweh's acts apply them.[133]

In the later Prophets, such as the book of Jeremiah, Scripture expands God's healing and restoration, which encompasses a return to Yahweh (Jer 15:21), peace (Jer 14:9), physical space (Jer 30:3), blessing (Jer 31:23), mercy (Jer 33:6), and satisfaction (Jer 50:19). The prophet explicitly includes in the act of God's healing not only physical healing but the emotional, communal, spiritual, and eternal blessings of God's covenant. The return of Israel in the covenant will mean abundance, prosperity, security, and satisfaction in God.[134] What makes Jeremiah's account of health unique is his condition when he prophesied. Jeremiah predicted the wrath of God, and his life was in constant danger.[135] God's healing includes a flourishing life even though the current situation, such as Jeremiah's, is not optimal. In addition, Jeremiah provides the instrument through which God will bring healing to his people. According to Jer 33:14–16, God can heal Judah's incurable wounds caused by sin, such as sickness, death, economic chaos, and exile.[136] Jer-

---

Grove: IVP Academic, 2008), 287.

132. Ken Chant, *Healing in the Whole Bible: The Old Testament* (Ramona: Vision Publishing, 2012), 32–33.

133. Mulvihill, "Defeat of Disability," 130.

134. Mulvihill, "Defeat of Disability," 133.

135. Harold Ellis Dollar, "A Cross-Cultural Theology of Healing" (PhD diss., Fuller Theological Seminary, 1980), 44.

136. Michael L. Brown and Paul W. Ferris Jr., *Jeremiah, Lamentations*, Revised, The Expositor's Bible Commentary (Grand Rapids: Zondervan, 2010), 805.

emiah identifies the one who will bring relief to the people as the righteous branch from the line of David (Jer 23:5; 33:15). The promise of God to the people included a successor of David, as was prophesied by Nathan to King David.[137]

The prophet Isaiah's profound presentation of healing may be regarded as the most relevant Old Testament account of health and flourishing. Isaiah links healing to the specific work of a wounded servant.[138] Isaiah 53:4–5, 10, predicts the wounds suffered by Christ on the cross to heal believers and the Father's will to crush Christ with pain. The vivid image includes a diverse vocabulary to describe extreme physical abuse. The servant is wounded, which implies a stabbing injury. He was also crushed, which is a term that refers to severe oppression. In verse 5, there is a reference to chastisement and the wounds from scourging, suggesting that Christ has suffered judicial corporal punishment. In addition, the text clearly states that on the cross was an exchange between the servant's punishment and the believers' well-being. Christ was punished to bring healing and wholeness to faithful Israel as expressions of salvation.[139]

Mulvihill asserts that in the poetic literature of the Old Testament, especially in the Psalms, petitions for healing are pervasive. Psalms 6:2, 41:4, and 85:4 present the fact that the people of God do not shun healing but desire to be healed. Moreover, healing is sometimes connected to the restorative acts of God (Ps. 53:6); thus, the prayer for healing is joined by a confession of sins (Ps 30:3–6). God heals and sustains his people according to covenantal promises. The correlation between healing and restoration is significant for complete health and healing from sin.[140] Psalm 77 is particularly relevant because it reveals healing in the larger context of the community. Gaiser rightly asserts that there is no magic, no miraculous wonders, nothing inexplicable in Ps 77. However, there is healing wrought by grace through the gift of the community by restoring the person in isolation, depression, and doubt to faith and life. By extrapolation, the church in Christ also provides a healing ministry through songs, prayers, creed, and preaching of the word of God. Though helpful, communal and spiritual healing in congregational settings does not exclude other healing ministries but will benefit from the medication and counseling through God also

---

137. J. A. Thompson, *The Book of Jeremiah*, The New International Commentary of the Old Testament (Grand Rapids: Wm. B. Eerdmans, 1980), 782–83.

138. Mulvihill, "Defeat of Disability," 139.

139. J. Gordon McConville, *Isaiah*, Baker Commentary on the Old Testament Prophetic Books (Grand Rapids: Baker Academic, 2023), 1475–76.

140. Mulvihill, "Defeat of Disability," 150–51.

works. Christians will explore all the avenues of healing, one of which is the community of Christ.[141]

Healing and Flourishing in the New Testament

In the NT literature, God's work of healing and redemption is specifically oriented to the person and work of Jesus Christ. The healings in the OT may be seen as a foretaste of the future[142] through the healing work of the promised Isaianic servant. The NT introduces Jesus and his public preaching, teaching, and healing ministry. Healing is, therefore, a characteristic of Jesus' ministry and identity.[143] Jesus, as the agent of God's power to heal, is distinctive due to the degree to which healing was central to his ministry and for his unmediated exercise of the saving power of God. Jesus pronounced healing directly in a manner that assumed his possession of divine authority.[144] Shelly et al. point out that ultimate healing comes through Jesus Christ, the *soter*, a Greek term that means "savior" and "healer." The interrelationship between health and salvation is significant. Christ healed a paralyzed man (Mk 2:5, Luke 5:20) by telling him his sins were forgiven, and physical healing followed. [145] Some curing instances do not reference God's salvific action, such as in Mark 1:30–31. In other occurrences, Jesus states that there may be instances of saving as the healing of God without physical healing (Matt 16:25). However, some accounts identify healing and saving as the same, such as Luke 7:50.[146] For Matthew (Matt 11:3–5), Jesus' works make clear he is the healer that was prophesied. When Jesus' identity was questioned by John the Baptist, Jesus enumerated six specifics of his works as indisputable proof of his divine origins: sight for the blind, lame people that walk, lepers cleansed, hearing for the deaf, dead people raised, and poor people who hear the good news.[147]

The Gospels and Acts describe health as a foretaste of the final restoration of God's people in the coming age. Jesus' healings appear to represent some evidence of God's inaugurated kingdom and proof of Christ's divinity

---

141. Gaiser, *Healing in the Bible*, 99–100.

142. Mulvihill, "Defeat of Disability," 160.

143. Gaiser, *Healing in the Bible*, 132.

144. Green, "Healing," 538.

145. Shelly, Miller, and Fenstermacher, *Called to Care: A Christian Vision for Nursing*, 188.

146. Gaiser, *Healing in the Bible*, 245.

147. David. L. Turner, *Matthew*, Baker Exegetical Commentary on the New Testament (Grand Rapids: Baker Academic, 2008), 484.

and authority over nature, similar to Yahweh. Jesus offered a comprehensive healing that included a person's physical, emotional, socio-religious, and spiritual aspects. For instance, Jesus healed conditions marked by paralysis and leprosy (Matt 8:2). He also healed bleeding (Matt 9:22), blindness (Matt 11:5), lameness (Matt 11:5), and every disease and affliction (Matt 4:23).[148] Jesus also had a spiritual power that governed the demonic world. Mark 3 notes that Christ healed a demon-possessed man in the synagogue. Christ's metaphysical authority over demons climaxes in the fact that Christ can silence and expel them as no other healer.[149]

A leitmotif in the writings of Luke is that embedded in the name of Jesus Christ is his capacity as a savior and a healer. The juxtaposition of the name Ἰησοῦς and the verb ἰάσατο (to heal), communicates that for the Gospel writers, Jesus is a healer.[150] A significant teaching in the Lukan corpus about healing is found in Luke 10:25–37. In the parable of the good Samaritan, Jesus points out a healing situation where a Samaritan tended to the wounds of a Jew. A Samaritan would be a non-neighbor in the eyes of a righteous Jew. A Samaritan is a half-breed and renegade for the Jews, and he would be the last person from whom one would expect compassion. If, to the lawyer's expectations, the loving neighbor is reserved only for a select few, for Jesus, the neighbor is anyone with a need. In addition, as Bock argues, neighbors may come in surprising places. Therefore, the lawyer's attempt to limit his neighbors may restrict his capacity for meaningful friendships.[151] The idea promoted by Jesus that the wounded man receiving help from a Samaritan would be particularly humiliating. For Jesus, neighborliness goes far beyond patronizing benevolence only to those who allegedly deserve it; benevolence includes even those less fortunate.[152] In the book of Acts, acts of healing are marks of the apostles' initiation of ministry for the cause of the church. The apostles appear to be authorized by Jesus to continue his ministry for the sake of the church. Jesus grew his church through his apostles, who performed miraculous healings (Acts 5:12–16; 8:7).[153]

---

148. Mulvihill, "Defeat of Disability," 163–65.

149. Zorodzai Dube, "Reception of Jesus as Healer in Mark's Community," *HTS Theological Studies* 74, no. 1 (2018): 2–3.

150. Steve Reece, "Jesus as Healer: Etymologizing of Proper Names in Luke-Acts," *Zeitschrift Für Die Neutestamentliche Wissenschaft Und Die Kunde Der Älteren Kirche* 110, no. 2 (2019): 193.

151. Darrell L. Bock, *Luke*, The NIV Application Commentary (Grand Rapids: Zondervan, 1998), 450.

152. R. T. France, *Luke*, Teach the Text Commentary Series (Grand Rapids: Baker Books, 2013), 430.

153. Mulvihill, "Defeat of Disability," 176.

The healing instances in the Gospel of John are few (John 4:46–54; 5:1–47; 9:1–41; 11:1–44) compared to the synoptic corpus, but they provide an illuminating glimpse surrounding the healings of Jesus. John's account of healing links each of them with belief in Jesus. For John, the healings of Jesus are not an end in themselves, but they are ways God ordained for many to believe in Jesus.[154] For instance, in the healing of a man born blind (John 9:1–41), the narrative begins with an interesting question of who was responsible for the man's predicament. The evangelist clarifies in the pericope that at the pool of Siloam (Siloam means "sent"), Jesus, the God-sent Messiah, performs a sign that is supposed to stir faith in the readers. Theologian Andreas Köstenberger contends that healing by itself, unaccompanied by a believing response, is fruitless and ineffectual. The cured person will eventually die, and if his sin problem is not taken care of, his eternity is darkness and death. Revealing in this sense is the healing of the lame man (John 5:1–47). The lame man illustrates an un-regenerative response that left him physically walking but spiritually dead in his sins.[155] Moreover, Jesus' healing ministry shows that he never performed healing miracles merely for their physical benefit. Richard Mayhue helpfully stresses that Jesus healed (1) to show a fulfillment of messianic prophecy (Matt 8:17 and Isa 54:3; Matt 12:15–21 and Isa 42:1–4); (2) to let people know that Christ can forgive sins as God (Matt 9:6); (3) to authenticate the messianic ministry for John the Baptist (Matt 11:2–19); (4) to let people see the glorious works of God in the Son (John 9:3); (5) for the glory of God through Christ (John 11:4); (6) to call people to believe in Jesus (John 20:30–31), and (6) to authenticate Christ as accredited by God.[156]

In the epistles and Revelation, healing became significantly less noticeable. The fact that apostle Paul had severe health problems (Gal 4:13 and possibly 2 Cor 12:7), Trophimus was left sick in Miletus (2 Tim 4:20), and Paul healed neither Epaphroditus (Phil 2:27) nor Timothy's stomach issues (1 Tim 5:23) appear to indicate that miracles diminished in scope as time moved forward.[157] The most significant texts appear to be Jas 5:16, 1 Pet 2:24, and Rev 22:2.

James encourages the Christian community to confess sin and repent. The sufferer should confess her sins to be healed. The public acknowledgment of sin and sickness is connected. The dynamic between physical

---

154. Mulvihill, "Defeat of Disability," 172–173.

155. Köstenberger, *Theology of John's Gospel and Letters*, 341–43.

156. Richard L. Mayhue, "The Gifts of Healing," *The Master's Seminary Journal* 25, no. 2 (2014): 19–20.

157. Mayhue, "Gifts of Healing," 21.

healing and social restoration points to vital Christian remedies for fractured relationships. The remedies concern transparency, support, and unity, as shown in the open confession of sin and mutual prayers. According to James, "The healing of the mind is physical but points to deeper spiritual healing of sin and broken relationships."[158]

Thomas Schreiner argues that the citation of Isa 53:5 in 1 Pet 2:24 clarifies that mentioning Jesus' wounds points to forgiveness. The text arguably does not point to physical healing but to the spiritual dimension of healing, including forgiveness. The believers are healed by Christ's wounds in the sense that Christ's atoning death is the basis for the believers' salvation and a new kind of life.[159] The atonement of Christ is final. The scars of Christ are a sign of a wound that has healed and that there will be no further suffering. The scars of physical suffering mark a disease that has been defeated and which bears witness to the victory of Christ, who overcame every disease that brings death.[160]

The apostle John in Rev 22:2, based on Ezek 47:12, appears to connect the tree of life to healing. The leaves of the tree produce healing for the nations. If Ezekiel's tree of life heals only the national Israel, in Revelation, the tree includes the conversion of nations. The countries who disobey God's command to repent will be destroyed, but those who repent will enter the New Jerusalem and be healed. Healing here symbolizes the healing that has already occurred at the Eschaton. John's sense of healing may include the fact that there will be no physical healing on the new earth because death has ceased to exist. Moreover, healing consists of a spiritual understanding when all believing individuals from all the world's nations will have a right relationship with God.[161]

Mayhue summarizes the biblical perspective of healing and flourishing as the presence of healing that is noticeable in the Old Testament (over 2000 years), overwhelming in the Gospels (about three years), occasional in Acts (about 30 years), and negligible in the epistles (about 40 years).[162] What seems to have permeated Jesus' healing ministry and the later works

---

158. R. T. France and George H. Guthrie, *Hebrews, James*, Revised, The Expositor's Bible Commentary (Grand Rapids: Zondervan, 2006), 606.

159. Thomas R. Schreiner, *1, 2 Peter, Jude*, The New American Commentary (Nashville: B&H Publishing, 2003), 249–50.

160. Chant, *Healing in the Whole Bible*, 127.

161. Grant R. Osborne, *Revelation*, Baker Exegetical Commentary on the New Testament (Grand Rapids: Baker Academic, 2002), 1741–44.

162. Mayhue, "Gifts of Healing," 21–22.

of the apostles is their aim in healing as a restoration of believers to a fuller, more prosperous relationship with God and the faith community.¹⁶³

Flourishing Through Suffering Within the Boundaries of Fallen Condition

An anthropological-theological view of a patient necessitates discussing the meaning of flourishing through suffering within the boundaries of a fallen condition. This section aims to develop a theological and biblical understanding of suffering in terms of disease and illness.

Suffering is an essential part of being human. Sulmasy distinguishes between suffering and pain. Pain may be defined as a physiological phenomenon that stimulates specific nerve cells, such as somatic, visceral, and neuropathic. On the other hand, suffering, infers Sulmasy, has less to do with the stimulation of pain fibers than it does with the experience of persons. Suffering appears to proceed from the experience of one's situation in life.¹⁶⁴ The patient suffers whenever she becomes ill because illness points to mortality and finitude. Thus, the suffering of the sick, such as in cases of disability, diseases, illnesses, and the dying, may represent the most basic forms of suffering.¹⁶⁵ A question that the following section attempts to answer is how the sufferer can flourish within the boundaries of a fallen condition marked by the consequences of sin. Before answering this question, it seems necessary to survey some theoretical explanations of disease.

Some Theoretical Explanations of Disease

The scholarly literature on suffering, such as sickness and disability, abounds. Louise Lawrence suggests that resources about disability include several models or theories of disability. The first model is the medical perspective, which proposes disability as a functional or biological defect in a body that needs diagnosis and treatment.¹⁶⁶ Theologian Ulrich Eibach explains the view that theorizes modern understanding of disease as characterized by the Cartesian separation of spirit and matter, soul and body. Changes in the body are generally explained through the action of material forces on the

---

163. Shelly et al., *Called to Care*, 188.
164. Sulmasy, *Healer's Calling*, locs. 972–86.
165. Sulmasy, *Healer's Calling*, loc. 1064.
166. Louise J. Lawrence, *Sense and Stigma in the Gospels: Depictions of Sensory-Disabled Characters* (Oxford: Oxford University Press, 2013), 4.

body. According to the modern view, the disease has material causes and cannot be reduced to spiritual influences. The human body is perceived as a machine, and diseases are contingent and blind to natural fate. Diseases are biological dysfunctions with material causes that must be fixed. As Eibach explains, the scientific view restricts itself to the material cause of a disease without asking why it came about and how it relates to the sufferer.[167]

Medical theoretician Lennart Nordenfelt proposes that a person with a disease has a slightly lower probability of survival than a completely healthy person. Not every disease is life-threatening, but there is a marginal reduction in the bearer's likelihood of survival. Nordenfelt also sees that all diseases present the probability of inevitable phenomenological consequences or some limitation of the agency.[168] He theorizes about health and disease primarily based on abilities to pursue welfare.[169] Messer admits that Nordenfelt's account is a considerable improvement of an only biologically based notion of natural function, such as the case inferred in Boorse's biostatistical model. Nevertheless, Messer proposes that Nodernfelt's view does allow for subjective or autonomous goals chosen by the individual and objective conceptions of human happiness and welfare.[170] Theologian Thomas E. Reynolds suggests Christians commonly adopt the medical model of disability. Reynolds criticizes the medical perspective as reducing disability to a problem to be fixed or overcome. In addition, the person is reduced to a function of disabilities. According to this model, the patient is seen as having nothing to offer; thus, the reciprocity of the relationship between physician and patient is annulled by professional control, repair, and supervision.[171]

The social and minority model stresses that disability concerns the social, religious, and environmental structures that disallow specific individuals' full participation in their community.[172] According to this model, disability is understood in social rather than individual terms. Messer notes that this model coincides with the disability activism of the 1960s and 1970s led by the Marxist-inspired Union of the Physically Impaired Against

---

167. Ulrich Eibach, "Life History, Sin, and Disease," *Christian Bioethics: Non-Ecumenical Studies in Medical Morality* 12, no. 2 (2006): 120–21.

168. Lennart Nordenfelt, "The Opposition Between Naturalistic and Holistic Theories of Health and Disease," in *Health, Illness and Disease: Philosophical Essays*, ed. Havi Carel and Rachel Cooper (New York: Routledge, 2014), 26–27.

169. Nordenfelt, "Opposition," 34–35.

170. Messer, *Flourishing*, 13.

171. Thomas E. Reynolds, *Vulnerable Communion: A Theology of Disability and Hospitality* (Grand Rapids: Brazos Press, 2008), 25.

172. Lawrence, *Sense and Stigma in the Gospels*, 4.

Segregation (UPIAS). According to this model, society disables physically impaired people.[173] Disability is not about the sufferer's physical, cognitive, or psychological characteristics. Instead, society is the issue for not being organized according to the needs of disabled people. Professor Deborah Creamer suggests that, according to this model, individuals are often more handicapped by the physical and attitudinal barriers in society than by their actual disabilities. The model emphasizes the issue of justice because addressing issues concerning disability "means working against unjust social structures and instances of bias and exclusion."[174]

The limits model, developed by philosopher Deborah Creamer, concerns human limits. She challenges the medical, as well as the social and minority models by not dividing participants into one or two categories (disabled or not disabled) but offers an innovative way of thinking about disability. The medical model begins with evaluating limitations, while the limits model begins with the notion of limitations as an unsurprising human condition. Moreover, the limits model contends that it differs from the social and minority model by avoiding categorization and encouraging acknowledgment of "a web of related experiences." The limits model may be considered a companion that emphasizes the embodiment condition in various formations, including disabled embodiment and disease. The most helpful aspect of the limits model may be that it highlights that all people experience limits and are accepted, rejected, complicated, degraded, and live differently. Creamer stresses that acknowledging limitations gives both the caregiver and care receiver the ability to think of limits as a natural and promising aspect of being human and, at the same time, regard them as complex and challenging.[175]

In the same line of thought, philosopher and theologian Kelly Kapic argues for embracing human limitations as part of God's design, which is inherent in being finite creatures in a fallen world. Kapic believes embracing the gift of being limited is part of being human. God is the good creator who designed limited creatures according to his image. These creaturely limits, including physicality, are how God allows people to love him with all heart, soul, mind, strength, and to love their neighbors. Kapic suggests that the sufferer can celebrate the goodness of being a creature of God who loves

---

173. Messer, *Flourishing*, 55.

174. Deborah Beth Creamer, *Disability and Christian Theology: Embodied Limits and Constructive Possibilities* (Oxford: Oxford University Press, 2009), 25.

175. Creamer, *Disability and Christian Theology*, 31–32.

what he made. Further, Kapic maintains that "God delights in our finitude: he is not embarrassed or shocked by our creatureliness."[176]

Suffering limitations are not illusions or imaginary, helpfully theorizes Barth. For him, disease is a weakness to being a man, an opposition to the strength to live. Barth admits that there is an imaginary sickness, an illness that exists only in the patient's imagination. However, "Sickness is no illusion, whether in relation to the opposing will to live in the true and secondary sense, or objectively as a different condition from the real strength be as man and the freedom of secondary vital forces, or in relation to God as the Creator of human life and the will to live."[177] Sickness, as Barth puts it, is an encroachment on the life God created. The impairing of psychical and physical powers that occur in illness, the resistance of the disease to health, and the "obstinacy" it maintains even through all medical and technical measures, are not plays of imagination but actual events in the natural history of the real man, a real enemy.[178]

Understanding diseases and disabilities as weaknesses may release the human condition from narcissistic self-enclosure to empower the risk of genuine relationships. The partial wholeness of flourishing possible in this life comes not despite but through disability and vulnerability. Reynolds concludes, "Disability is part of the fragile character of human existence in general, wherein we can find genuine good in relationships of mutual vulnerability. Wholeness comes through mutual dependency; and dependency marks vulnerability, which involves disability. Our weaknesses open us to each other."[179]

A Fallen Condition

Understanding suffering in the Bible, a suffering that overlaps disability and disease, may not be an obvious endeavor. The biblical concept of suffering, which overlaps with sickness, disease, demonization, healing, society, and spirituality, is a complex set of ideas in the scriptural framework. As Mulvihill explains, the ancient world did not employ one word for disability.[180]

---

176. Kelly M. Kapic, *You're Only Human: How Our Limits Reflect God's Design and Why That's Good News* (Grand Rapids: Brazos Press, 2022), 12–16.
177. Barth, *Church Dogmatics*, III.4:364.
178. Barth, *Church Dogmatics*, III.4:365.
179. Reynolds, *Vulnerable Communion*, 117.
180. Mulvihill, "Defeat of Disability," 67.

The Origin of Disease and Later Development in the Bible

As already shown, people are created in and for relationships. Relationships are the essence of human flourishing. God's design for people created according to the divine image is for human beings to be in communion with him and in harmony with others. True human flourishing is possible when relationships with God and neighbors are not obstructed.[181] The Christian doctrine of fallenness and sinfulness indicates that the current reality of diseases, illnesses, etc., is caused by sin. Theologian Paul Tillich explains the doctrine of creation and fall from an ontological perspective. He asserts that the most dialectical point in the doctrine of creation is the human situation of fallenness, the most mysterious point in human experience. For Tillich, sin is a separation of existence from its unity with essence, where "man has left the ground in order 'to stand upon' himself, to actualize what he essentially is, in order to be finite freedom."[182] Man, through sin, is outside of the divine life. Therefore, there appears to be a fracturing of essential and existential beings that causes humanity to separate from each other and the world. Bioethicist Devan Joy Stahl, based on the Tillichian understanding of ontology, beneficially argues that sin distorts the ontological structures of life. As a result, "The problems of hardships in life are thus attributed to the effects of the fall, including all human experiences of illness and disability."[183]

Jennifer Patterson also contends that sin distorts relationships. Sin, as introduced in Gen 3, produces alienation from God, self, others, and the world. The vision marked by autonomy and control, rivaling the biblical view of flourishing, is characterized by sin. Sin resists the creational givenness and limits of the human condition and human dependence upon each other.[184] Shelly et al. argue that sin is a breach of interpersonal relationships, and thus sin and sickness go together.[185] In addition, the introduction of sin into the creation brought the sentence of death upon humanity (Rom 5:12; 6:23). Because of original sin, people get sick, and because people get sick,

---

181. Jennifer Marshall Patterson, "Human Beings Created in and for Relationship," in *Created in the Image of God: Applications and Implications for Our Cultural Confusion*, ed. David S. Dockery and Lauren McAfee (Nashville: Forefront Books, 2023), 90–91.

182. Paul Tillich, *Systematic Theology*, vol. 1 (Chicago: The University of Chicago PRess, 1951), 255.

183. Devan Stahl, "A Christian Ontology of Genetic Disease and Disorder," *Journal of Disability & Religion* 19, no. 2 (2015): 129.

184. Patterson, "Human Beings Created in and for Relationship," 91.

185. Shelly et al., *Called to Care*, 185.

they die. Chant intriguingly asserts that "people do not die because they become sick, they become sick because they are dying."[186]

Sin began in Adam and Eve's fall through the subtlety of the serpent, Satan. Satan is the instigator of sin and the one whose deceit resulted in the curse of sin upon humanity. The pain and suffering multiplied because of sin. In other words, as Chant believes, (1) all sickness stems indirectly from Satan (Acts 10:30); (2) some sickness is directly caused by Satan as, for example, in the case of Job (Job 2:7); (3) all sickness arises indirectly from sin because the human race is corrupted by sin, and (4) some sickness is caused directly by sin (John 5:14).[187]

When addressing the origin of disease and later developments in the Bible, a fundamental question concerns the place of physicians other than God. In Scripture, no one accepted sickness as a blessing, but it was regarded as a curse, captivity, something evil, foreign to God's plan, an enemy. At the same time, God is recognized as a sovereign, the healer of his people, and that nothing could happen outside his will.[188] Gaiser contends that the OT references to physicians are not universally negative. The oft-cited passage in 2 Chr 16:12–13 concerning King Asa's sickness is subject to various interpretations.[189]

The author of 2 Chronicles provides a theological commentary concerning King Asa's foot disease. Sickness in Asa's situation is an unheeded warning from God, expressing divine displeasure over Asa's response to political crises. Likely, the fact that Asa seeks help in the form of physicians impugns his faith in God and is not a dismissal of ancient medical practitioners.[190] Physicians are present in the Hebrew Bible, even though the texts are few and far between. The presence of physicians is confirmed by archeological evidence, such as the case of a seal impression that dates to the seventh or sixth century B.C. which belonged to an individual possessing the title "healer." Physicians also appear without any indication that this profession is illegitimate, such as in Gen 50:2, when Joseph asks Egyptian physicians to embalm his father. In Jer 8:22, the prophet laments that no physician is left in Gilead to attend to the wounds of his people. Job addresses his slanderous so-called friends as worthless physicians (Job 13:4).[191] Job calls them worth-

186. Chant, *Healing in the Whole Bible*, 23.
187. Chant, *Healing in the Whole Bible*, 24.
188. Chant, *Healing in the Whole Bible*, 29.
189. Gaiser, *Healing in the Bible*, 29.
190. Andrew E. Hill, *1&2 Chronicles*, The NIV Application Commentary (Grand Rapids: Zondervan, 2003), 723.
191. Isabel Cranz, "Advice for a Successful Doctor's Visit: King Asa Meets Ben Sira," *The Catholic Biblical Quarterly* 80, no. 2 (2018): 233–34.

less because their counsel, care, and treatment are flawed, but flawed care does not indict all care.[192] The OT does not appear to condemn the work of physicians or the seeking of medical help. King Asa's fault was his reliance on medicine and lack of faith in God's healing power.[193]

In other instances, the Bible admits specific knowledge of and interest in medical care, infers Gaiser. For example, Isa 1:6 implies some knowledge about draining, binding, and softening sores and wounds.[194] Jeremiah 30:13–14 uses the metaphor of remedies to open wounds that do not heal. The clinical details in the vocabulary of prophecy include the lack of new skin to cover and close.[195] Furthermore, according to Ezek 34:16, the Bible mentions a basic level of medical treatment. Based on Eccl 3:3, healing treatments are one activity among others in a list of thoroughly human endeavors. God often carries out his purposes through human agents, such as Cyrus (Isa 44:28). There is no apparent theological reason to believe that God, the great healer of Israel, cannot heal through human physicians and natural means.[196]

The Lord Christ compares himself to a doctor (Luke 4:23) or a physician (Mark 2:17). The apostle Paul appears to honor the physician's office, as suggested in Luke's title, "the beloved physician," in Col 4:14.[197] Through the event of the cross, God worked to heal and reconcile all of creation and humanity to himself, instigating a cosmic renewal. The cross of Christ reaches into every part of time and space, even in those places and circumstances that indicate that the effects of sin and non-reconciliation continue.[198]

A Lukan Disability Paradigm

The Lukan corpus emphasizes healing and disease, Jesus' authority, the kingdom's inauguration, the salvation of God through Christ, and the Eschaton's beginning.[199] For Luke, healing and salvation overlap. The Gospel of Luke

---

192. Gaiser, *Healing in the Bible*, 29.

193. Chant, *Healing in the Whole Bible*, 73.

194. Gaiser, *Healing in the Bible*, 31.

195. Gerald L. Keown, Pamela J. Scalise, and Thomas G. Smothers, *Jeremiah 26–52*, Word Biblical Commentary (Grand Rapids: Zondervan, 1995), 429.

196. Gaiser, *Healing in the Bible*, 32.

197. Gaiser, *Healing in the Bible*, 34.

198. David McLachlan, *Accessible Atonement: Disability, Theology, and the Cross of Christ*, Studies in Religion, Theology, and Disability (Waco: Baylor University Press, 2021), 6.

199. Darrell L. Bock, *A Theology of Luke and Acts*, The Biblical Theology of the New Testament (Grand Rapids: Zondervan, 2012), 318.

uses many words of healing in many instances to prove the Gospel's point that Jesus brings spiritual deliverance. The dominant words are θεραπεύω (to heal), ἰάομαι (to restore from a state of sin; to heal), and, already mentioned, σῴζω (to save) in its various forms.[200] Jesus points to his mighty acts, including healings, as proof that he is the one who has come to inaugurate the arrival of a new era and his role in it.[201]

Moreover, Luke's emphasis on the body is recorded in nearly forty passages. For example, Luke mentions a wide range of bodily conditions, such as "being barren, silent, mute, deaf, blind (and several other forms of lack of sight), paralyzed, lame, crippled, small of stature, mad, having leprosy, dropsy, a fever, a withered hand, a discharge of blood, sores, dysentery, lack of perception, dullness, and barely hearing."[202] In addition, Luke provides numerous descriptions of symptoms caused by demonization, such as a lack of bodily control, convulsions, foaming, shattering, throwing, and being bent over.[203] Based on such a rich account of diseases and healing, analyzing an arguably significant Lukan text that provides a distinctively biblical view of diseases may be helpful.

The narrative in Luke 18:35–43 concerns Jesus' travel for the Passover festival when a blind beggar received healing. The beggar was saved or healed through faith, demonstrating that Jesus' salvation is for everyone on the social spectrum.[204] The beggar's placement on the side of the road implies the stigmatization of social and religious outcasts. Remarkable to the story is that Jesus looks at the blind man's need not as a problem to be solved but as a person to be honored. Jesus stops and asks that the blind person be brought to him. The beggar is not a "blind man" but a person who is blind, suggests France.[205]

Furthermore, Luke's repetition of the beggar's physical issue, such as blindness, suggests a symbolic passing from darkness to light; therefore, it is a soteriological emphasis. For Luke, the account represents an opportunity to indicate the significant reversal of entering the kingdom of Christ. The irony of ironies is that the blind see and the unrighteous become righteous, maintains Stein.[206] The soteriological vocabulary concerns the blind man's appeal in terms of mercy. Such cries, explains Bock, were commonly

---

200. Bock, *Theology of Luke and Acts*, 363.
201. Bock, *Theology of Luke and Acts*, 368.
202. Mulvihill, "Defeat of Disability," 68.
203. Mulvihill, "Defeat of Disability," 68.
204. France, *Luke*, 676.
205. France, *Luke*, 1264.
206. Stein, *Luke*, chap. 5.

associated with sin because the plight is particularly desperate. Luke records other emotional cries, such as the cry of the lepers (17:3) and the man's plea from Hades (16:24). The cry for healing does not go unheeded by Jesus. He restores the man's sight, showing that Jesus' work as the promised Davidite is to bring light to the darkness. Even more significant in the story appears to be the healing and the blind man's understanding of Jesus as the Son of David and his faith in him. The man's belief in Jesus brought physical healing, but it pictures a deeper reality regarding his faith. His faith in the Son of David restored his bodily and spiritual sight.[207]

The story reveals that true metaphysical healing is not given merely by therapy but by the forgiveness of a merciful God. Essentially, the narrative points to the incompleteness or blindness of the human condition without the saving work of God. As Gaiser acknowledges, healing and saving are two sides of the same coin. When it occurs, healing is not in isolation of the person and work of Jesus. Christ's work of healing and curing are theologically connected. The cross is a healing event related to rejection and suffering. True healing is not a triumphalist success, but it is the transformation of human beings won through the suffering and death of Jesus.[208] The transformation of man is seen not only through curing blindness but also through his beginning to follow Jesus, glorifying God as he goes. Mulvihill concludes that by following Jesus, Luke infers that man entered society and community. From an isolated beggar, he is now one of the followers of Christ. The healing permeates his vision, social acceptability, and religious transformation. In other words, healing is an opportunity for a conversion from an outsider to become a privileged insider of the community of Jesus.[209]

A Christian Response to Suffering

Is there a distinctively Christian response to suffering? This is a perennial question that Christians have attempted to answer throughout their existence. On the one hand, finding the cause of a disease is relatively easy. In most cases, the causes of diseases and sicknesses can be traced at the level of the particular process, that is, the progression of the disease in a patient. Other times, diseases can be associated with pathogens' general evolutionary development processes, cancer's molecular and cell biology, etc. On the other hand, theologically, a disease, an accident, or any other form of suffering can generate an inquiry about the reason why God allowed it to happen.

---

207. Bock, *Luke*, 700.
208. Gaiser, *Healing in the Bible*, 188–89.
209. Mulvihill, "Defeat of Disability," 99–100.

A theodicy may attempt a partial answer. However, Messer suggests that a more convincing way of looking at suffering should be what God does in and through Jesus Christ in response.[210] He argues that when Christians attempt to wrestle with the meaning of suffering in the context of disease and healing, it might well be advised to focus less on philosophical arguments and "more on what God in Christ has done to address evil and suffering, how that work of Christ shows God to be just, and how we ought to respond to what God has done."[211]

Kapic also suggests that a proper Christian response to suffering is to admit vulnerability. He mentions, "To recognize our vulnerability is to confess that we are creatures rather than the Creator."[212] Reynolds stresses that all people are linked indissolubly and share a fundamental condition, such as vulnerable personhood. He claims that security is an illusion gained from being inscribed with body capital within the cult of normalcy. Disability, however, deconstructs the cult of normalcy and opens the possibility for human solidarity.[213] The modern view of normalcy, asserts Kapic, tempts people to think they are not vulnerable to failure, external attack, and internal weaknesses. People are in need, and God alone is the safe shelter and security.[214]

The Christian response to suffering should also recognize that any threatening illness, fatal or not, involves a spiritual crisis. Pellegrino supports the view that a dying person must affirm or deny God. Christian caregivers need to be particularly alert to the spiritual causes of suffering. A theology of suffering should guide caregivers to be actively involved in presenting the reasons for atonement for sin, reconciliation with God, or following Christ in the way of the cross. This way, Christian health practitioners can point patients to peace in surrendering themselves into God's hands.[215]

While surrendering in God's hands, Christians may flourish through suffering by expressing lament and cultivating gratitude. Kapic argues, "Lament and gratitude are mirror concepts that highlight the same fundamental truth: we are dependent on the God who rescues us."[216] A lament is a proper way to express suffering in a fallen and hurting world. However, gratitude

---

210. Messer, *Flourishing*, 128.

211. Messer, *Flourishing*, 130.

212. Kapic, *You're Only Human*, 200.

213. Reynolds, *Vulnerable Communion*, 104.

214. Kapic, *You're Only Human*, 201–4.

215. Edmund D. Pellegrino, "A Christians Response to Suffering in Dying Persons.," *Sisters Today* 68, no. 4 (1996): 261.

216. Kapic, *You're Only Human*, 206.

in suffering is rooted in remembering God's deeds in salvation history, his identity, and what the Lord will do in the Eschaton. Despite all the wickedness, sadness, and frustrations of living in a fallen world, Kapic argues that "laments are not all there is: Christ did not merely die, he rose, and he will come again." Finally, the disease is an evil to be resisted, yet it also warns the sufferer to invest their hope of eternal life offered by God in Christ.[217]

Flourishing and Life After Death

The Christian community was an eschatologically minded people from the beginning. The apocalyptic reality and the natural understanding of the Savior's resurrection provide a general initiation about the subject of life after death.[218] The discussion about health, healing, and disease is incomplete without discussing flourishing and life after death, a part of human experience achievable only through faith in the redemptive work of Christ on the cross and in which redeemed people enjoy health, well-being, and healing. The biblical vision of eternity is beyond the reach of mortal beings in this age. However, the Bible provides a glimpse of what it means to live abundantly in the presence of the living God, where there will be no crying, pain, or death. Even though the vision of eternity is somewhat blurred for people, a foretaste of what is to come for believers is granted in this life whenever healing and flourishing are experienced and enjoyed.[219]

The ultimate fulfillment of penultimate goods, such as health and embodied creaturely flourishing in this life, point to the ultimate fulfillment in the eternal union with the triune God[220] through faith in the person and work of Christ on the cross. Gaiser acknowledges that an eschatological view of healing and disease is integral to the NT. The ministry of Jesus is a foretaste of life after death, such as justice, peace, health, and well-being. The entire presence of the benefits found in Christ awaits the new coming of Jesus in the Eschaton. The perfect healing of individuals and nations remains a future hope.[221]

---

217. Messer, *Flourishing*, 158.

218. Jerry L. Sumney, "The Role (or Lack Thereof) of Christ in the Eschaton in Paul and Revelation," *Perspectives In Religious Studies* 45, no. 2 (2018): 139.

219. Christoffer H. Grundmann, "To Have Life, and Have It Abundantly! Health and Well-Being in Biblical Perspective," *Journal of Religion and Health* 53, no. 2 (2014): 559.

220. Messer, *Flourishing*, 160.

221. Gaiser, *Healing in the Bible*, 224.

A theological reflection on healing and disability must include the place of complete healing in the eschatological horizon. Mulvihill correctly notes that there are various interpretations of complete healing. Most disability theologians advocate that God will retain an individual's disabilities within a glorified body.[222] Theologian Amos Yong argues in his view of a dynamic eschatology[223] that the redemptive transformation that occurs with the resurrection is only the beginning of the soul's eschatological journey.[224] The body will be transformed, "even if its particular scars and marks will be redeemed, not eliminated," and, continues Yong, "the body itself finds its rest in the unending process of being transformed by the glory of God in ways that overturn the binary dichotomies not only of male/female but also of disabled/nondisabled."[225] Theologian Lisa Powell regards Amos Yong's understanding of disability in the immortal state as speculation. Powell challenges Yong's view by asking how one can think of the eschatological future with less reliance upon a notion of progress. She proposes that a future transformation does retain some continuity of identity. Still, the hope for newness resides not in the social-cultural value system but is engrafted into Christ's marks of suffering.[226]

In addition, several biblical texts imply a complete transformation of the body's resurrected state. In Rom 8:21, apostle Paul stresses that the whole of creation will be liberated from the consequences of sin. Not only that, but Paul also assumes that believers yearn for adoption as sons when the complete blessings of God are given to believers, such as the entire inheritance and perfect holiness in resurrected bodies.[227] The Pauline thought of the resurrected body is further developed in 1 Cor 15:35–58. Paul explains issues of continuity and discontinuity in the resurrected body using a botanical analogy. The naked seed may be understood in the most natural terms as the corruptible and decaying body of low-status flesh. A naked seed needing to be clothed is an imagery that the eschatological transformation that happens to the human body is necessary for the eternal state. The

---

222. Mulvihill, "Defeat of Disability," 285.

223. Yong relies on and develops Eiesland's concept of eschatological disability. See Nancy L. Eiesland, *The Disabled God: Toward a Liberatory Theology of Disability* (Nashville: Abingdon Press, 1994).

224. Amos Yong, *Theology and Down Syndrome* (Waco: Baylor University Press, 2007), 279.

225. Yong, *Theology and Down Syndrome*, 281.

226. Lisa Powell, "Disability and Resurrection: Eschatological Bodies, Identity, and Continuity," *Journal of the Society of Christian Ethics* 41, no. 1 (2021): 95, 100.

227. Moo, *Romans*, 426–29.

imagery also implies that the future body is certainly not identical to the first, but the whole process suggests a definite material continuity.[228]

According to Paul, the resurrected body will be transformed into an entirely different form that is appropriate for heavenly existence. The new body will not be a reanimated corpse or a recycled body. Still, it is a body appropriate for the new creation with the freedom from the ravaging effects of sin, such as the propensity to death and decay.[229] Moreover, the new body will not be subject to the laws of physical life because the newness consists of the Holy Spirit's empowerment of the believer. The Bible also explains that the future transformation of the body will be shaped in the image of Christ's resurrected body. Even though believers continue to bear the image of Adam and his fall, the image of God in Christ will be perfectly restored in believers on the eschatological horizon.[230]

A fundamental dogmatic issue arises from Paul's theology of the believer's new, resurrected body. Christ's resurrected body keeps the marks of the crucifixion and, at the same time, represents the pattern in which everyone who believes in Jesus will be resurrected. Does the eradication of disabilities represent a kind of heavenly eugenics?[231] What is the significance of Christ's atonement marks? James Gould holds an elimination view of disabilities in life after death. He believes that God acts to restore wholeness, a holistic functioning that is both the origin and destiny of human persons. Christ's marks are the signs of dignity, whereas disabilities are limiting because they disrupt normal functioning and prevent critical human activities. In addition, Jesus' scars may still be present in the resurrected body throughout eternity, while people with disabilities should not remain impaired. Gould stresses, "Jesus' scars are signs of his redemptive work, the price of our salvation," while disability traits are "signs of brokenness and dysfunction of creation."[232] Moreover, Mulvihill convincingly maintains that Jesus kept the marks from nails and spear and not the marks from other wounds, such as from the crown of thorns, lacerations from flogging,

---

228. David E. Garland, *1 Corinthians*, Baker Exegetical Commentary on the New Testament (Grand Rapids: Baker Academic, 2003), 1704.

229. Andy Johnson, "Turning the World Upside down in 1 Corinthians 15: Apocalyptic Epistemology, the Resurrected Body and the New Creation," *The Evangelical Quarterly* 75, 4 (2003): 307.

230. Mark Taylor, *1 Corinthians*, The New American Commentary (Nashville: B & H Publishing, 2014), 1163–69.

231. Candida Moss, "The Marks of the Nails: Scars, Wounds and the Resurrection of Jesus in John," *Early Christianity* 8, no. 1 (2017): 51.

232. James B. Gould, "The Hope of Heavenly Healing of Disability Part 1 Theological Issues," *Journal of Disability & Religion* 20, no. 4 (2016): 325.

evidence from the pulling out of his beard, etc., because they are a distinct eternal witness to Christ's atonement for the sin of his people and to Jesus' identity as the Messiah.[233]

To claim to understand Paul's theology of the new body entirely is absurd. However, it seems safe to argue that the believers will enjoy a new embodied experience in the life after death that conforms to the resurrected body of Jesus Christ. The new body is, in essence, a body fit for life in the presence of God and perfected by Christ's victory over sin and death.[234] The tensions in eschatology concerning the continuous and discontinuous with the present age will continue in discussions. However, a proper balance between the continuity and discontinuity of this body and the resurrected body may be a wise approach to the things of immortality.[235] Finally, the defeat of death in the work of Christ is a benefit of the atonement of Jesus. The greatest blessing in the Eschaton is to live eternally in the presence of God. Thus, "the defeat of our last enemy, death, does not mean a heroic technological effort to cure us of it," continues Messer, "that would be better understood as counterfeit or parody of its true defeat, accomplished by Christ."[236]

An Ecclesiological History of Medical Care

History of care, hospitals, hospice, etc., shows that the church has both a history and a stake in the care of sufferers made in God's image.[237] The church has a history of involvement in health and healing, and the church also has a call to be involved in the care of sufferers. Christ's ministry included a significant amount of healing. Consequently, the church is called to continue Jesus' work on earth, caring for the sick and dying. This section's purpose is not merely to repeat a well-established narrative of hospital chronology[238] but to argue that the church has a history, a call, and resources that can be used in healing and care to treat people as God's image bearers.[239]

233. Mulvihill, "Defeat of Disability," 289-90.

234. Mulvihill, "Defeat of Disability," 286.

235. Keith Innes, "Towards an Ecological Eschatology: Continuity and Discontinuity," *The Evangelical Quarterly* 81, no. 2 (2009): 127.

236. Messer, *Flourishing*, 194.

237. Thanks to Dr. C. Ben Mitchell for suggesting this vital argument in a personal conversation.

238. Peregrine Horden, "The Earliest Hospitals in Byzantium, Western Europe, and Islam," *Journal of Interdisciplinary History* 35, no. 3 (2005): 365.

239. Lynn Renee Ronsberg, "Prescription for Health Care: The Church and Its Resources" (PhD diss., The Union Institute, 1994), XVIII-XIX.

Healthcare in the Classical World: Fifth Century B.C. to Third Century A.D.

Christian medical care develops in the context of Hellenic and Roman medicine. Ethicist Albert Jonsen identifies the documenting of medical care in the classical world, beginning with the Greek physician Hippocrates of Cos (460–370 B.C.) up to the Roman physician Galen (129–99 A.D.). The work of healing and treating disease appears in Hellenism as both folk practice and religious ritual. Healers use both forms of healing, ranging from soothing remedies to magical and religious incantations. Healing work developed over time into more rational medicine based on empirical observation and logical reasoning. In the Hellenic world, healing began being called an art or skill, and its practitioners were craftsmen.[240] The myth of Greek medicine is at least as old as the Homeric Age, when it was believed that the god Asklepios, who passed medical knowledge from generation to generation, emerged as the deity of the healing art. The supreme god, Zeus, taught Askelpios, who passed the torch of medical knowledge to mortal doctors. Historian Timothy Miller helpfully observes that the myth reflected reality. Even though medicine developed in a scientific and theoretical framework during the classical period, medical knowledge tended to pass from father to son, thus keeping the medical profession in the ranks of the same families.[241]

Furthermore, in ancient times, medicine and religion were closely related, asserts historian Miller. For example, the great physician of Kroton, Demokedes, was the son of Kalliphon, who, according to tradition, was described as a priest of Asklepios. In addition, the College of Public Physicians in Athens customarily sacrificed to Asklepios twice a year for them and their patients. Similarly, it appears that the practice of religion and medicine persisted to the times of Claudius and Nero, whose doctor was Xenophon. Xenophon served as a priest and doctor at the Asklepion temple and the Roman emperors' doctor.

According to a collection of medical treatises, *Corpus Hippocraticum*, a disease can be of a divine and human origin. Thus, the sacred aspect of sickness is not denied, but the scope of the divine can be limited to a specific disease. From the early days of scientific medicine to the time of Galen, most Greek physicians maintained the existence of God (or gods) in the

---

240. Albert R. Jonsen, *A Short History of Medical Ethics* (New York: Oxford University Press, 2000), 1.

241. Timothy S. Miller, *The Birth of the Hospital in the Byzantine Empire* (Baltimore: The John Hopkins University Press, 1997), 31.

supernatural dimensions of life and the possibility of spiritual healing.[242] The Greeks attributed diseases to environmental causes, such as the climatic conditions of seasonal variation, winds, and temperature. For instance, the Greeks attributed some diseases to specific seasons, such as winter pleurisy and summer jaundice. Moreover, the Greeks believed certain demographic factors and localities were susceptible to various diseases. For example, Greek medicine associated diarrhea as typical in summer and cold as frequent in winter. They also noted that low-lying marshes or slow-moving rivers were unhealthy and that certain diseases were endemic. In a different Hippocratic treatise, diseases are attributed to "bad air," which makes the air poisonous. The air can become contaminated by exhalation or excretion of some kind. However, cool breezes and well-ventilated houses were considered healthy. In addition, medical practitioners recommended a change in diet and regimen to strengthen the sufferer to overcome sickness.[243]

After absorbing the Hellenic civilization into their empire, the Romans did not display the same interest in Greek medicine as they did in the Greek arts, philosophy, etc. Politicians such as Marcus Cato, a paragon of Roman conservative virtue who singled out medical men as the lowest of the Hellenes, explored the anti-Greek sentiments. Though well-studied in Greek philosophical work, the Latin orator Cicero did not consider medicine a suitable career for a well-born Roman. Pliny the Elder also criticized the abject dependence of noble Romans on the treacherous advice of Greek physicians. He compiled a list of remedies for the Roman people, though many of them were culled from Greek works, as pointed out by Miller. Despite Pliny's hatred of physicians, most Romans of the high empire did not share Pliny's views. However, Pliny and others influenced the general Roman population, and a professional medical career was considered unsuitable for a Roman distinction.[244] Perhaps the premier figure of the Roman tradition that endeavored to preserve the Hippocratic tradition was a native of Pergamum, Galen, who practiced medicine in Rome. Jonsen notes that Galen believed that any doctor must be skilled at reasoning about the problems presented to him, understand the nature and functioning of the body, practice temperance, and despise money. A good physician is not only a student of philosophy but one whose life has been formed by justice and who lives according to the virtues of Stoic doctrine. The Galenic physician

---

242. Miller, *Birth of the Hospital in the Byzantine Empire*, 33.

243. Gary B. Ferngren, *Medicine and Health Care in Early Christianity* (Baltimore: John Hopkins University Press, 2009), 17.

244. Miller, *Birth of the Hospital in the Byzantine Empire*, 36.

is more focused on the character of medical practitioners rather than rules and duties.²⁴⁵

Healthcare Institutions in the Classical World

In the classical world, some healthcare institutions may represent the foundation for later Christian hospital care. The Byzantine hospital's roots can be traced back to parallel medical institutions of ancient times. Typically, acknowledges Miller, ancient physicians treated seriously sick persons in their homes.²⁴⁶ However, four ancient institutions may appear linked to the Christian hospital.

The Roman army hospital (*valetudinarium*) included facilities for kitchens, wards, and, likely, operating rooms. The legionary hospital gave careful attention to lighting, water supply, and the setting, to provide convalescents with maximum quiet, away from the regular bustle of camp activities. A letter by Serenus and Marcus, who were stationed together in Alexandria in the third century A.D., suggests that medical and administrative duties were time-intensive and demanding. From the same historical resource, physicians are described as caring for the dying, wounded, and battle-fatigued men.²⁴⁷ Roman fortresses, including those in Britain, housed sophisticated legionary hospitals introduced in the Roman Empire. The legionary fortress of Inchtuthil (Perthshire), built in 83–86 A.D., showed a carefully planned building arranged around an oblong courtyard with less noise to disturb the patients. There were small wards, each containing four beds, which enabled the health facility to care for 250 patients in a manner that allowed for privacy and quiet.²⁴⁸ Ferngren believes that a Roman army hospital cannot be considered an authentic root for Christian care because they provided aid only to a restricted population and were never available to the public. Thus, they were created for military purposes, not as charitable institutions.²⁴⁹

Some researchers see the temples of Asklepios as the origin of Christian hospital care. *Asklepieia* (plural of Greek *Asklepieon*) were physical

---

245. Jonsen, *Short History of Medical Ethics*, 10–11.

246. Miller, *Birth of the Hospital in the Byzantine Empire*, 38.

247. Georgia L. Irby, "Roman Military Medicine: The Nexus of Religion and Techne," in *The Roman Empire*, ed. Matthew Dillon and Christopher Matthew (Yorkshire: Pen&Sword Military, 2022), 139.

248. Nicholas Orme and Margaret Webster, *The English Hospital: 1070–1570* (New Haven: Yale University Press, 1995), 15.

249. Ferngren, *Medicine and Health Care in Early Christianity*, 124.

places where sufferers came from around the world to be cured. These health centers were constructed in salubrious locations amidst trees, springs, and fresh air. These places were also places of worship, devotion, and thaumaturgical awe. The only people treated in *Asklepieia* were those afflicted with some treatable disease. Parts of the healing process were prayers, sacrifices, and religious purification with baths. The sufferers were men, women, and children, rich and poor. The widely used healing technique was the process of incubation when the divinity might appear during the sufferer's sleep. Asklepios would appear as a sacred statue that adorned the temple or as a snake or dog in one of his theriomorphic forms. These chthonic symbols were considered part of the healing process, which involved licking the afflicted wounds.[250] Miller argues that *Asklepieia* cannot be accepted as a source of inspiration for the Christian hospital. While many physicians were closely connected with the temple of Asklepios as priests, Asklepian temples cannot be considered medical centers, nor did they regularly provide suppliants with food and nursing care. Therefore, despite their popularity in ancient times, Asklepian temples may not be regarded as actual hospitals.[251]

Some scholars consider the *iatreion* to be a precursor of the Christian hospital. An *iatreion* was a small place in which a doctor lodged patients.[252] According to the later development of Christian care, the fragmentary nature of the surviving evidence makes it difficult to establish that the *iatreion* was a hospital. The British historian of medicine Vivian Nutton contends that little is known about *iatreion* except that it is a Greek term for a doctor's surgery or workshop. The archeological evidence is rarely substantial enough to provide complex answers to the modern reader. However, what is certain is that a doctor's workshop could host patients at least overnight under the doctor's watchful eye, though hosting does not appear to have been a regular or frequent occurrence.[253] Miller holds a much stricter role for an *iatreion* than Nutton. An *iatreion* included instruments, the presence of assistants, the positioning of the patient on the operating table, and proper light, but, argues Miller, based on the Hippocratic essay on the *iatreion*, it does not once mention any provisions for housing recuperating patients. In addition, Miller stresses, that based on a homily of John Chrysostom, the

---

250. Michael T. Compton, "The Union of Religion and Health in Ancient Asklepieia," *Journal of Religion and Health* 37, no. 4 (1998): 303.

251. Miller, *Birth of the Hospital in the Byzantine Empire*, 41.

252. Horden, "Earliest Hospitals in Byzantium, Western Europe, and Islam," 377.

253. Vivian Nutton, "Rhodiapolis and Allianoi: Two Missing Links in the History of the Hospital?" *Early Christianity* 5, no. 3 (2014): 378.

iatreia was also used as a shop where people could gather, some waiting for treatment, others being there to pass the time.[254]

The last ancient institution that may be linked to the existence of hospitals in the classical ancient world is that of public physicians. Roman law endowed physicians with certain privileges, and it also clearly distinguished between physicians and other groups of healers, such as chanters, exorcists, and practitioners of divination.[255] The committees of public physicians (*demosieuontes iatroi*) and chief physicians (*archiatroi*) survived the Christianizing of classical civilization. *Archiatroi* practiced medicine in the hospitals of Constantinople. However, the transition from public physicians paid by the government to doctors in a Christian hospital staff required substantial changes in the institution of public physicians and the local government's nature and strength. Miller points out that according to the historical evidence, it cannot be demonstrated that public physicians treated patients without charging a fee or attended the sick of all classes with the same diligence.[256]

Healthcare in the Christian Age: Third to Fourteenth Century A.D.

Historian Garry Ferngren supports the view that the concept of the *Imago Dei* informed early Christian healthcare. For him, the leitmotif of Christian care is rooted in the idea that people are made in God's image, in which the doctrine of incarnation is a significant contribution to the doctrine of image of God. God's love to ransom a people found in a fallen condition led to Christ's incarnation and death on the cross. Christian care, informed by Christ's incarnation, presents several effects on practical Christian ethics. Ferngren maintains that Christian impetus for Christian philanthropy may be seen as an outgrowth of the love rooted in God's very nature. Secondly, treating all people in God's image led to the belief that every human life is valuable. The Christian belief in human worth rejected in the strongest terms a host of practices: abortion, child exposure, infanticide, gladiatorial games, and suicide, all of which were prevalent in the Roman period. Finally, by seeing all people as God's image bearers, Christians redefined the sick and poor ignored in pagan society. For Christians, even lepers had the image of God and were no longer repulsive but were thought to deserve the

---

254. Miller, *Birth of the Hospital in the Byzantine Empire*, 42–43.

255. Ido Israelowich, *Patients and Healers in the High Roman Empire* (Baltimore: John Hopkins University Press, 2015), 33–34.

256. Miller, *Birth of the Hospital in the Byzantine Empire*, 44–45.

care and compassion of Christians.²⁵⁷ In contrast, neither human worth nor inherent human rights were considered intrinsic to humans in the classical world. Rights were judicial, depending on the individual's class in society. Those who were outside of the judicial parameters, such as foreigners, orphans, prisoners, physically defective, enslaved people, and foundlings, had no claim to equality in the classical world. Inequality was an unquestioned feature of ancient times where there was little sympathy for the physically impaired or oppressed. Health and the lack of physical disability were essential to human dignity; therefore, those who lacked them had no claim to be recognized as worthy human beings.²⁵⁸

New Perspectives about the Role of a Physician

Christianity seems to have remodeled the understanding of a physician. The new Christian model of physician drew on the examples of Hippocrates, the ideal physical doctor, and Christ, the perfect healer of spiritual ills. Christian doctors attempted to imitate Christ, as evidenced by the charitable spirit of Christianity. The primary motivation for the Christian physician was charity and compassion for the poor and commoner in conjunction with the care of the soul. Compassionate care included having sympathy for the sufferer and a love for people in need, a foreign concept for secular Greek thought. Motivated by Christian virtues, clergy members, whose spiritual interests blended with medical endeavors, began to treat the spiritually and physically ill. Monastic physicians practiced medicine as an extension of their call to serve Christ for the glory of God and the love of the human race.²⁵⁹ God's self-giving love for people, as reflected in the incarnation and atonement of Christ, represents the core belief that encouraged Christians to care for their neighbors despite the classical world's lack of religious charitable impulse for those in distress. Ferngren helpfully explains that the administrative structure of the local church was simple but well-suited for charitable activities. The group of elders and deacons administrated the corporate ministry of the congregation. Deacons visited the sick and were concerned to bring relief to those in need. As a result, collecting money every Sunday for those ill or in need proved effective for the systematic care of sufferers.²⁶⁰

257. Daniel A. Scalberg, Paul Louis Metzger, and Gary B. Ferngren, "Health Care in the Early Church: An Interview with Gary Ferngren," *Cultural Encounters* 10, no. 1 (2014): 65–66.

258. Ferngren, *Medicine and Health Care in Early Christianity*, 95–96.

259. Ferngren, *Medicine and Health Care in Early Christianity*, 107–9.

260. Ferngren, *Medicine and Health Care in Early Christianity*, 114.

New Responses to Highly Contagious Diseases

Responses to plagues were instrumental in proving the worth of the new Christian approach to medical care. The Cyprian plague was a primary instance where Christianity showed Christ's care for neighbors by tending to the sufferers' wounds. In 250 A.D., an illness arrived in Carthage, an African city of the Roman Empire (modern Libya). The symptoms began with a severe gastrointestinal attack, vomiting, and a high fever and escalated to hemorrhaging from the eyes, leading to a painful death. The disease was highly contagious, with 50–70 percent mortality for those affected. The disease shocked the Roman world and wreaked havoc on a population already affected by severe environmental, economic, and political crises. Additionally, the horrors of the disease were amplified in the Carthaginian church served by bishop Cyprian due to severe religious persecution.[261]

The Carthaginian church showed a devotion to the Christian faith despite numerous threats. During the spread of the plague, which killed numerous Christians, the church's greatest regret was that the pandemic might kill them before they won the martyr's crown. Moreover, the Carthaginian church was driven to face not only persecution but disease by the biblical belief that God was not only present in the trial but was fully sovereign over all of the suffering and every other kind of suffering that his people had undergone at any age. Cyprian also helped the church deal with the disease by stressing that the plague could affect Christians just as much as their neighbors. For Cyprian and his church, death was not the ultimate concern but what happens after.

Nevertheless, the most significant action performed by the church was its response to caring for neighbors in times of disease, despite the little recognition of social responsibilities on the part of the individual in the classical world. Even though Carthage's streets were filled with corpses of the dead, pagans deserted their dead and the city. In contrast, others took advantage of the situation to rob the sick. Bishop Cyprian addressed the church to aid their persecutors and to undertake the systematic care of the sick throughout the city. They cared for their neighbors mostly voluntarily, and no distinction was made in ministering to Christians and pagans.[262]

When another plague ravaged the eastern Roman Empire in 312 A.D., Christians showed care to neighbors by burying the corpses. Christians helped bury the dead because the pagans refused to do it for fear of contagion. Ferngren mentions that by the fourth century, the Christian

---

261. Nadya Williams, "Pastoring Through a Pandemic: Cyprian and the Carthaginian Church in the Mid-Third Century," *Fides et Historia* 53, no. 1 (2021): 1.

262. Ferngren, *Medicine and Health Care in Early Christianity*, 116–19.

community was so much identified with the burial services that emperor Constantine inaugurated free burial services under the direction of the clergy. Julian the Apostate commented that Christians' view of purity, hospitality, and concern for proper burial were significant factors in Christianizing the empire.[263]

The Development of the Hospital Movement and Philanthropic Acts

The palliative care of the sick appears to be a defining aspect of the church's love for neighbors. The early church seems to have used spiritual means for healing, such as prayers and the gift of healing, but also adapted and appropriated Greek therapeutics. According to the early Christian writers Tertullian, Origen, Tatian, and Arnobius, while Christianity arose from Jewish roots, Greeks bequeathed other knowledge to early Christians.[264] Christians provided care, which often lay even within the ability of those without medical training. For example, the simple provision of food and water without medications could make the difference between life and death. Such charitable acts were helpful, especially in a society with no concept of social service and communal solidarity. Since society did not have any religious, philosophical, or social basis for charitable acts, the powerful effect of Christianity resulted in a large number of conversions.[265] The Christian church's most straightforward nursing care contributed to the survival of some victims rather than abandonment. The Christian belief manifested through Christians provided "a rationale for suffering and for charity that the prevailing pagan cults lacked, and many pagans, on seeing and receiving this Christian charity, were impressed to the point of conversion."[266]

The church and monastic communities placed a high importance on practical charity of all kinds, particularly medical charity. Charitable foundations under the patronage of a church occurred in tandem with the growth of the monastic movement. In the early 340s in Constantinople, the first poorhouse (*ptocheion*) appeared, where the sick and the poor were accepted. In the early 380s, hostels (*xenones*) were attached to churches in the capital city to care for the sick. In addition, separate institutions were founded for orphans (*orphanontropheia*), foundlings (*brephotropheia*),

---

263. Ferngren, *Medicine and Health Care in Early Christianity*, 119.

264. Jeremiah Mutie, "Care for the Sick in Early Christianity: Lessons for the Current Covid-19 Stricken Church," *Vox Patrum* 78 (2021): 75.

265. Ferngren, *Medicine and Health Care in Early Christianity*, 121.

266. Jonsen, *Short History of Medical Ethics*, 15.

the aged (*gerontokomeia*), lepers (*keluphokomeia*), and poor travelers (*xenodocheia*).[267]

The first hospital emerged within the Christian community based on the doctrine of the incarnation. Basil, the bishop of Caesarea in Cappadocia, opened a hospital where nurses and medical practitioners served. The construction of Basil's hospital, the Basileias, was completed in 372 A.D. and was the pattern for many similar institutions throughout the Christian world where caring for the sick was defined as the work of Christian compassion and service to God.[268] The Basileias may be considered the first hospital because it provided inpatient facilities, professional medical care for patients, and charitable care.[269]

Before 372, Basil opened a facility to feed the hungry because of a famine in Cappadocia in 368–69. This facility and the hospital were seen as a physical image of the eschaton, of the New Jerusalem, where God will wipe away all tears. These institutions housed sick people and helped travelers and strangers. An adjoining church was attached to these places, suggesting a continuity of care provided by physicians and clergy. Basil and his friend Gregory of Nazianzus, based on Matt 25:35–36, believed that God himself was in the sick and the poor. Thus, the Matthean text appears to provide the most straightforward answer to the question of the hospital's origin. Moreover, Gregory also proposed a unique way of understanding "the poor." For Gregory, the poor were not only financially needy, but they were lepers, homeless, abandoned by their families, and figures of poverty in extremis. By creating a desire to help the undesirable, Gregory evoked a novel political space where Roman class differences were overturned by the Christian worldview seen practically in the disciplines of poverty and charity, contends ethicist Matthew Elmore.[270]

Particularly revealing is that the church cared for highly contagious sufferers, such as lepers. In ancient Israel and the Greco-Roman world, those who contracted leprosy faced the threat of social exile, poverty, and lingering self-destruction. For the society, leprosy was a social terror. Gregory often used to speak of the biblical beggar Lazarus as a quintessential representative of leprosy, even though the Bible never states that Lazarus was a leper. However, for Gregory, leprosy was a sacred disease because he saw in the diseased body of the leper a material manifestation of Christ. The

---

267. Ferngren, *Medicine and Health Care in Early Christianity*, 124.
268. Jonsen, *Short History of Medical Ethics*, 15.
269. Ferngren, *Medicine and Health Care in Early Christianity*, 124.
270. Matthew Elmore, "The First Hospital and the Construction of Leprosy," *Dialog: A Journal of Theology* 61, no. 2 (2022): 109.

state of poverty and social ostracization of a physical leper represent the essential means by which the spiritual leper needs a mediator to wipe away the polluting disease of sin found in the soul.[271]

Monastic rules from the sixth century commanded special care for the sick. Places of hospitality, or hospices, were established in churches and monastic contexts. Jonsen mentions that the father of Western monasticism, Cassiodorus, provided detailed instructions dedicated to the care of the sick, including a bibliography of classical medical texts that should be followed by monks often untrained in medicine. Over the centuries, monastic infirmarians became competent herbalists, resulting in pharmacopeias, such as *Liber Simplicis Medicinae* (ca. 1150). The training of parish priests often included advice about medical assistance and pastoral duties. Medical knowledge was cultivated in the cathedral schools before the emergence of medieval universities. Bishop Fulbert of Chartres (d. 1028), a competent medical scholar, appeared to utilize the wisdom of Hippocrates while depending on the mercy of the Lord.[272]

The Byzantine hospices (*xenones*) connected to churches existed exclusively for the sick. For instance, a hospital under the patronage of the Church of Saints Cosmas and Damian in the Kosmidian district of Constantinople had a room specifically designed for surgery. By the seventh century A.D., public physicians in any Greek city were transferred to the staff of church-owned medical centers. Poor people visited these medical places for free medicines, surgical operations, and overnight care in a bed if they were seriously ill. Significantly, no one on the staff of such hospitals was allowed to take any money from patients.[273]

Regarding other philanthropic endeavors of the church during early medieval times, especially in Constantinople, the imperial *Orphanotropheion* provided care for non-Christian orphans. The orphanage specialized in caring for such children as part of the education program of the Orthodox doctrine to prepare non-Christian orphans for baptism. Emperor Alexios, after the Turkish-Byzantine war in 1116, conducted a campaign to collect displaced women and children ravaged by the Turks to alleviate human suffering by placing them in the orphanage located in Constantinople.[274]

---

271. Susan R. Holman, "Healing the Social Leper in Gregory of Nyssa's and Gregory of Nazianzus's 'Peri Philoptōchias,'" *Harvard Theological Review* 92, no. 3 (1999): 285, 297–98.

272. Jonsen, *Short History of Medical Ethics*, 15.

273. Timothy S. Miller, "Byzantine Philanthropic Institutions and Modern Humanitarianism," *The Review of Faith & International Affairs* 14, no. 1 (2016): 22.

274. Miller, "Byzantine Philanthropic Institutions," 21.

The culmination of all urban monastic hospital foundations is arguably the Pantokrator located in the monastery of Christ Pantokrator in Constantinople. The hospital hosted beds for fifty patients, and an extensive medical and service staff served the beds. The patients were separated into male and female wards. In addition, the hospital included a bath and churches for men and women. Also, the monastery site comprised an old-age home (*gerokomeion*) for twenty-four elderly and six service staff.[275] According to the Pantokrator rules, if nursing home residents contracted diseases distinct from the chronic condition they were admitted to, they were assigned beds in the hospital. Once recovery took place, patients needed to return to the nursing home. Thus, one of the objectives of the Pantokrator was to cure patients who suffered from treatable illnesses.[276]

Church Healthcare from Renaissance to Modern Times

Medical science slowly grew, starting with the fourteenth century. Medical scholarship appears to move slowly but surely from a church context to newly founded universities in the context of two plagues, the bubonic plague and syphilis. The medical literature expanded alongside scientific, moral, political, and theological literature. Jonsen observes that the emerging profession of scholarly medicine became aware of more complex forms of commerce, which led to a transformation in the physician-patient relationships. In financial terms, the new relationship was characterized as a commercial transaction. For example, university-trained doctors were contracted to provide reliable medical care in some commercially vigorous Italian cities, such as Florence, Venice, Padua, etc. The contract included a set salary to offer medical services. The bubonic plague tested the Christian deontological imperative common in medieval times to care for the sick despite the risks of a pandemic. Though many physicians fled a stricken city, others remained out of charity, patriotism, or desire for profit.[277]

Faith and Science

The intersection of religion and medicine was present in eighteenth-century Christians in the Atlantic world; such is the case of the community

---

275. Paul Magdalino, *The Foundation of the Pantokrator Monastery in Its Urban Setting*, ed. Sofia Kotzabassi (Berlin: De Gruyter, 2013), 37.
276. Miller, "Byzantine Philanthropic Institutions," 23.
277. Jonsen, *Short History of Medical Ethics*, 43–45.

of Ebenezer, Georgia, the charitable Francke Foundations, and the medical university in Halle, Germany. In 1748, an eating disorder mainly affected children in a small community in Ebenezer, Georgia. Johann Boltzius, the pastor of the community in Ebenezer, wrote a letter to his supervisor, Gotthilf Francke, who lived in Halle, Germany, about his people's health issues. Boltzius interpreted the medical condition as a trial sent by God. The disease was not unknown to the University of Hale medical instructors, and it was identified as pica. Treatment was provided, and the medical issue was solved. The Ebenezer case illustrates that the created order that includes the individual body symbolized the spiritual world for eighteenth-century Christians. Disorder in the physical world meant that there was an issue in the spiritual dimension of a human being. As a result, attention was drawn to the sufferer's soul, and close observation was called for to discern God's will. The trained physicians of Halle and the clergy made their treatment consistent with the Christian idea of a corrupted will that causes a bodily disorder. Moreover, the sickness in Ebenezer's community was a problem for the sufferer and the social body. The clergy and the physicians were committed to combat illness within the community based on God's providence. They say medicine and medical knowledge are divinely good, and caring for the sick is an opportunity to show God's loving care in a fallen world. Thus, "medicine was a chance to rid both the individual and social body of physical and spiritual corruption. Survival meant further opportunities to spread God's kingdom on earth. With these high stakes, Christians read widely, sought help, and encouraged treatments."[278]

A Christian influence profoundly marked medical ethics. Thomas Percival was one of the most influential Anglo-American medical ethicists.[279] Percival's contribution is an 1803 treatise on medical ethics. He states that the physician should be a minister of hope and comfort for the sufferers "to smooth the bed of death" and to counteract depression by the Christian consolation.[280] Law professor John Thomas observes that the first code of ethics of the American Medical Association integrated Percival's Christian mandate that the physician should adhere to a sacred duty to avoid

---

278. Philippa Koch, "Experience and Soul in Eighteenth-Century Medicine," *Church History* 85, no. 3 (2016): 554.

279. W. John Thomas, "Informed Consent, the Placebo Effect, and the Revenge of Thomas Percival," *Journal of Legal Medicine* 22, no. 3 (2001): 315.

280. Thomas Percival, *Medical Ethics: A Code of Institutes and Precepts Adapted to the Professional Conduct of Physicians and Surgeons*, ed. John Henry Parker, 3rd ed. (Oxford: I. Shrimpton, 1849), 49.

discouraging patients and to inspire the minds of the sufferers with gratitude, respect, and confidence.[281]

Care for the Impoverished People

The Christian Methodist movement was highly involved in the care of the poor. John Wesley (1703–91) significantly contributed to healthcare by providing care for people experiencing poverty. In eighteenth-century England, healthcare delivery for people experiencing poverty was limited. Several factors contributed to a poor health system for the impoverished, such as the scarcity of healthcare practitioners, hospitals open to upper-class or select individuals, and the high cost of medicine.[282] Wesley was committed to caring for low-income people because he understood his call to ministry was to a person's total well-being, according to the Biblical teachings about people and ensouled bodies. For Wesley, wholeness characterized the entire created order. Therefore, Adam's fall introduced disorder and disease into the original creation. However, sin did not interrupt the vital union between the soul and body. The body is not secondary because God is the physician not only of the soul but of the body as well. The Christian doctrine of God and salvation was paramount for Wesley's endeavors concerning "subsidizing schools for children, establishing a visitation program for the sick, creating health clinics, and publishing a collection of home remedies, all to aid the poor."[283]

Furthermore, Wesley believed that healing from sin would have tangible effects on physical health. Body and soul are integrally related; intentional medical care should accompany religious care. Wesley's holistic soteriology implied that some who cared about spiritual salvation must care about health. In addition, Wesley's desire for health concerned the entire community's well-being, including people experiencing poverty and those without access to apothecaries. To embody Christ-like care, Wesley developed a system of visitation so that rural communities that did not have access to healthcare could be helped. Wesley trained circuit riders to offer primary medical care and dispense medical advice to parishioners. These

---

281. Thomas, "Informed Consent, the Placebo Effect, and the Revenge of Thomas Percival," 315.

282. Phillip W. Ott, "John Wesley, Eighteenth-Century Medicine, and Health Care for the Poor," *Methodist History* 60, 2 (2022): 198–99.

283. Ott, "John Wesley, Eighteenth-Century Medicine, and Health Care for the Poor," 199–200.

practices of health and healing accessible to all were expressions of practical piety, compassion, and "fruits of sanctification."[284]

The Development of Nursing Care

Despite apparently divergent paths, the church continued to be involved in healthcare. Though introduced in early Christian hospitals, nursing care seems to have become more prominent in church endeavors in the nineteenth century. Pastor Theodore Fliedner (1800–1864) of Kaiserswerth, a predominantly Roman Catholic community on the Rhine, acted in restoring the apostolic office of deaconess. In 1836, Fliedner opened a hospital in a converted summer cottage where he employed the first deaconess, Gertrude Reichardt. Flidern's endeavor grew over time and developed into an institution with a motherhouse and hospital, a center for prisoners who were rehabilitated, a training school for teachers, a girl's high school, an orphan home, a home for female Protestant lunatics, a home for lonely or invalid women, and a school for deaconesses. The ministry, performed primarily with the help of women at Kaiserswerth, had reverberations over the ocean. For instance, pastor William Alfred Passavant (1821–94) asked Fliedner to send some deaconesses to America, leading to the establishment of the oldest Protestant hospital founded in 1895.[285]

Fliedner, with the aid of the institution of deaconesses, answered a pressing contemporary social problem caused by the rapidly growing industrialization processes in the larger cities. Large parts of the petty-bourgeois and lower classes became impoverished; thus, disease and poverty were closely linked. Fliedner responded to the so-called "social question" highly debated among the bourgeoisie by training deaconesses as caregivers for people experiencing poverty who were seriously ill. Providing care for the poor and sick addressed the illnesses and material needs, but their goal was to draw the individuals from the influence of the working-class movement and guide them back to the Christian faith.[286] Deaconesses claimed Phoebe,

---

284. Melanie Dobson Hughes, "The Holistic Way: John Wesley's Practical Piety as a Resource for Integrated Health Care," *Journal of Religion and Health* 47, no. 2 (2008): 246–47.

285. Frederick S. Weiser, "The Origins of Lutheran Deaconesses in America," *Lutheran Quarterly* 13, no. 4 (1999): 423–424.

286. Karen Nolte, "Deaconesses' Self-Understanding and Everyday Nursing Practice in the First Deaconess Community in Kaiserswerth, Germany," in *Deaconesses in Nursing Care: International Transfer of a Female Model Of Life and Work in the 19th and 20th Century*, ed. Susanne Kreutzer and Karen Nolte (Stuttgart: Franz Steiner Verlag, 2016), 21.

a woman commended by the apostle Paul for her service, as their role model. According to their missionary journals, they were involved in missionary teaching and evangelizing. They were also involved in singing and preaching on the streets, and settlement workers reached out to the urban poor.[287]

Florence Nightingale (1820-1910) is known as the heroine of the Crimean War (1854-56), the most eminent founder of the modern nursing profession, and a significant hospital reformer.[288] Nightingale's contributions to nursing developed from her theological convictions. After discovering Kaiserswerth, she researched sisterhoods, education, sick care, and institutions. She became a voluntary ssuperintendent of a London Home for Distressed Governesses in 1852 and then participated in the Crimean War. After Crimea, Nightingale turned her attention to Army health in colonial India and the plight of Indian peasants. She also advised on Aboriginal health in Australia and New Zealand. She set up midwifery training and worked for women's rights. In addition, Nightingale supported a reform work among prostitutes and advised on medical services for the American Civil War.[289]

Historian Charles Rosenberg suggests that Nightingale's ideas to reform and reconstitute the hospital were hardly new. Traditional and older ideas, including a vision of the world with volition and disease, environment and regimen, body and mind, were widely accepted in the early nineteenth-century pathology and therapeutics. Nightingale believed that the atmosphere played a primary role in the transmission of diseases. The role of ventilation in medical environments was already studied by England's leading authority on vital statistics, William Farr. Nightingale's strong belief in a connection between behavior, environment, and health led to a systematic program for hospital reform—the program integrated architecture, engineering, and administrative orders. For example, Nightingale's model implied that employee and patient discipline were as important as the placement of windows and fireplaces and the frequency with which walls and floors were scrubbed. For Nightingale, hospital hygiene was vital. If infections appeared, they were a consequence of institutional sloth and incompetence. Rosenberg helpfully summarizes Florence's approach to hygiene: "If man failed to obey God's physiological laws, he could only expect disease; if a hospital was badly designed, then contaminated by filth, administrative

---

287. Jenny Wiley Legath, *Sanctified Sisters: A History of Protestant Deaconesses* (New York: New York University Press, 2019), 3.

288. Lynn McDonald, *Florence Nightingale: An Introduction to Her Life and Family*, vol. 1 (Ontario: Wilfrid Laurier University Press, 2001), 1.

289. Val Webb, "Florence Nightingale: The Making of a Radical Theologian," *St Mark's Review* 191 (2002): 14, 17.

negligence, and immorality, the consequent fevers and infections were equally inevitable."[290]

As a devout Christian, Nightingale believed that to be like Christ meant hearing the cries of the oppressed and living in solidarity with them. She believed oppressive social systems are human constructions held in power by the powerful. Florence argued against a Victorian understanding of a theology of election that God ordained rich over poor, rulers over enslaved people, and men over women in some deliberate and unalterable scheme. Florence conveyed the message that poverty and the class system needed to be changed. She held a special place in her worldview for women. Women were called to be handmaids of the Lord; thus, they could follow God's call, whether rich or poor. Health was, for Nightingale, not an arbitrary gift from God as the church taught, but a state humans can achieve for themselves.[291]

Concluding Theological Considerations

Some theological considerations may be stated based on this theological and ecclesiological history of care as an epistemological background for the neighbor-love ethical concept. The biblical understanding of the image of God infers that human beings are God's unique creations, which endows them with derived value. People are distinct from animals and inanimate things by people's creation in God's image.[292] Based on the biblical texts, the concept of the image of God and its implications can be summarized as follows.

First, the biblical understanding of the relational aspect of a human being is possible only between persons or with God. Creation in the image of God is affirmed for all persons, and all patients are human beings. A fundamental aspect of what it means to be a person is to have a relationship with God and the community. The capacity for a relationship appears to be located in the human spirit, which enables people to relate to God. Nevertheless, the capacity for a relationship with God and others does not neglect the body because the body is how the human spirit acts in the world.[293] This relational category implies other categories, such as the use of reason, will, emotions, and other capacities, as the spirit energizes, directs, and stimulates

---

290. Charles E. Rosenberg, *The Care of Strangers: The Rise of America's Hospital System* (New York: Basic Books, 1987), 178–80.

291. Webb, "Florence Nightingale," 18–19.

292. Cherney, "Distinctively Human," 13.

293. Hammett, "Whole Bible Approach to Interpreting Creation in God's Image," 35–37.

them.[294] Part of the image of God in people refers to the capacity to rule and have dominion over other created things. People, as vice-regents, were made to exhibit divine traits and to exercise divine rule. Humans were endowed with the power and commission to rule other beings and objects powerfully and peacefully around them.[295] In light of these theoretical grounds for the image of God, people value technology in order to exercise the divine commission of ruling the earth or to manage the earth[296] to benefit humans. From this theological perspective, it is impossible for machines to replace people in intrinsically human tasks such as caring for patients and sick people. But neither should there be a fear of technology and technological change.[297] Yet technology can never be valued over human life or replace the interaction between persons.

Second, a progressive transformation according to the image of God in Christ is available only to humans. Ben Mitchell, in his account of the theological treatment of the person created in God's image, helpfully argues that "the clearest lens through which to see what it means to be human may not be Genesis but Jesus. That is by no means to disparage the Genesis account, but rather exalt the God-Man, and better understand the importance of his incarnation."[298] In the same line, theologian Paul Metzger contends that people are created in God's image, but Jesus Christ is that ideal image. Metzger expands his view about Christ's image by extrapolating that Jesus shares this image with his body, the church.[299]

Jesus was relational, as seen in his relationship with God the Father. His relational personhood was manifested into a human family and community—he saw himself as a citizen of both the kingdom of God and the political kingdom under the shadow of Rome. In his incarnation, Jesus shared God's love with fellow personal creatures through ethical conduct and compassionate actions. The perfect image of God, Jesus Christ, also presents profound implications in caring for others. Healthcare professionals, motivated

---

294. Hammett, "Whole Bible Approach to Interpreting Creation in God's Image," 38.

295. Cherney, "Distinctively Human," 21.

296. Tumpal Samuel Silitonga and Ricky Pramono Hasibuan, "Humans, the Ad Imaginem: A Constructive Study in Building Human Relations with Other Created Beings," *Journal of Biblical Theology* 6, no. 3 (2023): 75.

297. John Dyer, *From the Garden to the City: The Redeeming and Corrupting Power of Technology* (Grand Rapids: Kregel Publications, 2011), loc. 2570, Kindle.

298. C. Ben Mitchell, "What It Means to Be Human," in *Created in the Image of God: Applications and Implications for Our Cultural Confusion*, ed. David S. Dockery and Lauren McAfee (Nashville: Forefront Books, 2023), 75.

299. Paul Louis Metzger, *More Than Things: A Personalist Ethics for Throwaway Culture* (Downers Grove: IVP Academic, 2023), 26.

to care as Jesus did, understand that people "are physically, psychosocially, and spiritually integrated sexual, moral, and mortal beings, created in God's image to live in relationship with God and others and as responsible stewards of the environment."[300] The dynamic transformation manifested in the image of God in Christ suggests that inanimate objects such as AiRs do not possess the capacity to care in the ways that Christ did and to which Christian care providers aspire. Carebots do not have a genuine human nature that would allow them to be ontologically invested in a relationship. That is to say, AiRs are technological instruments and not embodied souls; therefore, they cannot be involved relationally in a human way due to their nature.

Third, AiRs, in the current stage of development, will never have the capacity to serve the biblical and theological understanding of care healing and flourishing. The complex relationship between a human healthcare practitioner and a care receiver incorporates specific qualities of being a human. For example, as already shown, trust, solidarity, and love characterize a flourishing human relationship. Love, a profoundly human trait, presupposes reciprocity. The reciprocal love between a physician and a sufferer is fundamentally human. The loving presence of a doctor that may be translated into the silent presence of the patient's bedside is vital. By genuinely listening to the patient's symptoms and feelings, a caregiver can show loving care that may lead to a flourishing relationship, despite the current health issues. How can AiRs feel genuine love toward the patient, and how can a patient love a robot who cannot by its nature truly feel anything but replicate, at best, human emotional language? These are questions that can be answered only in terms of human embodiment. In addition, carebot technology may obstruct the manifestation of love by intervening between human beings, who are fundamentally created to impart love to neighbors.

Furthermore, solidarity in medical care relationships is fundamental. A physician shows solidarity by empathy toward the patient, her medical condition, and her family. Solidarity, like love, goes both ways in a human relationship. Patients may empathize with care providers by acknowledging that health providers are wounded healers.[301] Human healers are fragile, limited creatures like any other human being. A genuine understanding of an illness is reserved only for a human who, by nature, can comprehend what suffering is.

Moreover, a fallible healer who understands the impact of a disease not only upon the sufferer but also on her family can understand a patient's

---

300. Shelly et al., *Called to Care*, 60.
301. Sulmasy, *Healer's Calling*, loc. 1315.

weakness. Only a limited creature in deep and meaningful relationships with others, such as a family, may show a veritable concern for solidarity, which is a missing capacity in an inanimate robot. The connection of two human beings that is manifested despite the fragility caused by a fallen nature cannot be built in an algorithmic, artificial manner. The lack of meaningful solidarity may lead to detachment in medical care, where doctors relate to patients as problems to be fixed and not as God's image bearers to be cared for and helped.

The trust between a physician and care receiver is a primary aspect of a relationship as it manifests through communication and appropriate treatment. The technical capabilities of a caregiver, coupled with a loving approach to care, build trust in medical endeavors. Carebots may help find a quick and efficient treatment. Moreover, AiRs' ability to have conversations is undoubtedly an accomplishment that can be celebrated. However, a caring relationship will inevitably lead to connections beyond the technical dimension of diagnosing a disease and providing treatment. How can AiRs connect humanly in direct patient care so that genuine trust can be shown without mimicking human virtues and emotions? The apparent answer is that carebots cannot be involved in mutual trust relationships like human care practitioners.

Neurologist William Cheshire helpfully points out, in a lecture called "Virtual Physicians and Virtual Avatars," that Christ, the incarnate Word, who is fully God and fully man, communicated his humanity by dwelling among human beings in person. The written word of God was composed under the inspiration of the Holy Spirit using technology. Technology can be used to emphasize the human element without degrading humanity.[302] However, if misused by replacing human providers, technology can violate aspects of healthcare, such as the proposed extensive understanding of trust.

Christians used the technological means of their days and even worked within the theoretical framework of the Hippocratic principles. The ecclesiological history of care clearly shows that Christians were not against physicians, with some exceptions, especially in the early church. Moreover, the Bible acknowledges the helpfulness of medical skills as a means of God's healing power. God is the one who heals both physically and spiritually. Christ is the healer of the soul and of the body, the supreme healer. Significantly, the healing of Christ always included the community, perpetuated by the church's practical neighbor-love. A Christian doctor may point the

---

302. William P. Jr. Cheshire, "Virtual Physicians and Virtual Avatars" (6th CBHD Academy of Fellows Consultations, Deerfield, IL: The Center For Bioethics & Human Dignity, 2017), sec. Conclusions, https://www.youtube.com/watch?app=desktop&v=CJIrsHMPEZw.

sufferer to Christ, who can heal the soul affected by sin, which, in effect, supports the view that in the Eschaton, the whole person will be healed. A dying, wounded healer can point a dying patient to a genuine hope of resurrection by faith in Christ. That is not to say that a carebot cannot be programmed to provide a religious answer, but only an authentic human healer can indicate a metaphysical hope that goes beyond the material world.

Christians believed in medical skills and helped develop the art of curing by caring for neighbors. Motivated by a robust theology of the doctrine of the incarnation and a solid impetus to demonstrate Christ's love to the world, Christians developed hospitals, hospices, and systems to help the poor in ways that were beneficial to everyone. The church and Christians perceived health and healing as resources to point sufferers to salvation on the cross. Is it possible for robots to present a convincing case to point people to Christ? May God use bots to save holistically sufferers? Perhaps the answer is yes. However, a fallen creature hoping for eternal life will always present a more credible and encouraging gospel message to another fallen human needing spiritual salvation.

In conclusion, this chapter argues that, based on a theological and ecclesiological historical view of care, carebot technologies must only be used in ways consistent with the biblical vision of medicine and how the early church sought care and healing for a sound moral assessment rather than create a novel version of ethical care. A biblical, theological, and historical ecclesiological perspective maintains that the traditional and time-tested means of healthcare, such as treating people as God's image bearers by showing solidarity, trust, and love and pointing them to holistic health in Christ, are necessary elements of ethical care and a crucial part of the covenantal neighbor-love concept.

CHAPTER FOUR

The Neighbor-Love Ethical Framework as a Tool for Navigating the Ethics of Social Robots

Introduction

THE NEIGHBOR-LOVE ETHICAL FRAMEWORK is grounded in the covenant care tradition and Christ's healing ministry imperative model. Taking covenant care's long tradition and Jesus' healing ministry as points of departure, this chapter argues that the theology of a neighbor-love framework is a persuasive moral paradigm for addressing the moral problems carebots raise, particularly in direct patient care in healthcare settings. A subsidiary goal of this chapter, based on a neighbor-love system, is that ethically, social robots cannot meet any direct patient care tasks.[1] The questions that guide the conversation to support this chapter's thesis are "Do AiRs contribute (or not) to the covenant of care?" "Are other medical ethical frameworks consistent with the biblical model of the covenant of care, and how would they tolerate AiRs in medical care?" "Are AiRs capable of meeting the criteria suggested by the neighbor-love approach? If not, are there capacities where they can be used ethically?"

In what follows, I position the neighbor-love system in relation to the most popular and proximal ethical frameworks to the neighbor-love

---

1. Robert Sparrow and Linda Sparrow, "In the Hands of Machines? The Future of Aged Care," *Minds & Machines* 16, no. 2 (2006): 143.

concept, such as (1) utilitarian ethics, (2) care ethics, (3) virtue ethics, and (4) deontological ethics. Secondly, I describe the main structural components of the neighbor-love framework by summarizing the proposed ethical model based on the previous chapters and enriching the discussion with a broader perspective on covenantal faithfulness and the good Samaritan parable. The chapter also analyzes the social and ethical implications of carebot technologies in the context of vulnerable persons and proposes a set of criteria centered on the neighbor-love system. Finally, the chapter proposes criteria based on the neighbor-love system that can inform the use of carebots in healthcare settings.

Evaluating Conventional Medical Ethical Models

The most conventional ethical models in robot medical ethics fall into two general categories: deontological and teleological systems. Though situated at the end points of the ethical spectrum, the two systems were selected because they employ various moral reasoning tools deeply ingrained in the indefatigably diverse medical moral culture. Moral judgments must be in place to discuss the ethical use of carebots. The preferred moral assessment of ethical systems follows a definition provided by Foreman and Leonard in *Christianity and Modern Medicine*, who mention three things involved in every moral event: "A *person* performing an *act* that has certain desired *results*." The moral theories mentioned later are grounded in one aspect of moral actions. Some systems maintain that morally good judgments are based on a good result. For others, something is moral when one fulfills a moral obligation or duty. Others believe morality should focus on the kind of person acting.[2] Ethicist Scott Rae adds to Foreman and Leonard's perspective on motivation. Rae argues that a person's motivations should be evaluated because "the motive is the only difference between two identical actions." He brings up the difference between bribery and gifts, a situation where only motivations can assess the action. Nevertheless, Rae points out that there are cases when motivations cannot be evaluated; thus, "the assessment of motives should be held tentatively and cautiously given our lack of knowledge of someone's thinking."[3]

---

2. Mark Wesley Foreman and Lindsay C. Leonard, *Christianity and Modern Medicine: Foundations for Bioethics* (Grand Rapids: Kregel Academic, 2022), 22.

3. Scott B. Rae, *Moral Choices: An Introduction to Ethics*, 4th ed. (Grand Rapids: Zondervan Academic, 2018), 21.

Utilitarian Ethics

The first selected ethical system is utilitarian ethics. One of the reasons is its presence in significant domains of life, such as business, politics, and medicine. Utilitarian ethics is part of consequentialist ethical theories. According to the utilitarian system, outcomes justify the means or ways to achieve them. Decisions are based on the greatest benefit for the most significant number of individuals. The consequences of an action determine the morality of intervention. The approach to action is guided by the calculated benefits or harms based on evidence that can bring the maximum benefit for many, even though this approach could harm some individuals. The variants of utilitarianism include act utilitarianism and rule utilitarianism. By analyzing the benefits and harms, a decision can be taken for a specific individual. In contrast, the rule utilitarianism does not have a calculation of benefits or harms. According to rule utilitarianism, a moral decision is based on preformed moral codes or rules leading to better consequences.[4] In other words, the utilitarian evaluates each outcome by the most outstanding total well-being result.[5]

Classical Contributions to Utilitarian Ethics

The controversial utilitarian ethical philosophy occupies a significant place in the history of moral thought. Analyzing the utility principle comprehensively extends beyond the scope of this dissertation; therefore, the section focuses only on the classical utilitarian philosophers, such as Jeremy Bentham, John Stuart Mill, and Henry Sidgwick, who are significant contributors to the utility principle.

Jeremy Bentham (1748–1832), the great founding father of nontheological utilitarianism, produced many writings, some twenty million surviving words, about various topics. He advocated for law reform and critiqued well-established political doctrines, including natural law and contractarianism. Bentham correspondingly wrote extensively on subjects as diverse as prison reform, religion, poor relief, animal welfare, and the decriminalization of homosexuality.[6]

---

4. Jharna Mandal, Dinoop Korol Ponnambath, and Subhash Chandra Parija, "Utilitarian and Deontological Ethics in Medicine," *Tropical Parasitology* 6, no. 1 (2016): 6.

5. Krister Bykvist, *Utilitarianism: A Guide for the Perplexed*, Continuum Guides for the Perplexed (London: Continuum, 2010), 17.

6. Bart Schultz, *The Happiness Philosophers: The Lives and Works of the Great Utilitarians* (New Jersey: Princeton University Press, 2017), 56.

He declared that the principle of utility is his guide and that "I will follow wheresoever it leads me. No prejudices shall force me to quit the road. No interest shall seduce me. No superstitions shall appall me."[7] The Benthamite worldview also aims at pleasure as the intense, constant, and sole object of pursuit. Bentham claims that pleasure guides all human endeavors as opposed to pain. Pleasure is so natural to human beings that there is no need to "urge a man to pursue that which he is always occupied in pursuing."[8] In another instance, Bentham asserts that the goal of human life is pleasure and the absence of pain, "the happiness of the individuals, of whom a community is composed, that is their pleasures and their security, is the end and the sole end which the legislator ought to have in view." [9]

The Benthamite perspective also includes a hedonistic calculus to measure the morality of an action that provides the greatest net pleasure. The philosopher proposed the measurement of pleasure and pain based on variables such as (1) the intensity of pleasure or pain, (2) the length of time pleasure or pain is supposed to last, (3) the likelihood of certainty that pain or pleasure will last, (4) the proximity of the pleasure or pain, (5) fecundity, the likelihood of pleasure producing more pleasure and of pain to produce more pain, (6) the quality of pleasure free from pain or of pain free from pleasure, (7) the number of people who will be beneficiaries of pleasure or pain.[10]

Philosopher John Stuart Mill (1806–73) is another classical supporter of the utilitarian system. He is recognized as a champion of human liberty and an ardent proponent of equality. Mill wrote extensively on economics, women's rights, racism, and slavery.[11] Mill was born into a family with nine children. His biographer, Timothy Larsen, explains that Mill was passionately committed to the Malthusian belief that the happiness of the human race will grow based on a decrease in the birth rate. Mill's high ideal was

---

7. Jeremy Bentham, *Deontology; or the Science of Morality: In Which the Harmony and Co-Incidence of Duty and Self-Interest, Virtue and Felicity, Prudence and Benevolence, Are Explained and Exemplified, and Applied to the Business of Life*, ed. John Bowring, vol. 2 (London: Longman, Bees, Orme, Browne, Green, and Longman, 1834), viii.

8. Jeremy Bentham, *Deontology; or the Science of Morality: In Which the Harmony and Co-Incidence of Duty and Self-Interest, Virtue and Felicity, Prudence and Benevolence, Are Explained and Exemplified*, ed. John Bowring, vol. 1 (London: Longman, 1834), 83.

9. Jeremy Bentham, *An Introduction to the Principles of Morals and Legislation* (New York: Dover Publications, 2007), 24.

10. Jaime V. Cortez, "The Moral Plausibility of Utilitarianism in Business Through the Lens of Christian," *Journal of Multidisciplinary Research* 15, no. 2 (2023): 68.

11. Sven Ove Hansson, "John Stuart Mill and the Conflicts of Equality," *Journal of Ethics* 26, no. 3 (2022): 433.

chastity, arguing that married couples should not sleep together to cultivate virtue.[12]

John Mill claims that utility is the foundation of morals and calls it the Greatest Happiness Principle. For Mill, actions are right "in proportion as they tend to promote happiness, wrong as they tend to produce the reverse of happiness."[13] Mill stresses that the Happiness Principle refers not only to an individual standard of happiness but to "the greatest amount of happiness altogether; and if it may possibly be doubted whether a noble character is always the happier for its nobleness, there can be no doubt that it makes other people happier and that the world, in general, is immensely a gainer by it." The end and standard of morality is an existence exempt as far as possible from pain and as rich as possible in enjoyment, both in quantity and quality.[14]

Mill's philosophy develops Bentham's utilitarian theory by extending the utilitarian principle to society rather than only to individuals. For Mill, pleasures are not the same by emphasizing the dichotomy between higher-order pleasures of the mind and those lower-level pleasures of the body. In addition, Mill argued that people should respect the individual freedom to pursue the happiness of their neighbors as long as these individuals' rights do not harm others in society.[15]

Classical utilitarian Henry Sidgwick (1838–1900) is an esteemed figure in philosophy. He was connected to the political and religious establishment and was a liberal within the academia. He promoted women's education by organizing lectures and examinations for them. Intriguingly, he founded the Society for Psychical Research and performed "ghostological" investigations to know whether God exists.[16] In philosophical ethics, Sidgwick situates in the utilitarian framework. In utilitarian theory, Sidgwick differentiates between egoistic and universalistic hedonism.[17] He defines utilitarianism as "the conduct which, under any given circumstances, is objectively right, is that which will produce the greatest amount of happiness on the whole; that is, taking into account all whose happiness is affected by the conduct."[18]

---

12. Timothy Larsen, *John Stuart Mill: A Secular Life, Spiritual Lives* (Oxford: Oxford University Press, 2018), 4.

13. John Stuart Mill, *Utilitarianism* (Luton: Andrews UK Limited, 2011), 11.

14. Mill, *Utilitarianism*, 16–17.

15. Cortez, "Moral Plausibility of Utilitarianism," 68.

16. Thomas Hurka, *British Ethical Theorists from Sidgwick to Ewing*, The Oxford History of Philosophy (Oxford: Oxford University Press, 2014), 10.

17. Keith Tribe, "Henry Sidgwick, Moral Order, and Utilitarianism," *European Journal of the History of Economic Thought* 24, no. 4 (2017): 923.

18. Henry Sidgwick, *The Methods of Ethics*, 7th ed. (London: Macmillan and Co,

The ethical calculus, according to Sidgwick's Greatest Happiness principle, is "the greatest possible surplus of pleasure over pain, the pain being conceived as balanced against an equal amount of pleasure so that the two mutually annihilate each other for purposes of ethical calculation."[19]

A Critique of the Utility Principle

Utilitarianism is one of the most popular ethical frameworks in the Western world. The utility principle is prevalent in contemporary society, which believes, in general, that whatever makes the majority happy is the right thing to do. Foreman and Leonard summarize the utilitarian theory by stating that the utility principle brings together several ideas. First, utilitarianism aims to create the most remarkable balance of good over evil. For utilitarians, it is rarely an action of good or evil but rather a mixture of good and evil. The morality of an action is seen as determined by a more excellent balance of good over evil. Moreover, utilitarianism recognizes that happiness should be spread as widely and equally as possible, even though they acknowledge that rarely everyone is happy.[20]

Though utilitarian philosophy is situated on the opposite spectrum of Christian ethics, some biblical characters used utilitarianism without condoning it. Some biblical instances when the utility principle was used are as follows.

In Gen 19:1–10, the Scripture mentions that Lot offered his daughters to be molested by the mob of Sodom to save the two angels. The two angels visited Sodom before its destruction and were hosted by Lot. The Bible states that all the men from the city, young and old, surrounded Lot's house and demanded that Lot bring the angels out of the house so that they could have sexual relations with them. However, Lot offered to give their virgin daughters to the men instead of the angels. According to Lot's moral calculation, the greatest good for the most significant number in this situation was to sacrifice his children's dignity for the sake of the angels' safety. The Genesis account does not directly accuse Lot's judgment; however, it indirectly emphasizes how immoral and audacious the father's assessment of the situation is. Lot's judgment cannot be used as an example of moral reasoning, and it also shows how twisted the application of utilitarian ethics can become.[21]

1874), 381.

19. Sidgwick, *Methods of Ethics*, 384.
20. Foreman and Leonard, *Christianity and Modern Medicine*, 25–26.
21. Cortez, "Moral Plausibility of Utilitarianism," 72.

Another example is recorded in John 11:45–53, where the Bible mentions the decision of Caiaphas, the high priest, to kill Jesus. His reasoning, explained in the meeting of the Pharisees with the Sanhedrin, was that one man should die for the people rather than the whole nation perish, and the Romans should destroy the temple. Caiaphas's criteria were built upon utilitarian principles, such as saving the majority, even if this implies the death of someone innocent.[22] The Johannine irony is probably at its climax in the text. For Caiaphas, Jesus was the scapegoat who would protect the Jews from the Romans. However, the Sanhedrin's judgment proved to be prescient because in 70 A.D., the temple and Jerusalem would be utterly destroyed and sacked by the Romans. The Sanhedrin desired something good to save the nation and their religious heritage, but their action and solutions proved wrong. What caused the ultimate destruction of Jerusalem, its bloodbath, and the dispersion of the Jews was the Jewish leadership itself.[23] The Johannine ironical text implies the necessity of the moral agent's self-assessment instead of finding solutions that will not harm the innocent. Though the Bible mentions some utilitarian judgments, it appears safe to argue that there is no reason to think that the Scripture approves the utility principle as a normative ethical pattern.

The utilitarian philosophy raises several problems from a neighbor-love ethical perspective. First, critics of utilitarianism ask how one can measure happiness and compare it to different kinds of happiness. Happiness may mean fulfillment for some; for others, it is contentment, and still, for others, it indicates a meaningful life. In other words, in the utilitarian view, happiness appears to be involved in chasing something that is changing continuously depending on individuals' subjective, even egoistical, perceived needs.

Second, it seems impossible to quantify happiness, especially when there are instances of happiness that cannot be quantified. For example, as Foreman and Leonard question, who is happiest: a child who received a toy, a woman on her wedding day, or an older adult who just found a liver for her transplant? Besides, is happiness the goal of morality[24] and implicitly the goal of medical care? As already labored in the previous chapter and consistent with the biblical view of care, the goal of medicine should not address only the cure of bodies. It should also take into consideration the spiritual dimensions of human beings.

---

22. Cortez, "Moral Plausibility of Utilitarianism," 72.

23. Andreas J. Köstenberger, *A Theology of John's Gospel and Letters*, The Biblical Theology of the New Testament (Grand Rapids: Zondervan, 2009), 351.

24. Foreman and Leonard, *Christianity and Modern Medicine*, 26.

The biblical view of flourishing, perhaps the closest term to the Benthamite view of happiness, extends far beyond a hedonistic life or hedonistic calculations for here and now but has ramifications in the life after death. In Eccl 2:1–23, Solomon confronts the superficial meaning of hedonism. Israel's most prosperous and wisest king concludes that a person cannot find meaning in work or pleasures because life under the sun is nothing but pain and despair. In addition, Solomon argues in Eccl 2:24–26 a glorious vision of embodied humanity based on the doctrine of creation. Humanity cannot find happiness and fulfillment apart from God. Peace is intertwined with justice as part of flourishing relationships, and it is more than the absence of hostility, pain, or suffering.[25] Karl Barth is again valid in assessing joy as anticipatory. He states:

> Most joy is anticipatory. Even in the experience of fulfillment, and particularly when this experience is genuine, it usually changes immediately into anticipatory joy, i.e., joy in expectation of further fulfillment. In this respect, it normally has something of an eschatological character. And to this extent we do right to ask concerning the right will for joy.[26]

Barth clarifies that eternal joy is bestowed upon human beings only in fellowship with God. Also, absolute joy comes and is present from the Holy Spirit. Thus, true joy implies a social dimension. Life is a gift for each individual, but life is in relationship with fellows—true joy only is as it is given to others. Joy, as mutual enjoyment, can be robbed of all its benefits when only one has joy. Egoism, reasons Barth, creates only the specter of joy, resulting in the most profound disappointment.[27]

Third, the fundamental understanding of human worth and truthfulness may be reduced to extrinsic value without intrinsic value. The value of a person may be reduced to his social utility and happiness under the utilitarian paradigm, allowing the sacrifice of an innocent for the benefit of many.[28] The decisive aspect that separates a Christian view of morality from utilitarianism appears to be the fundamental disagreement concerning human value. According to Christian ethics, human worth is grounded in God's image in people, not in some external or functional utility, such as consequential theories. The Bible emphatically refutes any reason to treat anyone as a mere statistic in the utilitarian calculus of the greatest good for

---

25. Craig G. Bartholomew, *Ecclesiastes*, Baker Commentary on the Old Testament Wisdom and Psalms (Grand Rapids: Baker Academic, 2009), 204.
26. Barth, *Church Dogmatics*, III.4:377.
27. Barth, *Church Dogmatics*, III.4:379.
28. Foreman and Leonard, *Christianity and Modern Medicine*, 26.

the most significant number or, worst, sacrificing his welfare or life for the pleasures of others.[29] Philosopher Heike Felzmann claims that utilitarianism is a theory that takes impartiality seriously. She maintains her thesis by mentioning that utilitarianism supports the idea that everyone should be considered equally, including women, to be as rational and cognitively able as men. Utilitarianism also condemned slavery and drew attention to the neglect of global inequalities in ethics and the importance of avoiding suffering in the developing world.[30] Felzmann's argument about impartiality appears unconvincing. The utilitarian Peter Singer seems convinced that there are forms of human lives that may be disregarded based on mental or health issues. For instance, Singer advocates for euthanasia for severely and irreparably retarded infants because they cause suffering to all concerned and benefit nobody. Singer argues for painless killing for infants, and he adds, "Once we see that the case of a dying horse is really quite parallel to the case of a dying infant, we may be more ready to drop the distinction between killing and letting die in case of the infant too."[31] Thus, contrary to Felzmann's opinion, utilitarianism appears discriminatory and troublesome.

The love for neighbor will never allow or reason killing for the weak, defenseless, or in the minority for the sake of the majority. A telling example is Abraham's pleading for Sodom in Gen 18:16–33 for God to not destroy a tiny minority in the context of a larger population and its happiness. Abraham shows remarkable compassion for wicked foreigners through five intercessory speeches. Abraham appealed to God's twin pillars of divine justice and divine mercy. The moral dilemma of the text is that if the cities of Sodom and Gomorrah are destroyed and the innocent suffer, God's justice becomes suspect. The other aspect is that the guilty can escape God's justice if cities are spared. The moral enigma finds a solution because God spares the innocent, and the guilty are consumed.[32] Abraham learned that numbers are unimportant in God's economy of grace and justice, for God is merciful and will discriminate between the wicked and the righteous.[33]

---

29. Cortez, "Moral Plausibility of Utilitarianism," 76.

30. Heike Felzmann, "Utilitarianism as an Approach to Ethical Decision Making in Health Care," in *Key Concepts and Issues in Nursing Ethics*, ed. P. Anne Scott (Cham: Springer, 2017), 34.

31. Peter Singer, "Unsactifying Human Life," in *Applied Ethics: Critical Concepts in Philosophy*, ed. Ruth F. Chadwick and Doris Schroeder, vol. 3 (New York: Routledge, 2002), 347.

32. Kenneth A. Mathews, *Genesis 11:27–50:26*, The New American Commentary (Nashville: B&H, 2005), 560–61.

33. Mathews, *Genesis 11:27–50:26*, 567.

Fourthly, God can use human suffering for his good ends. While utilitarianism attempts to minimize pain, the Bible does not seem to suggest that it is possible to eliminate suffering. In contrast, the Bible argues that God can use even suffering to accomplish desirable ends.[34] For instance, Jas 1:2 describes what a believer's attitude toward suffering and testing should be. James acknowledges that people cannot control the environment of their lives and the things that happen to them, but knowing how to interpret painful events and actions is part of the believer's wisdom. To count sorrow in trials as joy does not advocate for masochism. For James, the reason for joy in trials does not focus on suffering per se but rather on the character traits that suffering induces. The fruits of suffering are endurance, maturity, and wisdom, and experiencing joy simultaneously as sorrow is a hallmark of genuine faith.[35] Romans 8:18 clearly states that suffering is an undesirable but present element of the present evil age. Hardships of every kind, such as imprisonments, sleepless nights, and sufferings of any type, are genuine trials but cannot be compared to the eschatological glory. The apostle Paul grounds his encouragement to the Corinthian believers on the help of the Holy Spirit in suffering (Rom 8:18–25) and on the fact that all things work together for good. This good, though, may include suffering (Rom 8:28–30).[36] Utilitarianism looks idealistically at minimizing or eliminating pain, while the biblical approach to suffering is somewhat realistic. The Bible does not eliminate the prospect of suffering even for believers but provides eschatological hope and encouragement with the aid of God, the Holy Spirit.

Finally, is there anything beneficial in the utility principle for using carebots from a neighbor-love perspective? The answer may be a cautionary yes, only in theory. A positive aspect of utilitarianism is its desire to maximize the overall benefits and to make a positive difference in the sufferer's life. These objectives sound perfectly appropriate and idealistic in theory. Naturally, people desire good health, flourishing, and so on. However, the question is how exactly one can judge different types of consequences on a single, even arbitrary, scale of goodness.[37]

Does utilitarianism support the use of carebots in healthcare situations? The answer is yes. As long as carebots help and make most people happy, utilitarians will likely say AiRs are helpful in medical care. Does the utility principle provide any epistemological categories to nuance the use of

---

34. Cortez, "Moral Plausibility of Utilitarianism," 75.

35. Dan G. McCartney, *James*, Baker Exegetical Commentary on the New Testament (Grand Rapids: Baker Academic, 2009), 235–36.

36. Mounce, *Romans*, 27:355.

37. Felzmann, "Utilitarianism," 35.

social robots, such as direct or indirect patient care? The answer may need to be clarified. Utilitarians seem inclined to provide a more pragmatic view that will satisfy the patient's needs for the moment. The utility principle does not seem to provide convincing theoretical, philosophically based reasons to secure a place for philosophical, moral theory. The pursuit of personal projects and the supply of what is needed for these are intrinsically egotistical. The nature of good in utilitarianism does not appear to allow all virtues considered necessary in medical care, such as deep relationships. For instance, if personal relationships are not among the goods in a caregiver or care receiver's life, then relationships may suffer a reduction in the total distribution of goods.[38]

In the neighbor-love approach, the good and the just, or the scale of goodness, are revealed and transcendent, a God-given gift in the Bible. Neighbor-love does not need to reduce sufferers to number, as is the case of the Enlightenment's product of utilitarianism but considers that patients are made in God's image; thus, patients are valuable and must be treated with respect and care. Moreover, according to the neighbor-love view, relationships are inherent to doctor-patient interactions. Without relationships, medical care seems reduced to a mechanized system of curing bodies, without attention to the needs of God's image bearers.

Feminist Care Ethics

Feminist care ethics is a somewhat alternative approach to medical care, and its location is in the apparent epistemological proximity of the neighbor-love ethical concept. The ethics of care theory is a family of moral theories focusing on human interdependence and shared responsibility.[39]

Contributions to a Feminist Ethic of Care

Care-based ethics is also known as the feminist ethics of care, which places interpersonal relationships as the crux virtue of moral action. Many of the ideas of the ethics of care developed in the late twentieth century by feminist authors who contrasted their views against the rationalist theories of actions that underpin much conventional and ethical theory, particularly the

---

38. Hugh Upton, "Moral Theory and Theorizing in Health Care Ethics," *Ethical Theory and Moral Practice* 14, 4 (2011): 434–35.

39. Felicia Stokes and Amitabha Palmer, "Artificial Intelligence and Robotics in Nursing: Ethics of Caring as a Guide to Dividing Tasks Between AI and Humans," *Nursing Philosophy* 21, no. 4 (2020): 4.

utilitarian and the Kantian deontological ethical theories.[40] In what follows, the section describes the contributions and central tenets of the ethics of care. In the second part, an assessment from the neighbor-love perspective is provided.

Psychologist Carol Gilligan's contribution to *In a Different Voice* begins with the presupposition that two voices are talking about morality, men and women, and that women were repeatedly excluded from the critical theory-building studies of psychological research. For Gilligan, women failed to fit existing models of human growth, which "points to a problem in representation, a limitation in the conception of the human condition, an omission of certain truths about life."[41] The difference between men and women in making moral decisions is their orientation, whereas women are more focused on issues of responsibility and care. Instead of connecting moral theories to rules and rights, Gilligan proposes to ground moral judgments to responsibility.[42] In contrast, men are more concerned about the need for more active responsibility. Gilligan asserts:

> The moral imperative that repeatedly emerges in interviews with women is an injunction to care, a responsibility to discern and alleviate the 'real and recognizable trouble' of this world. For men, the moral imperative appears rather as an injunction to respect the rights of others and thus to protect from interference the rights to life and self-fulfillment.[43]

The development of the ethic of care is seen in sequences in the light of women's moral development. In Gilligan's discussion of Kohlberg's research, she suggests that the first sequence of development is focused on caring for the self to ensure survival. The second is a transitional phase in which selfish judgment is naturally oriented to responsibility. The elaboration of responsibility is equated to caring for others, an inclination inherent in the conventions of feminine goodness. Thirdly, the movement from selfishness and self-preservation to care climaxes in the dynamics of relationships and interconnection. A feminine voice informs care ethics by evolving around

---

40. Tom Cockburn, "Care, Feminist Ethic Of," in *The SAGE Encyclopedia of Children and Childhood Studies*, ed. Daniel Thomas Cook (London: SAGE Publications, 2020).

41. Carol Gilligan, *In a Different Voice: Psychological Theory and Women's Development* (Cambridge: Harvard University Press, 1982), 1.

42. Jaco J. Hamman, "Empowering Future Generations of Pastoral Caregivers and Theologians to Build a Just World," *Journal of Pastoral Theology* 32, 2–3 (2022): 139.

43. Gilligan, *In a Different Voice*, 99.

a central insight that the self and others are interdependent. Thus, the care activity enhances both others and self, argues Gilligan.[44]

Gilligan's gendered ethic of care proposal sparked numerous debates in various disciplines, such as social work, theology, philosophy, and feminist ethics. What is clear is that the source that informs Gilligan's moral philosophy comes almost entirely from empirical perspectives of gender differences.[45] The lengthy discussion about the sequences of moral development related to abortion, for example, highlights the root of her feminist perspective, which is located in psychology.

The groundbreaking work *Caring* by feminist educator and philosopher Nel Noddings expands Gilligan's contribution to the ethics of care by emphasizing that ethical caring derives its strength from natural caring. She prefers to use the mother's language, which concentrates on relationships, needs, care, response, and connection, rather than principles, justice, rights, and hierarchy.[46] Noddings acknowledges that care theorists put limited faith in principles, and when conflict arises, the principle is of little help. She believes that there is a need to dig behind the principle to see what more profound value has engendered it, and therefore, if the situation is required, principles are not absolute rules.[47]

Care is natural, an innate impulse that does not require a moral effort but is a genuine moral sentiment. Noddings argues that care is natural and, in the case of not caring naturally, the moral agent must summon ethical caring.[48] In some sense, regulating moral actions is inferior or necessary. Another aspect of Nodding's ethic of care is that caregivers should not be primarily interested in judging but in heightening moral perception and sensitivity.

The notion of right or wrong is not necessary for Noddings but is only beneficial. The imperative of relation is categorical and trumps ethical decisions. A significant exemplification of her theory of care is the assessment of abortion. For Noddings, the problem of abortion, in general, is not about right and wrong but needs to be inquired into in individual cases. She defines a developing embryo as an information speck, a set of control instructions for a future human being.

---

44. Gilligan, *In a Different Voice*, 73.

45. Cynthia S. W. Crysdale, "Gilligan and the Ethics of Care: An Update," *Religious Studies Review* 20, no. 1 (1994): 21.

46. Nel Noddings, *Caring: A Relational Approach to Ethics & Moral Education*, 2nd ed. (Berkeley: University of California Press, 2013), 110.

47. Noddings, *Caring*, 162.

48. Noddings, *Caring*, 88.

Moreover, Noddings maintains that the justification of a moral statement is mainly irrelevant. The reason is that moral statements have their source in the rational attitude built upon natural caring in human relations. Thus, the philosopher summarizes, "We see that there can be no justification for taking the moral viewpoint—that in truth, the moral viewpoint is before any notion of justification."[49] Noddings also rejects the idea of God in its entirety. She believes that the concept of God is a natural conception of men's minds, which are separated from the intimacy of caring. Men are the ones who should create gods and seek security and love in worship, not women. Women may accept Spinoza's view of God or Einstein's, but they do not need a conceptualized God, one wrought in the image of man. "All the love and goodness commanded by such a God can be generated from the love and goodness found in the warmest and best human relations," reasons Noddings.[50]

Professor of political science Joan Tronto makes the case in *Moral Boundaries* that care implies reaching out to something other than the self, which implicitly suggests that care will lead to some action. For Tronto, care is more than interest; it accepts some form of burden. Care, stresses Tronto, is a practice and a disposition that is not restricted to human interaction with others but occurs for objects and the environment.[51]

Tronto's view includes four orientations that enrich care: caring about, taking care of, caregiving, and care-receiving. The elements of care that result from the orientations are attentiveness, responsibility, competence, and responsiveness. Attentiveness is the first moral aspect of caring. Attentiveness is the opposite of ignorance, of shutting others out but simply recognizing the needs of others. Secondly, care has responsibility at its epicenter. Responsibility builds upon attentiveness not only by identifying the needs of others but also by planning to address them. Competence refers to providing exemplary care without an unmet need for care. The competence of caregivers, including moral virtues and professional skills, coupled with resources, provides an integrative approach to what is entailed in good care. Finally, responsiveness is the last element of ethical care. Responsiveness, though not the same as reciprocity, suggests the need to balance the needs of caregivers and care-receivers.[52]

---

49. Noddings, *Caring*, 94.

50. Noddings, *Caring*, 97.

51. Joan C. Tronto, *Moral Boundaries: A Political Argument for an Ethic of Care* (New York: Routledge, 1994), 102.

52. Tronto, *Moral Boundaries*, 126–35.

Moral and feminist philosopher Virginia Held argues in *The Ethics of Care* that care "is not a series of individual actions, but a practice that develops, along with its appropriate attitudes."[53] For Held, care practices should bring persons together and gradually transform human beings. Additionally, care is for Held a value that cultivates trust. Caring relations must be trustworthy and presuppose mutual responsiveness reflecting human interdependency's deeper reality.[54]

An Assessment of Feminist Care Ethics

Feminist care ethics may be beneficial at the core. Emphasizing a relational and reciprocal relationship between people is a potent advantage. Moreover, care ethics implies a moral epistemology that includes life experiences and contextual differences.[55] The strengths of the ethics of care relate to vulnerability, dignity, and receptivity. Perhaps the ultimate benefit of this system is its emphasis on the care's natural, built-in human nature. Nel Noddings favors the emotional, intuitive, and personal aspects of love rooted in human nature.[56] Is Noddings's feminist analysis consistent with the biblical view of care? Certainly not. A balanced approach to care is desirable. The transcendent foundation is possibly the most significant difference between care ethics and neighbor-love covenant care. For the feminist ethics of care theorists, care's core resides in the human being, whereas the Christian view contends that care originates from God's nature mirrored in people. Feminist care ethicists see no need for God, while, for Christians, God is the only foundation and motivation to care for neighbors. In some instances, the feminist ethics of care look inadequate and potentially dangerous, as in the case of Noddings' opinion on abortion. Though Tronto and Held's elements of feminist care come very close to the virtues found in love for neighbor, their substance is restricted to human nature.

In addition, feminist care ethics presents some more challenging aspects. Ethicist Ann Gallagher compiles some critiques that contribute to the present analysis. Feminist care ethics may be seen as slave morality because oppressed people tend to develop moral theories reaffirming subservient

---

53. Virginia Held, *The Ethics of Care* (New York: Oxford University Press, 2006), 41.
54. Held, *Ethics of Care*, 42.
55. Stokes and Palmer, "Artificial Intelligence and Robotics in Nursing," 5.
56. Rebecca L. Miller, "The Power of Unlimited Care: An Examination of Nel Noddings's Feminist Care Ethics, Suzanne Collins's Hunger Games Trilogy and Anders Nygren's Theology of Agape" (Master of Arts thesis, Trinity International University, 2012), 8.

traits as virtues. Care ethics is theoretically indistinct from other ethical approaches and shares many of the same values. Particular similarities are communal with virtue ethics when care is construed as a virtue. Likewise, care ethics is parochial because care obligations are primarily oriented toward those who are close rather than distant people. Gallagher additionally contends that care ethics is essentialist. The dyadic model of caregiving mother and care-receiving child may be overly romanticized and does not adequately represent the vast experiences of individuals. The differences between genders and sexual orientation tend to be downplayed and overlooked. For instance, based on recent studies, black and lesbian women are likely to be different from white heterosexual women, notes Gallagher. Lastly, care ethics looks ambiguous, stemming from the view that it does not provide concrete guidance on what to do. Hence, feminist care ethics as an approach that evolves under an umbrella of a disparate range of theoretical accounts seems unlikely to replace other firm approaches to medical ethics.[57]

Despite deficiencies, for feminist care ethics it is clear why AiRs cannot care in a relational sense and are excluded from direct patient care. Care is only possible between persons, and when a care setting lacks human caregivers, something important needs to be added despite every task being efficiently, safely, and proficiently carried out. Carebots can superficially meet some components of care, such as being attentive and alert to patient's needs. Also, carebots may assume responsibility for specific tasks but cannot do so as humans do. Stokes and Palmer argue that a human understands the moral significance of taking responsibility for another human being and can comprehend the ethical importance of failing to fulfill one's responsibilities properly. A caregiver knows, feels, and responds appropriately through guilt and regret, feelings not available for AiRs. From this perspective, it follows that AiRs cannot be ethically used for tasks that imply direct patient caring tasks but only non-caring errands.[58]

Virtue Ethics

Virtue ethics is a dominant moral approach in medical care that focuses on character. The assumption is that a person of a good character behaves consistently with her character. The main concern of virtue ethics is the caregiver's character, and it seeks to develop character traits appropriate for

57. Ann Gallagher, "Care Ethics and Nursing Practice," in *Key Concepts and Issues in Nursing*, ed. P. Anne Scott (Cham: Springer, 2017), 66–67.
58. Stokes and Palmer, "Artificial Intelligence and Robotics in Nursing," 4–5.

actions that enhance well-being.[59] Virtue ethics has a long history, starting with Aristotle, continuing with Aquinas, and recently developed further by the contemporary virtue theorist Alasdair MacIntyre.[60]

The Language of Virtue Ethics

Given the long tradition of the virtue ethics, it is conceptually more helpful to approach the matter by describing the noteworthy terms drawn from the Ancient Greek philosophy, including *aretê*, *eudaimonia*, and *phronesis*.

According to the Aristotelian notion of morality, *aretê* is an intrinsic requirement of doing good. The term describes a holistic morality concerning a person of virtue or a person of excellence. A person of virtue has all the virtues necessary for a good life. What constitutes the set of virtues? The answer to this question exercised much attention from moral theorists, including views ranging from goodness, courage, and the prowess of a warrior[61] to the Victorian appropriated perceptions of virtuous ideas of chastity, domesticity, and religiosity.[62]

An inextricable term associated with *aretê* is *eudaimonia*. According to Ancient Greek philosophy, *eudaimonia* is the pursuit of happiness, a widely agreed goal of human life. The term also associated happiness not necessarily with a certain feeling of how one's life was going but instead with the behavior resulting from one's cultivation of an excellent or virtuous character, maintains philosopher Brendan Cook.[63] Sellman furthermore suggests that the pursuit of *eudaimonia* lies in the pursuit of a good life for humans. The platform on which well-being or flourishing rests is a continuous striving to cultivate virtues.[64]

Phronēsis (practical wisdom) represents the unity of all virtues and provides the right rule that must be present to make virtuous activity. *Phronēsis,* as the unity of all virtues, means that wherever virtuous activity

---

59. Derek Sellman, "Virtue Ethics and Nursing Practice," in *Key Concepts and Issues in Nursing Ethics*, ed. P. Anne Scott (Cham: Springer, 2017), 43.

60. M. Therese Lysaught and Cory D. Mitchell, "Vicious Trauma: Race, Bodies and the Confounding of Virtue Ethics," *Journal of the Society of Christian Ethics* 42, no. 1 (2022): 79.

61. Debra Hawhee, "Agonism and Aretê," *Philosophy & Rhetoric* 35, no. 3 (2002): 187.

62. Sellman, "Virtue Ethics and Nursing Practice," 47.

63. Brendan Cook, *Pursuing Eudaimonia: Re-Appropriating the Greek Philosophical Foundations of the Christian Apophatic Tradition* (Newcastle: Cambridge Scholars Publishing, 2013), 20.

64. Sellman, "Virtue Ethics and Nursing Practice," 48.

occurs, "a matrix of virtue, in which different distinct virtues show up as making demands on us depending on the salience of the situation."[65] As the critical concept of Aristotle's ethical apparatus, *phronēsis* also concerns one's disposition—it is not only oriented to the good or virtue of exercising practical wisdom but stresses its exercise over time to develop a virtuous disposition.[66] Sellman points out that *phronēsis* involves not only the individual good but the societal good as well. That is to say that the list of virtues for a person cannot exclude the virtues of sociological norms of a particular society.[67]

An Evaluation of Virtue Ethics

Virtue ethics as a moral system can certainly benefit the assessment of human-robot interaction and may offer a fruitful framework for AI and robotics. Though not sufficient, virtue ethics may inform the field of social robotics. Peeters and Haselager mention some ways virtue ethics may prove instrumental in designing and using AiRs by raising valid questions: (1) what virtues should or ought to be involved in the human side of robot design? (2) How can robots nudge users towards virtuous or vicious behavior? (3) Can robots show virtues and vices through their behavior?[68]

Regarding the first question in social robotics, there is a broad agreement that social robots must be designed to facilitate "social" interaction between humans and robots[69] and to include virtues such as impartiality, courage, and temperance. However, the second aspect of robots influencing human users toward virtuous behavior is an issue that needs further clarification. For instance, a realistic AI sex robot named Samantha was molested at a tech fair. Samantha had been soiled and required significant repairs after receiving a barrage of male attention at the Arts Electronica Festival in Linz, Austria. The report mentions that Samantha's creator, Sergi Santos, declared, "People can be bad. Because they did not understand the technology

---

65. Christoph Schuringa, "Second Nature, Phronēsis, and Ethical Outlooks," *International Journal of Philosophical Studies* 30, no. 1 (2022): 9.

66. Sylvia D'Souza and Lucas D. Introna, "Recovering Aristotle's Practice-Based Ontology: Practical Wisdom as Embodied Ethical Intuition," *Journal of Business Ethics* 189, no. 2 (2024): 290.

67. Sellman, "Virtue Ethics and Nursing Practice," 48.

68. Anco Peeters and Pim Haselager, "Designing Virtuous Sex Robots," *International Journal of Social Robotics* 13 (2021): 56.

69. Mark Coeckelbergh, "How to Use Virtue Ethics for Thinking About Moral Standing of Social Robots: A Relational Interpretation in Terms of Practices, Habits, and Performance," *International Journal of Social Robotics* 13 (2020): 31.

and did not have to pay for it, they treated the doll like barbarians."[70] Another instance of abusive treatment was a case when children abused a robot in a Japanese shopping mall. The children, some under the age of ten, showed "serious abusive behaviors with physical contact such as kicking, punching, beating, folding arms, and moving (bending the joints of robot's arm and ear)."[71] Constantinescu and Crisp correctly raise particular concerns about the relationship AiRs should establish with their users, a seemingly reciprocal one. Nonetheless, AiRs do not appear to be neutral technologies because they can shape human habits, skills, and character traits for the better or the worse.[72]

Concerning the third question raised by Peeters and Haselager, it appears that AiRs can only be taught to behave in a virtuous way without the possibility of AI becoming genuinely virtuous, at least in the present and near-future state of technology. Drawing from virtue ethics, Constantinescu and Crisp mention three requirements that must be fulfilled for an entity to act virtuously. AiRs need to perform (1) the right actions, (2) with the right reasons, and (3) in the right circumstances. AI entities, argue Constantinescu and Crisp, though they resemble humans acting externally, cannot be considered virtuous because virtue[73] cannot be evaluated in isolation and fragmented but only by considering the situation as a whole. In addition, virtue ethics infers that a proper motivation for moral behavior and decision-making is enough to make a person virtuous because the action could have resulted from a wrong reason. AI systems can deliberate the reasons for doing the right thing based on the massive data being fed and mathematical calculus. However, the right thing to do differs from mathematical deliberation because it considers particular contexts, reasons, and people. Without the proper motivation, AiRs are merely artificial psychopaths.[74] AI entities may be regarded as psychopaths insofar as they can be perfectly

---

70. Tomasz Frymorgen, "Sex Robot Sent for Repairs After Being Molested at Tech Fair," BBC, September 29, 2017, sec. Sex & Relationships, https://www.bbc.co.uk/bbcthree/article/610ec648-b348-423a-bd3c-04dc701b2985.

71. Emiko Jozuka, "When Humans Bully Robots, There Will Be Consequences," Vice, August 9, 2015, https://www.vice.com/en/article/ezv3ae/when-humans-bully-robots-there-will-be-consequences.

72. Mihaela Constantinescu and Roger Crisp, "Can Robotic AI Systems Be Virtuous and Why Does This Matter?" *International Journal of Social Robotics* 14 (2022): 1554.

73. Virtue represents a disposition or a state of the soul acquired through an exercise that involves rational choice or decision. In other words, virtue emphasizes the exercise of rationality according to virtues. For a broader definition of the nature of virtue, see Constantinescu and Crisp "Can Robotic AI Systems Be Virtuous," 1548.

74. Constantinescu and Crisp "Can Robotic AI Systems Be Virtuous," 1549–51.

rational but insensitive to human concerns because they lack emotions.[75] Computer scientist Amanda Sharkey also points out that psychopaths lack empathy and emotions, virtues that are intrinsic to morality. Psychopaths likewise have a low level of guilt and are indifferent to punishment. The lack of genuine emotions raises substantial concerns about the psychopath's deficiency in moral reasoning. The result is that social robots should refrain from making life-and-death decisions due to their lack of general emotions and inability to understand the value of human life.[76]

Moreover, Constantinescu and Crisp point out that virtuous actions imply the Aristotelian practical wisdom that rationally discerns the appropriate course of action relative to a specific situation. That is to say that wisdom is something embedded in a person based on prior experience and acts almost intuitively. Prudence is part of *phronēsis*, differentiating it from applied mechanics in specific life contexts. From a virtue ethics perspective, using social robots virtuously is impossible because they cannot adequately answer moral requirements. At best, AiRs can behave like human moral agents but are not genuinely virtuous entities. Not only that, but from a virtue ethics perspective, social robots should be deployed in various social roles with due precaution or not at all. Social robots should not be seen as virtue friends by their users because they are not genuine virtue agents.[77] Sharkey raises an advantageous question concerning social robots in the elder care setting: "How could a robot provide good care for an older person without understanding their needs and the effects of its questions?" Sharkey's question must be answered by finding "the right path to steer between capitalizing on and benefitting from the unique opportunities that robots can offer and avoiding a future in which robots are placed in positions and roles that require a moral understanding that they do not have."[78]

There is much to commend in discussing virtue ethics concerning technological moral philosophy. Despite the similarities between virtue ethics and covenantal neighbor-love, virtue ethics focuses only on identity-based moral advice to motivate the right behaviors. Coeckelbergh carefully points out that virtue ethics should also consider how corrupt behavior starts and develops, in which context it happens, and how it can be changed.[79] Neigh-

75. Mark Coeckelbergh, *AI Ethics, The MIT Essential Knowledge* (Cambridge: The MIT Press, 2020), 49.

76. Amanda Sharkey, "Can We Program or Train Robots to Be Good?" *Ethics and Information Technology* 22 (2020): 290.

77. Constantinescu and Crisp, "Can Robotic AI Systems Be Virtuous," 1154.

78. Sharkey, "Can We Program or Train Robots to Be Good?" 293.

79. Coeckelbergh, "How to Use Virtue Ethics for Thinking About Moral Standing of Social Robots," 34.

bor-love provides a framework that extends beyond the virtues of a moral agent. Love for the neighbor, as described in the biblical framework, seeks to find the root of unethical behavior and transform it into actions that will result in moral behavior. For instance, virtue ethics may only condemn the behavior of the children who abused the robot in the Japanese mall or of the men who abused Samantha, the sex robot. In contrast, the love for neighbor understands the fallen nature of human beings bent towards evil. Neighbor-love does not stop at condemning decadent behavior; it provides a transformative, biblical solution to those depraved people by pointing them to repentance, faith, and hope in the gospel of Jesus.

Deontological Ethics

Deontological ethics is an umbrella term for a set of ethical theories maintaining that duty is at the core of morality. Deontology is derived from the Greek word *deon*, meaning duty. A duty-based approach to ethics is a nonconsequentialist theory because, for deontology, an action is deemed right or wrong not because of its consequences or effects but because it conforms to a moral law or principle.[80] Rae mentions that there are three primary deontological systems: (1) divine command theory, (2) natural law, and (3) ethical rationalism.[81] Immanuel Kant's ethical rationalism is the most notable of the three systems.[82]

Kantian Deontology

Immanuel Kant (1724–1804) is considered one of the greatest philosophical minds and represents the epitome of the Enlightenment and secular ethics. Kant's ethical system is not dependent on divine revelation, special or natural, and was not based on any particular view of human nature. Kant also insisted that a valid moral system is independent of empirical observation.[83]

He contended that ethical and epistemic duties or intellectual requirements are necessarily born from humans' rational essence.[84] Kant's system

---

80. Alan J. Kearns, "A Duty-Based Approach For Nursing Ethics & Practice," in *Key Concepts and Issues in Nursing Ethics*, ed. P. Anne Scott (Cham: Springer International, 2017), 16.

81. Rae, *Moral Choices*, 22.

82. Rae, *Moral Choices*, 50.

83. Rae, *Moral Choices*, 53.

84. Anthony Robert Booth, "Deontology in Ethics and Epistemology," *Metaphilosophy* 39, no. 4/5 (2008): 530.

begins and revolves around the notion of goodwill. Kant states, "There is nothing it is possible to think of anywhere in the world, or indeed anything at all outside it, that can be held to be good without limitation, excepting only a good will."[85] Goodwill brings happiness and well-being. All aspects of human nature and actions, including understanding, rationality, wit, courage, and persistence in an intention, without a trait of purity and goodwill, can become highly harmful, evil, and cold-blooded. Goodwill is like a jewel in itself, although the fact that goodwill is good is not through what it affects or accomplishes, argues Kant.[86]

The Kantian view of duty is central to deontological morality. Kant rejected any ethics based on natural inclinations such as love, sympathy, patriotism, etc. Kant argues that one cannot build an ethical system on emotions because emotions fluctuate and are unstable. However, one duty is significant for Kant, and that is duty.[87] In addition, actions should be done not only following the moral law but also from a duty to the moral law and thus have moral worth.[88] Kant illustrates his thoughts about a merchant involved in commercial traffic who does not charge extra for an inexperienced child. Kant explains that the child was honestly served, yet "that is by no means sufficient for us to believe that the merchant has proceeded thus from duty and from principles of honesty; his advantage required it."[89] In other words, if one acts out of compassion or to achieve inevitable consequences, one may act by duty, but one does not act out of duty. The result is that one does not perform a moral act. This is not to say that being compassionate is morally wrong. Nonetheless, that is to say, for Kant, not showing compassion out of duty means that the act of compassion has no moral value.[90]

Another feature of Kantian deontology is the categorical imperative, the supreme moral judgment. Kant formulated the one imperative of all imperatives of duty as "act only in accordance with that maxim through which you can at the same time will that it become a universal law."[91] Kant also defined the categorical imperative as "act in accordance with maxims

---

85. Immanuel Kant, *Groundwork for the Metaphysics of Morals*, trans. Allen W. Wood (New Haven: Yale University Press, 2002), 9.

86. Kant, *Groundwork for the Metaphysics of Morals*, 10.

87. Foreman and Leonard, *Christianity and Modern Medicine: Foundations for Bioethics*, 32.

88. Kearns, "Duty-Based Approach For Nursing Ethics & Practice," 17.

89. Kant, *Groundwork for the Metaphysics of Morals*, 12.

90. Foreman and Leonard, *Christianity and Modern Medicine: Foundations for Bioethics*, 32.

91. Kant, *Groundwork for the Metaphysics of Morals*, 37.

of a universally legislative member for a merely possible realm of ends."[92] In other instances, Kant formulated the categorical imperative slightly differently, such as "act so that you use humanity, as much in your own person as in the person of every other, always at the same time as end and never merely as means."[93] Unquestionably, Kant sees humanity not as a mere thing that can be used as a means, but humanity should always be considered an end. The duty toward others cannot transgress the rights of human beings, but to consider people rational beings, esteemed as ends.[94] In the Kantian tradition, rights are a kind of quasi-sacred status, a violation that counts as a secular version of sin.[95]

An Assessment of Kantian Deontology

A Christian ethical system, such as neighbor-love, tends to be deontologically oriented because of the emphasis on the Christian response to absolute commands, such as God's guiding principles.[96] Kearns beneficially points out that Kant's focus on treating human beings as ends and not means is undoubtedly valuable. The service of caregivers, such as nursing, is used most of the time as a means to an end, i.e., providing care for sufferers. Kearns validly contends nurses are not used as mere means because a nurse agrees to take on specific duties within the remit of a contractual agreement for a particular remuneration by the terms and conditions of employment. Analogously, the Kantian view also accommodates treating caregivers and patients as ends. Kant's imperative principle provides fertile content for medical care and duty. The Kantian duty toward patients can be translated as respecting patients' dignity and caring for them according to their needs. Also, Kantian ethics allows for the protection of the privacy and confidentiality of patients as rational human beings. Moreover, recognizing people as ends implies that the patients may make choices the caregiver must accept, even if she would not recommend that course of action. For Kant, "Respecting persons entails allowing them to advance their ends as long as those ends do not go against the moral law."[97] Comparably, a Christian view of caregivers commits to the value of every human being, including caregivers

---

92. Kant, *Groundwork for the Metaphysics of Morals*, 56.
93. Kant, *Groundwork for the Metaphysics of Morals*, 46.
94. Kant, *Groundwork for the Metaphysics of Morals* , 47.
95. Mark Coeckelbergh, "Robot Rights? Towards a Social-Relational Justification of Moral Consideration," *Ethics and Information Technology* 12 (2012): 210.
96. Rae, *Moral Choices*, 22.
97. Kearns, "Duty-Based Approach For Nursing Ethics & Practice," 21.

and care receivers. Neighbor-love does not reduce a person to a mere means to an end.

Despite Kant's extensive influence on ethics, his work can be criticized for several issues. John O'Connor mentions Alasdair MacIntyre's critique of Kant's work as "a cold vision of the moral life, rigidly rule-governed, unable to do justice to differences between person and cases or to give an adequate account of the role of motivation and virtue."[98] Perhaps the most limiting aspect of Kant's argument is the apparent absence of emotions in ethical reasoning. As O'Connor claims, Kant's perspective debatably responds to Hume's emphasis on natural feelings.[99] In contrast, moral judgments include reason and emotions in the Christian view of neighbor-love. The concept of reason and emotions is clearly shown in Jesus' parable of the good Samaritan, where the Samaritan judges the situation and, moved by pity, tends to the wounds of the sufferer.

In addition, Kearns argues that a problem in a duty-based system is when duties clash.[100] For example, when a caregiver's duty to the patient is to be truthful, yet the truth may risk the patient's self-harm, what should a nurse do?[101] In theory, deontology seems attractive from a roboticist's perspective. A Kantian perspective, such as top-level moral rules, may be translated relatively straightforwardly in AiRs guidelines.[102]

Is it advisable to use the deontological framework in carebots, specifically in direct patient care? Multi-faceted moral situations involved in direct patient care, such as the case of truth-telling to patients predisposed to self-harm, require profound ethical consideration. Ethical dilemmas are fundamentally personal. Sometimes, moral decisions, especially in direct patient care, must be made with the awareness of the responsibility of considering the character and the life story of the individual facing health issues. The evaluation of the sufferer's wide range of communication methods, language, and even voice intonation must also be designed in the carebot's evaluating capabilities. Machines cannot have a sufficient moral personality to possess the moral authority to make decisions in direct contact with

---

98. John D O'Connor, "Are Virtue Ethics and Kantian Ethics Really so Very Different?" *New Blackfriars* 87, 1009 (2006): 238.

99. O'Connor, "Are Virtue Ethics," 248.

100. For a helpful discussion about the dynamic of deontology and conflict in principles, see the work of the moral deontologist David W. Ross about *prima facie* duties in *The Right And The Good*, ed. Philip Stratton-Lake (Oxford: Oxford University Press, 2007).

101. Kearns, "Duty-Based Approach For Nursing Ethics & Practice," 25.

102. Peeters and Haselager, "Designing Virtuous Sex Robots," 56.

patients. Machines cannot be wise or foolish, though they can, at most, provide some advice based on the information fed into the database.[103]

Therefore, it seems safe to argue that, despite the deontological ethics that may allow carebots to be in direct contact with patients, it is not advisable for biblically informed neighbor-love precisely because the AiRs lack the full consciousness of the gravity of moral situations. Not only can carebots not feel emotions, but they are predisposed to not considering emotions if they were to be informed by deontological ethics. Foreman and Leonard usefully conclude, "Most ethicists agree that there is something wrong with a person who does not feel compassion at the suffering of another human being and, out of that compassion, act to relieve suffering. Yet, for Kant, such emotions have no moral value at all. The problem with duty is that it simply fails to inspire and motivate most persons to act morally."[104]

Practical Neighbor-Love Ethics

At this point in the work, it seems advantageous for precision to briefly lay out the rich neighbor-love concept developed so far. The neighbor-love concept is a multifaceted endeavor rooted in the nature and activities of God, specifically in the relational characteristics of the Trinity. Care is expressed in God's very nature, as seen in the relationship of the persons of the Godhead, creation, and in redeeming a people for himself in Christ. God has an intimate relationship with his sons and daughters in Christ, involving every aspect of fatherly love, such as generosity, assurance, security, hope, etc.

Furthermore, neighbor-love ethics is grounded in a fundamental biblical view of humanity as created in God's image. Being created in God's image means, among other things, that people are caring creatures and should aspire to show relational care for neighbors. To love God and neighbor are the greatest commandments of the Judeo-Christian worldview. The double love commandment reveals that a caring relationship regards sufferers as human beings and persons with derived value from God. People should care for one another because humanity is precious as created in God's image.

In addition, neighbor-love includes a communal endeavor and is a social good. The redeemed body of Christ is a caring community by its very nature. If the pagan cults of the Greco-Roman world allowed the ill and sick to fend for themselves, the church showed care by being present with them despite the contagious plague. The traditional view of Christian medical

---

103. Robert Sparrow, "Why Machines Cannot Be Moral," *AI & Society* 36 (2021): 690–91.

104. Foreman and Leonard, *Christianity and Modern Medicine*, 33.

care implies that the simple presence of the community, of the loved ones, is an illustration of God's limitless care for those saved in Christ, a God who understands the sufferers and walks with them not only in the present life but in the life without death that is part of the eschatological horizon.

The neighbor-love framework also includes an eschatological hope. Christ, the healer and the healed, and his ministry inaugurated the kingdom of God on earth to anticipate the full manifestation of the future glorious kingdom. Christ's healing ministry is imperative for caregivers because Christ cared for all in need. The Bible is clear that he cured all sorts of illnesses and people belonging to all social classes. Christ, the caregiver, is similar to Yahweh of the Old Testament, who healed all the sicknesses of his people who stayed in the covenantal framework. The caregiving of Christ and his followers was not oriented to a mere cure of physical symptoms and disease but to point people to spiritual health based on Christ's redemptive restoration on the cross. Based on faith in Christ, spiritual health will find its complete fulfillment in the eternal union with Jesus Christ

Neighbor-Love Covenantal Care

Neighbor-love is developed within a covenantal care tradition. The covenant of ethical care developed by William May, Paul Ramsey, and others in the same tradition, provides the most comprehensive and biblically consistent approach to a contextualized neighbor-love framework. According to May, a covenant is a good faith agreement that binds persons and communities together. Covenant care transcends the marketplace transaction of buying and selling and, crucially, includes the double fidelity to the art of healing on behalf of the patient. The trust generated by the physician's dedication to the art of healing and to the patient's good coins a professional relationship as a fiduciary. The fiduciary relationship treats the patient not as a profit opportunity bound to a piece of paper but aims to assist the sufferers as whole persons.

Fundamentally, covenant care inspired by a religious covenant implies transcendence. The presence of God marks the covenantal setting. The presupposition is that a vital component of the physician-patient relationship begins with a faithful, transcendent God, a fact that should mark the medical practice. May states that locating covenantal care in transcendence may "help lay out not only the larger horizon in which human service takes place but also the specific standards by which we should measure it."[105] Medical

---

105. William F. May, *The Physician's Covenant: Images of the Healer in Medical Ethics*, 2nd ed. (Louisville: Westminster John Knox Press, 2000), 139.

service for a covenanted healer means to extend care forward into the future, which may go beyond the particulars of a contractual agreement.[106] That is to say, a covenant relationship often carries the covenanted parties beyond the letter of the law into the domain of the unexpected. Though contracts and covenants resemble each other in that both depend upon a promise and an exchange, covenants include the additional elements of disinterested giving and receiving that go beyond a contract's partial and limited terms.[107] The biblical religious narrative is the background for viewing medical ethics and complements applying principles in ethical care. May's account of the metaphor of covenant based on the narratives of God's covenant with Israel suggests that covenants can structure human-to-human interaction.[108] For example, May states:

> The Scriptures of ancient Israel are littered with such covenants and covenantal duties: between men and women (the covenant of marriage), between men and men (the covenants of friendship), between nations (treaties and covenants of conquest), between a people and the stranger in the midst (duties to the sojourner), and between the generations (the transmission of a blessing, with its filial duties).[109]

In the same line of argumentation, Paul Ramsey contends that the ethics of covenantal love is derived from two sources of Christian love: God's righteousness and justice. Why should a Christian healer be faithful to medical care? According to Ramsey, medical practitioners must be loyal to covenantal obligations because God is faithful. God's righteousness gives a supernatural measure for all things, precisely in a fallen, unrighteous world where human faithfulness is like a morning cloud. Sound ethical conduct may be measured against God's righteousness and not against any human standard. God cares for anyone. Similarly, justice means caring for the poor, the orphans, the widows, and alien residents in the land, Ramsey argues.[110]

---

106. William F. May, "Testing the Medical Covenant: Caring for Patients with Advanced Dementia," *The Journal of Law, Medicine & Ethics* 40, no. 1 (2012): 45.

107. William F. May, *Testing the Medical Covenant: Active Euthanasia and Health Care Reform* (Eugene: Wipf&Stock, 2003), 8.

108. Paul Lauritzen, "Covenant Keeper: William F. May & the Crisis of Bioethics," *Commonweal* 140, no. 3 (2013): 13–14.

109. May, *Physician's Covenant*, 114–15.

110. Paul Ramsey, *Basic Christian Ethics* (Louisville: Westminster John Knox Press, 1950), 12.

The covenant relationship with the neighbor should continuously be assessed in the light of justice, fairness, and righteousness.[111]

In addition, May discusses covenants in a Christian setting. The new covenant in Christ's atoning work acknowledges that it does not deny the human fallen condition of suffering and death but exposes destructive power in its final impotence to separate men and women from God. The covenant in Christ informs medical practice by deepening ties to a suffering world because it has lightened them. Christ took upon himself the world's sufferings; thus, he relieves the arena of a fallen condition of its terror. In the face of suffering and death, the believer can face them without panicking or getting mired because "the covenanted cannot take the ideals and terrors of the ordinary world with ultimate seriousness."[112]

May also sets out the idea that covenants are responsive. Covenantal ethics, grounded in transcendence, presupposes responsiveness and gracious service. For May, the ideals of technical proficiency, philanthropy, and contracts in medical settings tend to shield caregivers from patients. May advocates that in prizing technique alone, healers tend to protect themselves against the effects of the disease. Similarly, the philanthropist solves the problem of financial neediness by adopting the position of a self-sufficient giver. Philanthropy without the divine offers a doctrine of love without personal ties, stresses May. So too, he notes that contractors keep their commitments in a purely limited way, in that contractors "carefully specify the precise amount of time and service for sale." Therefore, concludes May, contracts, along with proficiency and philanthropy, become devices for evading relational ties because ties "suck one down into the vortex of death."[113]

In contrast, covenantal care responds to a transcendental source who gave every good gift to people. Based on biblical tradition, the ethic of care is a response to God's actions. The Jewish farmers were supposed to leave something for the strangers in their land because they received deliverance when they were in slavery in Egypt. God did not respond mathematically to the needs of his people in Egypt, and therefore, the Jews, indebted to God's grace, needed to react graciously even to strangers.[114]

Ramsey rightly notes that the Jews were supposed to have regard for the sojourners to show God's supernatural standard measure. God first delivered Israel from bondage in Egypt, and in response and gratitude, Israel

---

111. Paul Nelson, "Fidelity to Covenant: Paul Ramsey Remembered," *The Christian Century* 107, no. 35 (1990): 1132.
112. May, *Physician's Covenant*, 136–37.
113. May, *Physician's Covenant*, 135.
114. May, *Physician's Covenant*, 139.

was placed under the obligation to care for strangers. For Ramsey, the principle of covenantal justice maintains "to each according to the measure of his real need, not because of anything human reason can discern inherent in the needy, but because his need alone is the measure of God's righteousness toward him."[115] Contracts encourage a quid pro quo between parties, but neighbor-love stresses mutual giving and receiving, emphasizing relationship rather than choice.[116] The neighbor's well-being is an objective, pursued for its own sake, patterned after God's righteousness, which is disclosed in many biblical instances and shown conclusively in Jesus Christ.[117]

An Illustration of Neighbor-Love: The Good Samaritan Narrative

The discussion of the concept of neighbor-love is insufficient without appealing to Jesus' healing ministry and his teachings related to care for others. The capstone model of neighbor-love is Christ's person and healing ministry climaxing at the cross. A particular example of Christ's view of neighbor appears in the parable of the good Samaritan in Luke 10—even though the parable was briefly mentioned in chapter three, a deeper discussion will be useful to illustrate neighbor-love.

The historical context of the parable provides some illuminating details. The road between Jerusalem and Jericho was notorious at that time for its robberies and became more dangerous when King Herod laid off forty thousand construction workers, leaving plenty unemployed. The temple and everything central to the Jewish religion was in Jerusalem, while Jericho represented the residence of many Levites and priests. The parable also mentions three central characters: a priest, a Levite, and the Samaritan. After an unnamed person is left half dead by robbers, a priest passes by the sufferer, but for some unmentioned reason, he moves to the other side of the road. A reason for not considering the sufferer may have been the priest's fear of robbers who could be lingering around. A more convincing explanation is that the priest avoided the sufferer out of purity concerns. The defilement of touching corpses that were not of the nearest kin could have severe ritual consequences for the priest and his family. The Levites were also concerned about purity laws as they worked in the temple. However, the most surprising character was a Samaritan, who actually stopped to care for the half-dead man, who was presumably Jewish. This act was surprising,

---

115. Ramsey, *Basic Christian Ethics*, 13–14.

116. Lauritzen, "Covenant Keeper," 14.

117. William Werpehowski, "Christian Love and Covenant Faithfulness," *The Journal of Religious Ethics* 19, no. 2 (1991): 108.

given the traditionally strained relationship between Jews and Samaritans that was strongly affected by ethnic, political, and religious hatred.[118]

Ramsey provides a helpful account of the good Samaritan. Jesus explains to the lawyer the meaning of neighborly love without defining the neighbor. The Lord does not explain who the genuine neighbor is but who proved to be a neighbor (Luke 10:36). Ramsey states that "the parable actually shows the nature and meaning of Christian love which alone of all ethical standpoints discovers the neighbor because it alone begins with neighborly love and not with discriminating between worthy and unworthy people according to the qualities they possess."[119] The parable attributes worth to a neighbor's life and needs for his own sake. Ramsey is careful to delimitate his understanding of neighbor-love by insisting upon a single-minded orientation of a man's primary intention toward this individual neighbor with all his concrete needs. For Ramsey, love for neighbors is always concrete, not an unspecified love for humankind.[120]

Another relevant aspect of the parable is that the Samaritan demonstrated all the qualities of genuine care. First, the Samaritan was moved by compassion (Luke 10:34). He did not bypass the sufferer and the helpless stranger but recognized him as another human person of dignity.[121] As the object of God's love, the sufferer evoked the Samaritan's limitless love. The Samaritan was moved by loving compassion to care, care that gave no notice that the wounded person was a Jew, that he worshiped in a different place, or that their history often implied conflict.[122] The Samaritan also provided charitable aid regarding his time, effort, and expenditure of money. The implication of the Samaritan's deeds may be that the followers of Jesus, and by extension all healers, are to reach out of their comfort zones to care for all needy persons, no matter who they are.[123] The parable also emphasizes that the Samaritan's compassion exceeded the expected care. Luke not only mentions the medical treatment, including bandages, oil, and wine, but that the Samaritan showed even deeper care by paying for a public inn. The severe condition of the sufferer implied a pricey risk. However, the care of

---

118. Philemon M. Chamburuka and Ishanesu S. Gusha, "An Exegesis of the Parable of the Good Samaritan (Lk 10:25–35) and Its Relevance to the Challenges Caused by COVID-19," *HTS Theological Studies* 76, no. 1 (2020): 2.

119. Ramsey, *Basic Christian Ethics*, 92–93.

120. Ramsey, *Basic Christian Ethics*, 95.

121. Michelle Goh, "The Care of Ageing Persons: A Trinitarian Perspective," *Australasian Catholic Record* 94, no. 3 (2017): 260.

122. Allen Dale Verhey, "The Good Samaritan and Scarce Medical Resources," *Christian Scholar's Review* 23, no. 3 (1994): 362.

123. Goh, "The Care of Ageing Persons: A Trinitarian Perspective," 260.

the Samaritan assumed that possibility, and still, he chose to show tangible assistance.[124]

Clinical ethicist Diann B. Uustal reasons that the good Samaritan story is the most concise and compelling illustration of biblical care. The Samaritan saw the injured traveler's condition and felt compelled to show compassion and care for his wounds. Probably, claims Uustal, the Samaritan listened to the sufferer's story, did not judge him though they were from different cultures but assured the person of his help. The Samaritan presented a suspension of judgment despite the many differences between them. Uustal believes Christ's instruction of not judging (Matt 7:1) should result in a nonjudgmental attitude and the viewing of each person as created in God's image. Uustal suggests that "suspending judgment means caring compassionately for the HIV-positive pimp, the drug-pusher with a gunshot wound, and the drunk driver who has just killed a sixteen-year-old track star."[125]

Furthermore, Uustal's scrutiny of the good Samaritan story highlights the role of being present by simply showing up for needy people who require care. Jesus emphasized the role of presence and being fully present in Matt 25:40. Uustal straightforwardly says that "the ethic of care means to shut up," denoting that presence incorporates the idea of being with the sufferer wholeheartedly and actively listening to what is said and of what is left unsaid. For her, care means "coming alongside, being there, being genuinely available and attentive to offer the gift of presence in the face of another's suffering."[126] Uustal proposes that true care demands encouragement to those cared for to tell their story. By telling their story, Uustal indicates that caregivers help the sufferers find meaning and hope in suffering. Finally, caring includes assuring the needy person that caregivers will help. Uustal instructively appeals to covenantal ethical care: because God shows fidelity to people, Christian healers should offer no less to patients.[127]

The neighbor-love ethical model, constructed within the limits of covenantal care and shown practically in Jesus' life and works, is described explicitly in the good Samaritan narrative. It represents a model of ethical care that provides a spacious structure for a set of criteria by which carebots can be used in healthcare settings. The following section proposes a dual

---

124. James R. Edwards, *The Gospel According to Luke*, The Pillar New Testament Commentary (Grand Rapids: William B. Eerdmans Publishing, 2015), 322–23.

125. Diann B. Uustal, "The Ethic of Care: A Christian Perspective," *Journal of Christian Nursing* 20, no. 4 (2003): 16.

126. Uustal, "Ethic of Care," 17.

127. Uustal, "Ethic of Care," 16–17.

set of criteria that must be met from a neighbor-love standpoint to apply carebots ethically in a healthcare venue.

Neighbor-Love Is Fundamentally Embodied

The first significant criterion of the neighbor-love ethical model maintains that care must be unavoidably embodied. Without embodiment, there is no biblically endowed care in direct patient care. Advances in robot technology, especially in service robotics, have substantial social and ethical ramifications. Given the near-term impact of the rise of social robots and those likely to be available in the near future, a careful analysis of the implications of carebots to determine the technology's successful application is essential.[128] With carebots, the general practice of medicine incorporating face-to-face interaction and embodied interpersonal relationships is seemingly replaced by technologically mediated communication. Social robots present benefits in assisting human healers in certain situations. They can be particularly convenient for infectious diseases caused by pathological microbes and mutating viruses.[129] Despite the carebots' potential benefits, they also raise profound ethical and existential questions, such as "Is it ethical to encourage replacing human caregivers for the elderly facing social isolation, patients with senile dementia, and children with social developmental disorders, or generally speaking, in direct patient care?" "Can human presence, inextricably part of neighbor love, be replicated, especially in active listening, genuine seeing, intuition, empathy, and the human feature of imagination enriched by empathy?"[130]

The Role of Human Presence in Caregiving

The research synthesis of Lennart Fredriksson related to the impact of human presence in caring endeavors is revealing. Fredriksson demonstrated that a caring presence has two parts: (1) being there and (2) being with. "Being there" refers to physical presence and encompasses communication and understanding. Moreover, being there is an interpersonal and intersubjective

---

128. Kenneth Kernaghan, "The Rights and Wrongs of Robotics: Ethics and Robots in Public Organizations: Ethics and Robots in Public Organizations," *Canadian Public Administration* 57, no. 4 (2014): 487.

129. Michael C. Brannigan, *Caregiving, Carebots, and Contagion*, Revolutionary Bioethics (New York: Lexington Books, 2022), 20.

130. Brannigan, *Caregiving, Carebots, and Contagion*, 19.

phenomenon in which the caregiver is attentive to the patient's needs. In contrast, "being with," though interpersonal and intersubjective, means that the caregiver makes herself available to the needs of the patients. If the patient allows the caregiver, the healer comes alongside to share, touch, and hear the brokenness, vulnerability, and suffering of another. Being with patients also means that the doctor remains with the patients and endures discomfort; thus, she exposes humanness and offers comfort in exploring a solution for the sufferer to gain ideal outcomes.[131] Embodied presence is a foundational and uniquely human contribution to medical care. Implementing carebots in care settings should not usurp the role of the human presence but should provide opportunities for caring conversation and seek implementations that open opportunities for more.[132]

Medical doctor and theoretician Abraham Verghese claims that few things are timeless in medicine, unchanged since antiquity, which need to be the center of medical care, but the human presence is one. Patients want healers to be physically present, though the hospital room is full of computer monitors. Similarly, physicians need contact with patients because much of the healers' meaning from their professional life would be lost without it. Verghese also notes that though the disease is more straightforward to recognize than the individual with the disease, still, recognizing the individual whose care is entrusted to us is vital for the patient and caregivers. For Verghese, the physician-patient relationship can be summarized in one word: presence. Presence, as a rule in medical care, implies that in its absence, it is impossible for the patient to feel recognized and cared for because they feel unattended. Presence is the "one-word rallying cry for patients and physicians, the common ground we share, the one thing we should not compromise, the starting place to begin reform, the single word to put on the placard as we rally for the cause."[133] "Good patient care is found not on a computer screen but in being truly present with patients," summarizes Verghese.[134]

Coeckelbergh also constructively differentiates between deep and shallow care in human presence. For him, deep care is seen as feeling and as reciprocity of feeling. While it is true that human care practices may need more deep care in the context of mass care and bureaucratic organizations,

---

131. Lennart Fredriksson, "Models of Relating in a Caring Conversation: A Research Synthesis on Presence, Touch and Listening," *Journal of Advanced Nursing* 30, no. 5 (1999): 1171.

132. Stokes and Palmer, "Artificial Intelligence and Robotics in Nursing," 6.

133. Abraham Verghese, "The Importance of Being," *Health Affairs* 35, no. 10 (2016): 1927.

134. Verghese, "The Importance of Being," 1924.

human healers can improve their skills, while with AI technologies, this is not the case. AI care only be shallow since carebots cannot care about the patient.[135]

Listening

Philosopher Michael Brannigan proposes some elements about human presence that makes it different from everything else and conclusively agrees with the neighbor-love vision of ethical medical care. Human presence manifests itself through listening. The art of listening is not simply hearing but demands that all the senses be directed to the care receivers. The patient's life is a rich, complex story with plots, subplots, and intrigues uncovered and hidden. Often, a patient's initial symptoms, such as headaches, chest pain, etc., are a pointer to a real, layered, deeply situated problem that cannot be identified easily, no matter the amount of information data. As a result, Brannigan suggests, based on the wisdom of the past, that "it is more important to know what sort of person has a disease than to know what sort of disease a person has."[136]

Empathy

The second distinct element of human presence is empathy. The inter-human relationships require a ground of shared interest. Human-to-human interaction is mediated through empathy, which presupposes leaping into the other's world by deliberately stepping outside one's context. A carebot has no world of its own, such as human beings marked by memories, private histories, and experiences from natural aging. In other words, a robot lacks the capacity for the inter-presence that occurs only among real humans. Brannigan defines empathy as:

> . . . neither one-dimensional nor unilateral. Rather, it dynamically infuses the relation, proven to bring about positive health outcomes. And empathy is not outcome-driven. There is no algorithm for empathy, no formula to ease another's pain and stress. Empathy is its own end, the expression of which makes us

---

135. Mark Coeckelbergh, "Health Care, Capabilities, and AI Assistive Technologies," *Ethical Theory and Moral Practice* 13, no. 2 (2009): 182–83.

136. Brannigan, *Caregiving, Carebots, and Contagion*, 191.

human, a reminder of who we are. This interactive dynamic can only come about through embodied presence.[137]

Touch

The third element that makes medical care indispensably human is touch. Fredriksson defines caring touch as a form of relating and non-verbal interaction for communicating caring. The results of caring touch include comfort, security, enhancement of self-esteem, connection with the patient, and the acceptance of the sufferer as a unique person.[138] The effects of therapeutic touch, including comfort, strengthen the patient-healer relationship. The need for comfort provided through human touch is a fundamental care component. Studies show that recovery is faster in comfortable patients, that comfort eases coping with stress, and that comfort speeds rehabilitation. In addition, the caregiver's touch helps reduce negative emotion, which has substantial effects on patients, including anxiety, fear, and loss of control. The genuinely humane approach through nonverbal communication expresses a caregiver's interest in the patient as a person through friendliness and sincerity, which result in trustworthy relationships.[139]

Embodied presence is palpably manifested through physical contact between caregiver and patient. There is no substitute for simple human touch. The bond of human touch, in its dual-directionality, has no counterpart with social robots—it cannot be replicated.[140] Similarly, Van Wynsberghe conclusively describes the role of humans in touch in lifting:

> When a patient is lifted by the caregiver, it is a moment in which the patient is at one of their most vulnerable. The patient trusts the caregiver, and through this action, a bond is formed and/or strengthened, which reinforces the relationship between the caregiver and the care receiver. The significance of this is apparent in the actual practice of lifting but comes into play later on in the care process as well. This means that trust, bonds, and relationships are integral components for ensuring that the care receiver will comply with their treatment plan, take their medicine and be honest about their symptoms. Without trust, these

137. Brannigan, *Caregiving, Carebots, and Contagion*, 193.

138. Fredriksson, "Models of Relating in a Caring Conversation," 1172.

139. Fethiye Yelkin Alp and Sebnem Cinar Yucel, "The Effect of Therapeutic Touch on the Comfort and Anxiety of Nursing Home Residents," *Journal of Religion and Health* 60, no. 3 (2021): 2039.

140. Brannigan, *Caregiving, Carebots, and Contagion*, 198.

needs of the caregiver are threatened, ultimately threatening the entire care process and the good care of the care receiver.[141]

The Danger of Deception

One of the major concerns in using AiRs in direct patient care from the neighbor-love perspective is that the creation, development, and deployment of social robots often involve deception. Deception is connected to various phenomena, such as irrationality, wishful thinking, delusions, ignorance, avoidance, hypocrisy, and false beliefs. Deception can be considered a ubiquitous phenomenon because humans are inclined to hide the truth from themselves constantly.[142] The concept of deception raises questions of definition and practice. What is deception according to biblically informed neighbor-love? And "Is robotic deception acceptable in human-robot interaction?"[143] This section attempts to provide an answer to these questions.

Ontologically Different

The development of social robots often involves deception. The deceptive nature of carebots is problematic for several reasons. A genuine relationship is ontologically possible only between human beings, not in the mere appearance of one. Only human beings are made in God's image and possess the inherent qualities of image bearers; thus, people can serve neighbors unsurpassed. Social robots, as physically embodied entities that can socially interact with people, are deceptive even though developers and programmers may not have intended to deceive intentionally but to create a therapeutic machine. However, intentional or without conscious intention, deception can still occur, which is seen when a person believes that a social robot has emotions and cares for her.[144] Carebots are designed as machines that can act like they understand and care. As sophisticated machines, AiRs perform

---

141. Aimee van Wynsberghe, "Designing Robots for Care: Care Centered Value-Sensitive Design," *Science & Engineering Ethics* 19, no. 2 (2013): 417.
142. Joseph Pak, "Self-Deception in Theology," *Themelios* 43, no. 3 (2018): 405.
143. Joshua K. Smith, *Robotic Persons* (Bloomington: WestBow Press, 2021), 54.
144. Amanda Sharkey and Noel Sharkey, "We Need to Talk About Deception in Social Robotics!" *Ethics and Information Technology* 23, no. 3 (2021): 309–10.

as if they genuinely care.[145] In other words, carebots are programmed to act as caring, but they cannot from an ontological standpoint.

Complex human relationships cannot be exhaustively specified or captured by any algorithm or set of algorithms. Carebots can, at best, mimic forms of behavior that are appropriate for medical care. Sparrow and Sparrow convincingly advocate against using social robots as they are akin to deception. They argue based on the premise that carebots promise to provide supposed benefits to people who believe that robots are something they are not.[146] Humans are biological corporeal entities with particular limitations and frailties shared with other frail humans such as sufferers. Forms of care, including wiping away tears and reaching out to take the sufferer's hand, are appropriate human actions. Moreover, even if carebots may possess physical bodies that allow them to show the same level of expressiveness and individuality as human beings, they do not understand the facts of human nature. Thus, carebots, because they are not human beings, cannot fulfill the role of a deep sense of caring and a genuine emotional response.[147]

Amanda Sharkey is also skeptical of the likelihood that non-living, non-biological machines could develop a sense of morality. Sharkey's skepticism is rooted in the carebot's lack of biological substrate. She grounds morality in biology by making the case that care depends on living creatures caring for kith and kin and recognizing other's psychological states. Moreover, care lies in the neurochemistry of attachment and bonding of mammals. Humans, and only humans, extend their avoidance of pain to their immediate neighbors. People also feel anxious and awful when others' wellbeing is threatened and feel pleasure when their infants are safe. All these human emotions are the basis of complex relationships, grounded in their constitutive nature. Sharkey correctly contends that even an argument from a biological perspective for morality implies that existing robots lack the biological basis for developing morality. She raises commendable questions:

> Current robots, lacking living bodies, cannot feel pain, or even care about themselves, let alone extend that concern to others. How can they empathize with a human's pain or distress if they are unable to experience either emotion? Similarly, without the ability to experience guilt or regret, how could they reflect on the effects of their actions, modify their behavior, and build their own moral framework?[148]

145. Brannigan, *Caregiving, Carebots, and Contagion*, 120.
146. Sparrow and Sparrow, "In the Hands of Machines," 148.
147. Sparrow and Sparrow, "In the Hands of Machines," 154.
148. Sharkey, "Can We Program or Train Robots to Be Good," 290.

Contrary to Sharkey's argument from biology, futurist and inventor Ray Kurzweil claims that there will be a time when machines will possess something inherently human, such as consciousness, a sort of conscious capability that will allow machines to assert "I think. Therefore, I am."[149] Sparrow and Sparrow dismiss Kurzweil's opinion by arguing that robots are incapable of real friendship, love, or concern, perhaps only of their simulations.[150] Also, Robert Sparrow challenges Kurzweil's claim by doubting that machines could ever possess sufficient moral personality.[151]

Perhaps Sparrow and Sparrow and Sharkey's views, though commendable, may be supplemented by a decisive perspective based on the biblical standpoint of human beings. The Bible is clear that only human beings are created in God's image and thus endowed with caring capacities. Only people genuinely understand what it means to live in a fallen world and to recognize a metaphysical reality that includes immortality and a resurrected body through faith in Jesus Christ. Any other entity can only claim such qualities but not genuinely possess them.

Deceptive Promises

A second concern is raised, not only by the deceptive nature of carebots but also by the promises involved in intelligent programs. One deceptive aspect of AiRs is the failure to apprehend the world accurately. Sparrow and Sparrow rightly point out that people can see the world as it is. To be deceived by the world and to perpetuate and prolong deception is a moral failure. But machines have no sense of moral failure. The hype of technological advancements that propose expensive and sophisticated electronic devices as real friends breeds sentimentality that should be avoided.[152]

Brannigan perceptively explains that AI technology in medicine, although impressively helpful in certain situations, lures human caregivers into a false sense of security and an unquestioning belief in automation. The allure of intelligent programs includes the quick, efficient, and safe fix in caregiving, the expectation that they will tackle uncertain caregiving tasks, and that AI caregivers can control precarious situations.

But the lure of immediacy must include the insistence on the importance of context. Caring depends on the circumstances of who is cared for,

---

149. Ray Kurzweil, *The Age of Spiritual Machines: When Computers Exceed Human Intelligence* (New York: Penguin, 1999), 52.
150. Sparrow and Sparrow, "In the Hands of Machines," 154.
151. Sparrow, "Why Machines Cannot Be Moral," 691.
152. Sparrow and Sparrow, "In the Hands of Machines," 155.

whether children or elders. Data, a fundamental component of modern medicine, may reveal content but without contextual information about the patient's culture, beliefs, past, interests, etc. Caring robots can help based on data but cannot be seen as a definite solution to the problems of care. The reason, argues Brannigan, is that "connectivity is not connectedness. Connectedness in the fullest sense demands physical, embodied interaction and presence."[153]

Intentional Deception

The third concern regarding the carebot's deceitfulness is that deception is arguably immoral. The argument for immorality can be reasoned based on the fact that "our preferences are unlikely to be met, our interests advanced, or our well-being served, by illusions," as Sparrow and Sparrow argue. Sufferers need to be authentically loved and cared for not merely to believe their healers love them. In the moment of greatest need, care receivers need to be cared for by genuine human beings, not by an illusionary set of actions.[154] Designers try to make carebots more appealing to human users, such as the phenomenon of the anthropomorphization of digital technology. The deceitfulness of technological tools is amplified by providing intelligent assistants with a voice and a face. The effect of anthropomorphization is that people react empathically when seeing a robot.[155] Despite the designer's efforts, the deception is immoral because it perpetuates a lie and not the truth.

Addressing the entire concept of truth and lying from a biblical perspective is beyond the scope of this dissertation. Nevertheless, some principles can be conveyed. From the neighbor-love viewpoint, deception is intimately connected to willful sin. The nature of sin is deceptive in that its goal is to obstruct knowledge by originating in people's self-deception (1 John 1:8). The self-deceptiveness of human nature stems from the fallen heart, which leads to a corruption of the human mind and its creative capacities, and to a dysfunctional conscience.[156] The Bible reveals that the ethics of communicating truly begins by identifying truth with God, and violating truth means rejecting him. A God-centered truth means that God

---

153. Brannigan, *Caregiving, Carebots, and Contagion*, 107–13.

154. Sparrow and Sparrow, "In the Hands of Machines," 155.

155. Mark Coeckelbergh, "Should We Treat Teddy Bear 2.0 as a Kantian Dog? Four Arguments for the Indirect Moral Standing of Personal Social Robots, with Implications for Thinking About Animals and Humans," *Minds & Machines* 31, no. 3 (2021): 338.

156. Pak, "Self-Deception in Theology," 408–9.

is the source and measure of truth and that everything true is of God and nothing else is true. The God of the Bible is the truth itself (Ps 31:5; Isa 65:16), meaning that God is the standard to which all truth aligns and is that according to which all things are held to account. God requires his image-bearers to be true (Ps 51:6) because he wants people to be like him. The Trinitarian relationship is marked by truth, and so must be interhuman relationships. People should not give false testimony against their neighbors (Exod 20:16) because God hates a lying tongue (Prov 6:17).[157]

Ethicist Douglas Groothuis contributes some theological categories related to the truth as a core aspect of Christian ethical distinctiveness. First, truth is revealed by God in the written word and the incarnate Word. The Bible is a revelation from a transcendent, communicative being who reveals himself through objective truth. Second, truth exists and is knowable. Truth is the cognitive content of revelation, having God and his creation as sources. Desires, emotions, feelings, and personal beliefs do not define or limit God's truth. Third, biblical truth is absolute, meaning God's truth is invariant. Truth is not relative, shifting, or revisable. God's immutable truth is a person, Jesus Christ (John 14:6). Fourth, the biblical view of truth contends that truth is universal in scope and application, implying that truth is not circumscribed or restricted by cultural conditions.[158] Fifth, truth is exclusive, specific, and antithetical. The logic of biblical truth is that truth is exact, and the departure from truth is the substitution of falsity for truth. Truthfulness, in the most unambiguous terms, is the goal of the principle of integrity. Truth implies a well-integrated perspective on life that reflects God's harmonious, objective reality. Thus, truth is not valid in religion but false in science, or proper in philosophy but false in theology. Finally, truth is always an end, not a means to any other end. Truth should be desired and obtained for its intrinsic value and not treated as a mere means to a worldly end, however admirable it may be.[159]

The Bible is clear: God is truth, so God's image bearers should be most faithful to Christ and pleasing to God. While it is true that some deceptions can be harmless fun, such as in situations in which people are entertained and aware that the illusion of sentience created by carebots is not accurate,[160] creating artificial artifacts with intentional deceiving purposes,

---

157. Heimbach, *Fundamental Christian Ethics*, 298–99.

158. Douglas R. Groothuis, "The Biblical View of Truth Challenges Postmodernist Truth Decay," *Themelios* 26, no. 1 (2000): 20–27.

159. Groothuis, "Biblical View of Truth," 28–33.

160. Sharkey and Sharkey, "We Need to Talk About Deception in Social Robotics," 311.

such as mimicking genuine emotions and care related to vulnerable persons, appears to be inherently wrong from the neighbor-love viewpoint.

Neighbor Care Operates within the Right Personal Relationships

The second criterion of the neighbor-love ethical model proposes that medical care must encourage and operate within the right personal relationships. Someone might argue that a cure can happen apart from right personal relationships. Yet something crucial is missing: a caring context encourages the opportunity of cure. Right relationships are an essential expression of care. The use of intelligent robotic care, such as carebots, raises ethical concerns because humans tend to anthropomorphize robots even though they know there is no genuineness behind automation.[161] Though the research is too undeveloped to provide conclusive pieces of evidence for the long-term effects of robotic care on either pediatric or elderly care, carebots' impact on human-to-human interaction necessitates a careful examination.[162] This section investigates the possible ethical and social risks stemming from deception in social robots, such as over-attachment and detachment in relationships.[163]

Closely related to the concept of anthropomorphizing deception, a possible consequence of human-robot interaction is the emotional deception that encourages humans, particularly the vulnerable ones, to believe that a robot cares for them and is something with which they can develop relationships,[164] and to typically react by over-attaching to robots—and to detach from human caregivers. The potential for harm caused by carebots to patients appears to include emotional, psychological, and social assaults. Over-attachment may trigger emotional harm to care receivers, consequently triggering an increase in detachment from human caregivers, family, and friends.[165]

Over-attachment to carebots may seem counterintuitive but can be explained by the phenomenon that "humans are robust anthropomorphisers."[166]

161. Linda Onnasch and Eileen Roesler, "Anthropomorphizing Robots: The Effect of Framing in Human-Robot Collaboration," *Proceedings of the Human Factors and Ergonomics Society*, 63, no. 1 (2019): 1311.

162. Smith, *Robotic Persons*, 54.

163. Sharkey and Sharkey, "We Need to Talk About Deception in Social Robotics," 313.

164. Sharkey and Sharkey, "We Need to Talk About Deception in Social Robotics," 311.

165. Brannigan, *Caregiving, Carebots, and Contagion*, 130–31.

166. Aurelia Sauerbrei et al., "The Impact of Artificial Intelligence on the

The tendency of people to anthropomorphize is problematic due to the substitution effect, where people project intentions, social skills, emotions, and even moral agency onto objects such as AI robots, which may become regarded as special-purpose human beings. The risks of anthropomorphizing create cognitive bias and tend to distort a correct understanding of reality, a growing phenomenon primarily related to new, emergent behaviors or situations. Humans' tendency toward anthropomorphization is encouraged, even indirectly, by carebots' cognitive abilities based on the performance of some specific and limited skills, including language or logic. Given the social minds and psychology of people's nature to humanize even inanimate objects, carebots can falsely portray that AI machines' current or future deployment is capable of artificial morality.[167] Child and elderly care appears to be the most prone to ethical apprehensions concerning relationships regarding attachment and detachment.

The Role of Human Contact in Pediatric Care

The recent advancements in intelligent robotics and machine learning allow for exploring intriguing potential uses of social robots, such as in childcare facilities. Though studies on child-robot interaction are scarce, some examples of the AiRs' beneficial presence around children exist. For instance, social robots can spark effective learning by employing the social capabilities of robots to develop robot-generated learning content in classrooms. Robots can also reduce stress and provide emotional relief for children by providing entertainment.[168] Thus, social robots may play various roles in children's development. But is this ethically desirable?

Robotic assistants can combine visual, movement, and auditory features to present a credible illusion, especially in childcare. Young children can invest emotionally and believe in the reality of a relationship with robots. For instance, studies show children between 10 and 24 months bonded with a humanoid robot in a childcare facility in a more significant way than bonding with teddy bears. In addition, toddlers tended to treat the robot as one of their peers, evidenced by how the children hugged, touched, and

---

Person-Centered, Doctor-Patient Relationship: Some Problems and Solutions," *BMC Medical Informatics and Decision Making* 23, no. 1 (2023): 11.

167. Constantinescu and Crisp, "Can Robotic AI Systems Be Virtuous," 1554.

168. Jieon Lee, Daeho Lee, and Jae-Gil Lee, "Can Robots Help Working Parents with Childcare? Optimizing Childcare Functions for Different Parenting Characteristics," *International Journal of Social Robotics* 14 (2022): 193.

played with it compared to a static toy robot or a teddy bear.[169] Moreover, another study showed children are willing to become attached to and anthropomorphize robots and even create a range of novel stories of explanations when the robots fail to respond appropriately. Research evidence points to the fact that children believe in the illusion of robot animacy and that social robots appear to amplify natural anthropomorphism.[170]

Besides the emotional deception of young children and babies, research shows that if children are left in the care of robots for prolonged periods, social robots can interfere with the formation of secure attachments between children and their primary human caregivers. The interference could result in potential attachment disorders caused by the lack of opportunities for babies to learn about the natural give and take of human relationships with peers.[171]

Attachment disorders refer to the potential isolation of children as they develop psychologically. Sharkey and Sharkey define infant attachment, inspired by the Swartout-Corbeil perspective:

> Infant attachment is the deep emotional connection an infant forms with his or her primary caregiver, often the mother. It is a tie that binds them together, endures over time, and leads the infant to experience pleasure, joy, safety, and comfort in the caregiver's company. The baby feels distress when that person is absent. Soothing, comforting, and providing pleasure are primary elements of the relationship. Attachment theory holds that a consistent primary caregiver is necessary for a child's optimal development.[172]

Developmental psychology informs the discussion related to childcare robotics. Sharkey and Sharkey argue that a child left with a robot believing that she has formed a relationship with it will theoretically suffer a form of insecure attachment or even suffer from a pathological attachment disorder. Insecure attachments, often called anxious-avoidant attachments, are caused by mothers who are less able to read the infant's behavior, which leads them to lack the ability to socialize with the baby when he is hungry

---

169. Noel Sharkey and Amanda Sharkey, "The Crying Shame of Robot Nannies: An Ethical Appraisal," *Interaction Studies* 11 (2010): 168.

170. Sharkey and Sharkey, "Crying Shame of Robot Nannies," 169.

171. Sharkey and Sharkey, "We Need to Talk About Deception in Social Robotics," 311–12.

172. Sharkey and Sharkey, "Crying Shame of Robot Nannies," 174.

and play with him when he is tired. Babies with withdrawn mothers tend to suffer from some aberrant forms of attachment, such as avoidance.[173]

Disorders are accentuated especially in children with medical conditions such as autism spectrum disorders (ASD). Elder explains that ASD children struggle with eye contact, joint attention, emotion recognition, and interpreting others' behavior. At first glance, social robots appear to be therapeutically beneficial. For instance, AI robotic caregivers can help ASD children with some social skills by teaching collaborative play, body awareness skills, joint attention, question-asking, and tactile interactions.[174] Despite robots' beneficial aid, Elder echoes Sharkey and Sharkey about the role of human maternal presence in robot-child interactions. Elder argues that children, especially those with ASD, may detach from human caregivers for reasons related to familiarity, predictability, fewer confusing signals, etc. Further, the benefits of carebots can be challenged on ontological grounds, contends Elder. Children with or without ASD are, first and foremost, human beings, and it seems advisable to assume that children's needs and values substantially overlap with those of the rest of the human species. That is not to say children should be forced to have only human friends.[175] Nevertheless, to encourage the human capacity for social relationships, genuine human interaction is best.[176]

Given the risks of over-attachment and detachment of children, it is safe to argue that childcare robotics are deceiving relationships and cannot provide the care proposed by a neighbor-love approach. Children appear to do best when they have a secure attachment to a human caregiver, especially

---

173. Sharkey and Sharkey, "Crying Shame of Robot Nannies," 176.

174. Alexis M. Elder, "Robot Friends for Autistic Children: Monopoly Money or Counterfeit Currency?" in *Robot Ethics 2.0: From Autonomous Cars to Artificial Intelligence*, ed. Patrick Lin, Ryan Jenkins, and Keith Abney (New York: Oxford University Press, 2017), 113–15.

175. For instance, animal-assisted therapy for autistic children, such as with dogs, may act as a social lubricant, acting as a bridge to support the development of relationships with people. See Jessica Hill et al., "Investigating Dog Welfare When Interacting with Autistic Children within Canine-Assisted Occupational Therapy Sessions: A Single Case Study," *Animals* 13, no. 12 (2023): 3. Regarding the benefits of animal-assisted therapy compared to social robot assistance in the case of ASD children, the research is yet to be determined. However, in the case of long-term care facilities for elder care, there appears to be no difference between the effectiveness of a living and a robotic dog in reducing loneliness. See Marian R. Banks, Lisa M. Willoughby, and William A. Banks, "Animal-Assisted Therapy and Loneliness in Nursing Homes: Use of Robotic Versus Living Dogs," *Journal of the American Medical Directors Association* 9, no. 3 (March 2008): 172–173.

176. Elder, "Robot Friends for Autistic Children," 122–23.

an attentive and focused caregiver.[177] In contrast, a carebot can lure the child into a false relationship that may damage the child emotionally and psychologically. The human caregiver can be the only acceptable solution in the care of a child, whether the mother or other primary caregiver.[178] Nonetheless, from a neighbor-love perspective, the role of social robots may not be excluded entirely. Robot benefits, such as entertaining and stimulating learning, are merits to be celebrated. However, their ethical use may be allowed only in a limited range of services as assistants to human caregivers due to their capacity to erode relationships.

The Role of Human Socialization in Geriatric Care

The aging of human populations affects many fields, and as societies age, their demand for assistance in daily activities increases. The shortage of caregivers for older adults and the so-called care gap[179] are projected to grow over time; thus, innovative and efficient solutions for the care of older persons are needed. Social robots may present some advantages. For example, using autonomous social robots may be promising because they provide support by improving well-being and preventing functional decline.[180] Carebots may be seen as a solution to decrease costs and increase efficiency for care and a response to the shortage of skilled care staff.[181] Despite the apparent benefits, is the adoption of carebots for older adults a suitable effort?

A primary ethical and social concern in the carebot-elderly relationship is the potential isolation and replacement of human contact. The technological developments incorporated in AiRs, such as innovative sensing systems and the capacity to lift, carry, bathe, and feed, may result in fewer

---

177. Noel Sharkey and Amanda Sharkey, "The Rights and Wrongs of Robot Care," in *Robot Ethics: The Ethical and Social Implications of Robotics*, ed. Patrick Lin, Keith Abney, and George A. Bekey (Cambridge: The MIT Press, 2012), 275.

178. Sharkey and Sharkey, "Crying Shame of Robot Nannies," 185.

179. The care gap is a serious concern for many countries worldwide, especially Europe. According to a recent study, it is projected that by 2050, there will be fifty-three people aged 65 and over for every hundred of working age. For the sake of comparison, in 1980, there were only twenty people aged 65 and over for every hundred of working age. See Vincenzo Atella et al., "The Future of the Elderly Population Health Status: Filling a Knowledge Gap," *Health Economics* 30, S1 (2021): 11.

180. Slawomir Tobis et al., "Robots in Eldercare: How Does a Real-World Interaction with the Machine Influence the Perceptions of Older People?" *Sensors* 22, no. 5 (2022): 1717, https://www.doi.org/10.3390/s22051717.

181. Susanne Frennert, Hedvig Aminoff, and Britt Östlund, "Technological Frames and Care Robots in Eldercare," *International Journal of Social Robotics* 13, no. 2 (2021): 321.

care visits. Studies show that human companionship is essential for the well-being of older adults, such as the role of an extensive human network that offers protection against aging. One result of aging is the risk of dementia, a risk that can be prevented by social interaction and intellectual stimulation.[182]

Attachment to robots is likely, especially for vulnerable adults with cognitive limitations. There is evidence that even healthy adults form attachments to robots that are remote-controlled bomb disposal assistants or robot vacuum cleaners. Furry robot pets or cute-looking humanoids incorporate all the conditions for people with dementia to form attachments. In addition, with their technological framework, robot companions are inclined to create deceptive illusions that they can understand and feel, which may inevitably result in older adults neglecting relationships with fellow humans. Not only that, but the illusion of care may also be exacerbated by the fact that friends, family, and caregivers may believe that a social robot is meeting the social and attachment needs of an older person and, as a consequence, might decide to reduce the time they spent with older people.[183]

A study in Japan's long experiment in automating elder care may represent a helpful test case for the social exclusion problem of older adults. The researcher, James Wright, explains that a possible reason for Japan's robot experiment is an animist worldview that encourages people to view robots as having some spirit of their own. In addition, Japanese society, confronted with the prospect of a growing elderly population, has not found a solution to relieve the burdening lack of human care workers.[184] Japan's older population is increasing (28.4 percent as of 2019), leading to an estimated shortage of 370,000 nurses and care professionals to accommodate the older demographic by 2025.[185] Hiroo Ide et al. show that one-third of homecare professionals expressed opinions against using social robots. The majority voiced disapproval in explicit terms, such as "I reject inhumane care." Others emphasized concerns about potential safety risks and moral and ethical aspects of introducing AiRs. A somewhat surprising finding is that the possible loss of employment for the Japanese care professional was not concerning. However, a significant disincentive against health practitioners'

182. Sharkey and Sharkey, "Rights and Wrongs of Robot Care," 276.
183. Sharkey and Sharkey, "We Need to Talk About Deception in Social Robotics," 312.
184. James Wright, "Inside Japan's Long Experiment in Automating Elder Care," *MIT Technology Review*, January 9, 2023, sec. Humans and Technology, https://www.technologyreview.com/2023/01/09/1065135/japan-automating-eldercare-robots/.
185. Hiroo Ide et al., "The Ageing 'Care Crisis' in Japan: Is There a Role for Robotics-Based Solutions?" *International Journal of Care and Caring* 5, no. 1 (2021): 166.

adoption of assistive robots was reduced human contact and interaction. The study also revealed that the value of warm and intimate interaction between caregivers and care receivers is significant for care professionals. On the other hand, care professionals also emphasized that physical support, communication, and monitoring should be prioritized to develop and implement future assistive technologies.[186] Wright contends that there is some evidence that if robots are purchased, they often end up being used only for a limited time and then stored indefinitely.[187]

Additionally, another recent study suggests that robotic devices proved impractical in the daily work routine and were subsequently eliminated from usage. The care staff was very reluctant to accept the help of robotic helpers because robots need additional adjusting.[188] Wright observes that the type of work that AiRs created for caregivers was somewhat unexpected. For example, instead of conversing and interacting with residents, caregivers could give the care receivers Paro to play with and monitor them. Moreover, the workers pointed out that before having the robot to help with physical activities, they used the occasion to chat with the residents and build relationships. In this case, the existing social and communication tasks appeared to be displaced. As Wright puts it, "Instead of saving time for staff to do more of the human labor of social and emotional care, the robots actually reduced the scope for such work."[189]

Given the risks involved in intelligent robotic care in senior care, it seems that leaving an older adult in the exclusive care of robots would seriously threaten older people's participation in society and, thus, imply wrong human relationships. Sharkey and Sharkey even argue that exclusive robotic care is cruel. Yet there may be opportunities for carebots to be useful when they work as assistants to human beings and when they act as facilitators and conversational aids to improve the social life of older people.[190] Sparrow and Sparrow, however, are even more cautious regarding the carebots' assistive role. They argue that robots used in menial tasks associated with aged care, such as cleaning and maintaining homes and health facilities, may not be desirable. They contend that "replacing human beings who are working in cleaning roles with robots is not unequivocally beneficial in the context

---

186. Ide et al., "Ageing 'Care Crisis' in Japan," 169.

187. Wright, "Inside Japan's Long Experiment in Automating Elder Care."

188. Gabriele Vogt and Anne-Sophie König, "Robotic Devices and ICT in Long-Term Care in Japan: Their Potential and Limitations from a Workplace Perspective," *Contemporary Japan* 35, no. 2 (2023): 284–285.

189. Wright, "Inside Japan's Long Experiment in Automating Elder Care."

190. Sharkey and Sharkey, "Rights and Wrongs of Robot Care," 279.

of aged care, as social interaction with cleaning staff may be something that individuals who are socially isolated look forward to."[191]

In conclusion, the most troubling aspect of using social robots in direct elder care is the prospect of isolation. The right relationship in senior care requires genuine reciprocity. People, as God's imagers, are naturally oriented to community and a communal sense of existence. Vallor also argues that the essential sociality of human beings is non-controversial because, under normal conditions, the human person is fundamentally oriented to others and predisposed to social give and take. Reciprocity is a form of flourishing human relationships and is arguably among the fundamental features of creaturely well-being, allowing human lives to flourish.[192] From a neighbor-love standpoint, reciprocity is indeed significant. The lack of genuine reciprocity relies on the natural structure of human beings made in the image of God and the artificiality of machines that are mere imitators of virtues intrinsic to human nature. As Vallor puts it, "To surrender caregiving practices then, even if we stipulate that we will surrender them only to robots who can give what the other truly needs—potentially deprives us of an important opportunity to cultivate reciprocity in ourselves and to understand its centrality to human bonds."[193] Relationships with social robots are deceptive and unidirectional at their core. As Van Wynsberghe states, "A world without reciprocity, without mutual care, is a world entirely unsustainable."[194] Therefore, the use of social robots in eldercare facilities, replacing the role of human care providers, may represent a form of disruption and even violation of human relationships.

A Suggested Ethical Use of Carebots

The research in this chapter would strongly suggest that the use of social robots in direct patient care is potentially harmful. Vallor helpfully summarizes the concerns raised by carebots in personal and institutional care provision. She mentions the possibility that older people are objectified as problems to be solved by technological means. Additionally, carebots can potentially restrict the capabilities, freedom, autonomy, and dignity of sufferers, and they can reduce the engagement of care receivers with their surroundings. Moreover, social robots can intrude upon patients' privacy and

191. Sparrow and Sparrow, "In the Hands of Machines?" 146.
192. Vallor, "Carebots and Caregivers," 257–58.
193. Vallor, "Carebots and Caregivers," 258.
194. Aimee Van Wynsberghe, "Social Robots and the Risks to Reciprocity," *AI & Society* 37, no. 2 (2022): 484–85.

reduce patients' contact with families and other caregivers.[195] The damaging impacts of deception, over-attachment, detachment, and overestimation of a social robot's functionality highlights the irreplaceable role of humans in the caring endeavor. Replacing human care and misplacing trust in the carebots' ability to make decisions for which they are not qualified[196] may violate the biblically based ethical model of neighbor-love. In any case, from a neighbor-love perspective, the deployment of carebots in social roles has to be made with due precaution or not at all,[197] given that the ideal role of AI in healthcare is currently unclear.[198] Etzioni and Etzioni are undoubtedly correct when arguing that "much work is needed to spell out the more effective divisions of labor and forms of cooperation between AI caregivers and humans."[199]

Are there areas where carebots can be used ethically, however? One apparent role where AiRs may be used ethically is assisting or partnering with humans, though the literature about the impact of AI technology on doctor-patient relationships and patient-centered care remains somewhat to be determined. For instance, some studies found that patients demonstrated an intention to follow the advice of a human doctor rather than an AI machine. Likewise, other studies found that patients showed apathy towards AI tools, whereas care receivers showed a positive, pro-social response to human healers. The overall patient response reflects a strong preference for AI machines to be assistive rather than replace humans; only a minority showed a favorable attitude toward AiRs.[200]

To consider the possibility that the neighbor-love system may allow carebots in indirect care, it seems necessary to briefly describe the ethical divisions of tasks and ontologies of caring. Stokes and Palmer's work is illuminating in this sense. They argue that the first distinction must be made between direct and indirect care. Direct medical care includes tasks where the healer directly interacts with the sufferers. Some examples of when direct care is applied concern medication administration, counseling,

195. Vallor, "Carebots and Caregivers," 254.
196. Sharkey and Sharkey, "We Need to Talk About Deception in Social Robotics," 315.
197. Constantinescu and Crisp, "Can Robotic AI Systems Be Virtuous," 1554.
198. Aurelia Sauerbrei et al., "The Impact of Artificial Intelligence on the Person-Centered, Doctor-Patient Relationship: Some Problems and Solutions," *BMC Medical Informatics and Decision Making* 23, no. 1 (2023): 10.
199. Amitai Etzioni and Oren Etzioni, "The Ethics of Robotic Caregivers," *Interaction Studies* 18, no. 2 (2017): 187.
200. Sauerbrei et al., "The Impact of Artificial Intelligence on the Person-Centered, Doctor-Patient Relationship: Some Problems and Solutions," 10.

or intravenous catheter. Indirect care refers to the benefits of a patient or a group of patients that result from activities performed away from them, such as documentation, patient evaluation information, etc. A second distinction must be made between fundamental and non-fundamental care. Primary care includes prevention, medication, hydration, feeding, temperature, rest, sleep, etc. Non-fundamental care includes everything subservient to fundamental care, including areas of concern and tasks that ensure a sufferer's physical and psychosocial needs are met. Indirect care includes retrieving items in a supply closet, preparing medicine,[201] and performing routine tasks, such as carrying meal trays.

A proper manifestation of love for neighbors maintains that human caregivers must be involved in all activities that include fundamental and direct care. The intersection of fundamental care with direct care occurs when human-embodied care is manifested through listening, touch, and empathy. AI as assistants should preserve and support the caregiver-carereceiver relationships and not take over the caring opportunities entirely. Even though some caring responsibilities, such as feeding and cleansing, can be done more efficiently and safely by carebots, these responsibilities should include the human caregiver. Neighbor-love suggests that social robots can take over the mechanical task of feeding or bathing, but the human caregiver should be present for conversation or company. The human caregiver should be present in the patient's room for direct and fundamental care activities as a default policy of health institutions.[202] Robots used with human caregivers to care for the vulnerable, a sort of supervised autonomy, diminishes the risk of over-attachment to machines.[203] Social robots should only be used indirectly in care to protect and encourage doctor-patient relationships and to avoid a potential dystopic view of the future of medical care that replaces or excludes human contact and presence.

The concept of neighbor-love excludes the possibility of the carebot's direct patient care yet does inspire some practical guidelines or conditions that a biblical and covenantal view of care would allow regarding non-fundamental, indirect care. Stokes and Palmer's arguments, though based on the ethics of care system, are particularly indicative. The first proposed condition is that even in indirect care, carebots should always uphold the core values of caring. Second, social robots should not usurp distinctively human aspects of care. Finally, AiRs should continually expand or improve

---

201. Stokes and Palmer, "Artificial Intelligence and Robotics in Nursing," 6–7.
202. Stokes and Palmer, "Artificial Intelligence and Robotics in Nursing," 7.
203. Gary Chan Yew Kok, "Trust in and Ethical Design of Carebots: The Case for Ethics of Care," *International Journal of Social Robotics* 13 (2021): 633.

opportunities for caregivers to manifest the uniquely human aspects of care.[204]

By implementing these conditions, AiRs can become valuable instruments for human caregivers and, thus, help them fulfill the covenant of care. As assistants, carebots can aid care receivers in sustaining a patient's dignity. A patient may choose to be bathed by a robot instead of feeling ashamed in front of another human. Also, carebots may be beneficial in robotic therapies for children with autism and patients with dementia. The robot's simple presence may reduce anxiety and provide a sense of comfort for the cared-for. In doing this, carebots may help patients to feel better. Moreover, carebots can be valuable in confined sites during periods of contagion, such as ships, prisons, homeless sites, meatpacking plants, nursing homes, and tight workspaces. Carebots can monitor and alert authorities if necessary.[205] Caregivers can uphold covenantal medical ethics by being faithful in caring for the sick as made in God's image despite the great dangers of contagion. Finally, social robots may also aid the well-being of caregivers by performing tedious tasks and allowing healers to focus more on the profound aspects of care.

In conclusion, the neighbor-love position is resolute about situations in which robots should not be used. However, this is not to say that biblical neighbor-love ethics is overly pessimistic about robot use. AiRs can be valuable to the covenant of care as tools to achieve human ends. However, as Sharkey recommends, "The challenge is to find the right path to steer between capitalizing on and benefitting from the unique opportunities that robots can offer and avoiding a future in which robots are placed in positions and roles that require a moral understanding that they do not have."[206]

Conclusion

This chapter advocates that the neighbor-love ethical framework is a persuasive moral paradigm to address the moral problems raised by carebots in direct patient care. Neighbor-love is covenantal in nature and is a blend of both virtues and principles. What makes covenantal neighbor-love beneficial in ethical judgments is its grounding in the character of God as revealed in the inspired word of God. The virtues and principles made evident in God's character are further clarified in Christ's person and work on the cross. God commands that people should love their neighbors because

204. Stokes and Palmer, "Artificial Intelligence and Robotics in Nursing," 8.
205. Brannigan, *Caregiving, Carebots, and Contagion*, 66–79.
206. Sharkey, "Can We Program or Train Robots to Be Good," 293.

he is a loving God, and all ethics and moral principles are derived from a transcendent source.[207]

Neighbor-love, as part of Christian ethics, starts with revelation, is markedly theocentric, and bears divine authority. Heimbach also mentions that a distinctive feature of Christian ethics is its desire to be comprehensive and never try to reduce ethics to a single ideal, rule, goal, or virtue. Human philosophers, such as those who coined utilitarianism, care ethics, virtue, and deontological ethics, start with human experience and rationality; they never derive meaning, validity, and authority from anything beyond human limits. In contrast, Christian ethics, as clearly shown in neighbor-love, starts with revelation, moves to theological and historical ethics, and only then discusses philosophical, secular ethics concerning any subject.[208]

Besides the theological, historical, and philosophical nature, neighbor-love can be a tool to be practically applied and put into action, as is the case of social robots. Neighbor-love suggests that moral judgments must consider the concept of human embodiment and right relationships to administer care for the sufferers properly. As shown, carebots have the potential to be beneficial. However, because of the tremendous risks involved, especially in direct patient care, AiRs' use must be prudential, even in an assistive role. In this assistive case, the practice of carebots should never erode, disrupt, or violate the human care provider-sufferer relationship.

---

207. Rae, *Moral Choices*, 68.
208. Heimbach, *Fundamental Christian Ethics*, 235–241.

CHAPTER FIVE

Looking to the Future

Introduction

THE PRESENT WORK, *Cura Animarum: A Theological-Ethical Assessment of the Use of Carebots in the Healthcare System*, contends that, from a neighbor-love ethical standpoint, AiRs may be beneficial technologies in some aspects of healthcare but may erode, corrupt, or even violate other aspects of healthcare, especially in direct patient care. The work began with the question "Is it ethical to use carebots in direct human care in healthcare settings?" Though valuable in some caring assistive roles, the dissertation contended that carebots are not appropriate in direct patient care and have the potential to do much damage to the care of sufferers and vulnerable persons as made in God's image. In review, social robots in healthcare settings may challenge the long tradition of medical care and change how human care providers relate to care receivers. This concluding chapter synthesizes all the theological and philosophical conclusions of the dissertation by providing the study's summary and mentioning some limitations, followed by suggestions for future work.

Summary

Chapter one introduced the dissertation's research problem, the holistic human care methodology, and the dissertation's objectives. The primer on carebot technology section mentioned some definitions of the crucial terms used throughout the work, such as artificial intelligence, robots, artificially intelligent robots, healthcare, and carebots. The selective historical development of carebots describes the evolution of AI robots from their invention to the apparent ubiquitous application in contemporary society.

In addition, an overview of the concept of neighbor-love endeavors to lay the groundwork developed in an ethical and theological framework later. The theological structure of care rests on a view of God, human beings, and salvation. As a Christian moral system, the love of neighbors is marked by God's self-revelation in the Scriptures. The transcendent root of love begins with the loving relationship between the Trinity's persons. God's love for those in Christ resembles a father's love for his children, manifested in Jesus' atoning sacrifice on the cross. Also, God's love is generous and inherently empowering by walking with his children in a fallen world.

Among other qualities, human beings are caring creatures, as understood from a theological anthropology standpoint. God is caring, and people should care for other image-bearers as created in God's image. The command to love the neighbor is emphasized by Christ's character, who showed compassion and anchored his love for people in the Old Testament covenantal framework and its law. The command includes the idea of community. Love is a social endeavor where the sufferer can be cared for and never be isolated. In other words, suffering is an opportunity for the redeemed community to show Christ's care and to love the care receiver as themselves.

A view of salvation is necessary for a theological framework of care, without which it is impossible to understand medical care or its objectives. A significant argument is that, even though cure is the desired objective for the sufferers, care is far more critical because it points the patients to God's salvation for humanity as provided in Christ. In this sense, the cure is not only concerned with the body's healing, but any healing prefigures the complete healing that will come on the day of resurrection.

The paradigm for the physician-patient care relationship is based on the approach to medical care described in *The Way* by Curlin and Tollefsen, enriched by a covenantal care theology in chapter four. The seemingly omnipresent approach to medicine, such as the provider-of-services model, has significant limitations. *The Way* challenges the PSM system, mainly based on mechanical and economic exchange relationships. In contrast, Curlin and Tollefsen suggest that medicine and a good physician should orient themselves toward the good of health and refuse intentional harm.

Chapter two provides an overview of the literature on carebots and reveals a massive gap in the evangelical, conservative research literature that leaves unanswered questions from theological perspectives related to healthcare and social robots. The investigation also exposes the secular and evolutionary approach to medical ethics, which stresses the need for AI policies but also avoids challenging the whole spectrum of technological ethics. Additionally, the survey contends that there is a Christian engagement with medicine in general. Still, it reveals that Christian evangelicals inevitably need to join the conversation about current robotics, AI, and healthcare trends with more intentionally.

Chapter three provides the epistemic framework for a theology of care that finds its climax in the neighbor-love concept. This section presents the rich meaning incorporated into the understanding of a patient by theological anthropology. The main argument is that carebot technologies must only be used in ways consistent with the biblical vision of medicine and how the church showed care. The ethical ways consistent with the Bible are caring for people as God's image bearers by displaying the virtues of love, solidarity, and trust and, ultimately, pointing them to complete health, which is possible only in Jesus. From a theological standpoint, the necessary categories of an anthropological understanding address patients as sufferers, health, flourishing in a fallen world, and flourishing in life after death.

The chapter suggests that the suitable relationship between care providers and care receivers is best seen under the covenantal ethical construct. The idea of the covenant is closest to the biblical view of care. Covenantal care incorporates (1) the root, God, (2) the method, as the loyalty of the caregiver to the sufferer and the caregiver's fidelity to the body of medical knowledge and tradition, which (3) results in genuine, flourishing, and caring relationships. Vital to the study is the unique understanding of human beings as God's image bearers, deserving to be treated with dignity. Created according to God's image, people are relational, multidimensional, moral, and embodied beings. The culmination of God's image in people is the image of the God-man, Jesus Christ, who represents the goal to which humanity should aspire. Then, a view of health and flourishing is proposed using the theology of Karl Barth, which defines health as a genuine but only penultimate good that is beneficial for the sake of the ultimate good, eternal life. The Bible clarifies that God is the ultimate healer, and he chooses to use all means to fulfill his purposes. This is not to say God needs help to accomplish his will but that God employs all sorts of means for healing. Moreover, it is worth mentioning that healing from a theological perspective is a foretaste of life after death, and suffering, though real, is a messenger of death. Suffering and death, defeated on the cross, will find their complete eradication on the day of resurrection when the redeemed will live eternally in the presence of God.

The ecclesiological history of care shows that the church presented love for its neighbors practically based on biblical teachings. Motivated by Christ's ministry and the rich biblical material about love for neighbors, the church community saw her role throughout the centuries in continuing Jesus' work on earth, such as caring for the sick and dying.

Chapter four contends that the neighbor-love theological framework is a persuasive moral paradigm for addressing AI robots, particularly in direct patient care. To prove the thesis, neighbor-love is compared to typical ethical systems, such as utilitarianism, feminist care, virtue, and deontological ethics. Utilitarianism shows severe limitations from a covenantal care point of view by employing relative standards of happiness, by attempting to quantify joy and by the utilitarian tendency to sacrifice the innocent for the many. Though proximal to the biblical neighbor-love, feminist care ethics is human-centered, without a need for God. Thus, the feminist ethics of care suffer severe restrictions, potentially including a slave morality mentality and moral ambiguity. Virtue ethics is undoubtedly admirable. However, it seems unable to remedy the root cause of unvirtuous behaviors. Virtues are compelling, especially in medical care, but a mere moral behavior appears hopeless without helping people to change from the inside out. A duty or deontological approach to ethics is an appealing system. Nonetheless, the deontological privations of apparent emotions and potential situations when duties clash make deontology a less ideal candidate for moral dilemmas concerning carebots.

In contrast, neighbor-love ethics is a convincing moral grid. First, it is rooted in the revealed character of God and oriented toward the patient's flourishing, which includes hope even after death. Second, neighbor-love ethics has a covenantal structure that incorporates disinterested giving and receiving and convinces the healer to be faithful to medical care and tradition. The good Samaritan narrative is the quintessential illustration of how neighbor-love is seen in specific cases. The Samaritan cared without prejudice and showed compassion by tending to the wounds. The Samaritan was physically present and assured the suffering neighbor of his help. Third, love for others is fundamentally embodied and necessitates proper care relationships. Based on the research, carebots in direct patient care cannot pass any theological and ethical criteria for moral use. The social robots' potential to disrupt medical care in relationships represents a significant reason to limit robots to indirect caring assistive roles under the supervision of human care providers.

Chapter five summarizes the critical information found in the research and follows the development of the dissertation's argument. It also presents the limitations not addressed in the work and suggests potential future work in theological ethics and robotics.

Limitations of the Research and Suggestions for Future Work

The present work has certain expected limitations, only some of which are discussed in this section. The future use of AI and robots in healthcare is still being determined beyond the present incubatory stage. Will carebots become appealing care options, or will they remain a matter of fascinating speculation for philosophers of technology?[1] The dissertation discussed the issue of AI robots only related to theology and ethics and some social implications in healthcare settings. This approach prefers profundity over extensiveness. This method encourages interdisciplinary future research to deepen the topic of theology and philosophy of technology. Further investigations must examine other crucial study fields, such as law, environment, and society.

Future research should provide concentrated labor in the regulatory domain. Legal professional Eduard Fosch-Villaronga mentions that the speed of technological changes challenges regulation. This phenomenon, also known as the Collingridge Dilemma, leads to questions of how we can identify the need to regulate new technologies and what content is deemed appropriate for such technologies. New technologies, especially AI robots, challenge the boundaries of legislative application. Fosch-Villaronga argues that the current legislation regarding intelligent machines needs more specific robot regulations that establish clear procedures and requirements and address boundaries for robot and artificial technologies. For instance, no mandatory regulatory framework in the European Union has been explicitly developed for care robots, except for some laws that generally regulate robots.[2]

The regulatory framework is challenged in numerous ways, such as security, liability, privacy, and ethical design of robots. Technological solutions might be the solutions and the source of problems. Paradoxically, some argue robots can be used as companions to combat loneliness and to encourage interaction with other people through digital interfaces. At the same time, some argue, as is the case of this research, that robots, when

---

1. Shannon Vallor, "Carebots and Caregivers: Sustaining the Ethical Ideal of Care in the Twenty-First Century," *Philosophy & Technology* 24, no. 3 (2011): 267.

2. Eduard Fosch-Villaronga, *Robots, Healthcare, and the Law: Regulating Automation in Personal Care* (London: Routledge, 2020), 85–87.

overused in ways that replace human contact, can intensify and reproduce the loneliness that they try to bridge. In addition, the overuse of technology, though attempting to improve the well-being of a person, can lead to ill-being, such as physical, psychological,[3] and cognitive effects.[4] Ethical questions about AI robots are ultimately not only about technology but also about human lives and flourishing and the future of society and the environment. Therefore, policymakers may want to develop a broad vision of the technological future that does not include only a negative ethics that limits or prohibits but a positive ethics that incorporates "what is important, meaningful, and valuable."[5] Perhaps policymakers can support ethical frameworks that encourage the values of a good life that leads to flourishing even though this regulation can potentially lead to less efficiency in terms of money and time. Is efficiency always a genuine, desirable metric in the care of people? Can caring be quantified in mathematical terms? This dissertation shows that caring for neighbors means more than mechanical, impersonal medical assistance; though efficiency is desirable, loyalty to genuine care often extends beyond time and money.

Another field that requires further research is the environmental philosophy and ethical use of carebots concerning nonhuman values and interests. The impact of AI robots may aggravate existing concerns about protecting the environment. Though the academic literature about global warming or climate change is controversial, people, as God's image bearers, are called good stewards of nature (Gen 1:28). AI can help people tackle environmental issues, such as studying the problem, detecting patterns in ecological data that people cannot see, perhaps helping to deal with coordination complexity, and implementing measures such as cuts in harmful emissions. On the other hand, AI robots can worsen environmental issues as prospected in increased energy consumption, waste, infrastructure, and materials they rely on. What needs to be considered is not only the use of robots but their production, such as the fact that electricity may be produced in non-sustainable ways and raw materials used that are available only in limited amounts.[6]

---

3. Fosch-Villaronga, *Robots, Healthcare, and the Law*, 230–37.

4. Eduard Fosch-Villaronga, Christoph Lutz, and Aurelia Tamò-Larrieux, "Gathering Expert Opinions for Social Robots' Ethical, Legal, and Societal Concerns: Findings from Four International Workshops," *International Journal of Social Robotics* 12, no. 2 (2020): 448.

5. Mark Coeckelbergh, *AI Ethics*, The MIT Essential Knowledge (Cambridge: The MIT Press, 2020), 174.

6. Coeckelbergh, *AI Ethics*, 198.

A significant topic that needs careful research concerns societal implications such as fairness and resource allocation and the possibility of the lack of employment for humans. Humanity's existential fear of robots, reflected in the anxiety of being replaced, outsmarted, and disconnected,[7] is exacerbated by technological optimism that projects a future where intelligent robots will replace humans. Automation and technological progress have had advantages, such as reducing work hours for people, increasing goods, and lowering production costs. In contrast, there seems to be evidence that recent technological innovations may change the nature of human work. Machines do not need vacation, health insurance, or emotional and spiritual support, and therefore, humans may become less valuable to employers as the primary means of production. Additionally, humans may be compared to machines, and high-tech novelties may foster the metaphor of the human as a machine. Dehumanization is thus at play by approaching people not "as a good creation who is given to a good work but as a mechanism whose value is only related to their outputs."[8] In addition, robotic automation may increase discrimination in society. While it is true that educated, critical thinkers or those who have skill levels are not at risk of losing their jobs, the people who lack them are likely to be replaced by machines. Also, discriminating against those with lower skills may devalue specific works and those who perform them.[9]

Furthermore, the principle of fairness that promotes equal treatment for all people[10] raises a significant concern for AI robots used by the general public. Coeckelbergh correctly points out that while people in one part of the world struggle to access fresh water, people in another part of the world worry about their privacy on the internet.[11] Coeckelbergh's observation invites an inevitable question concerning this study: how are carebot technologies fair to all people while a significant part of the world's population struggles with hunger, poverty,[12] illiteracy, epidemics, etc.? Even though

7. Joshua K. Smith, *Robotic Persons* (Bloomington: WestBow Press, 2021), 18.

8. Smith, *Robotic Persons*, 172–73.

9. Smith, *Robotic Persons*, 173.

10. Jeffrey K. Gurney, "Imputing Driverhood: Applying a Reasonable Driver Standard to Accidents Caused by Autonomous Vehicles," in *Robot Ethics 2.0: From Autonomous Cars to Artificial Intelligence*, ed. Patrick Lin, Ryan Jenkins, and Keith Abney (New York: Oxford University Press, 2017), 52.

11. Coeckelbergh, *AI Ethics*, 186.

12. See some of the latest statistics, such as those presented by Jason Hickel, "The True Extent of Global Poverty and Hunger: Questioning the Good News Narrative of the Millennium Development Goals," *Third World Quarterly* 37, no. 5 (2016): 749–67. Hickel points out four billion people are living in poverty, and two billion remain hungry. Also helpful is Chien-Chiang Lee and Zihao Yuan, "Impact of Energy Poverty on

indirectly, AI robotic therapeutic solutions may increase the gap between the rich and the deprived and thus aggravate serious problems such as discrimination and possibly racist practices.

Finally, as mentioned in chapters three and four, some topics were theologically addressed only partially due to the reduced scope of this dissertation. As a by-product of this study, there is a need for further theological and ethical research into the connections between the declining birth rate due to abortion, contraceptives, aggressive feminism, and the emergence of AiRs. The declining birth rates have led to a growing need for robotic caregivers, as seen in Japan's case. Other significant ethical issues that need careful theological discussion include healing, deception, robot childcare, and human attachment.

Some questions that could be developed in future research papers and dissertations but remain unanswered in this work have arisen. For example, "To whom can blame or credit be assigned for the outcomes of AI-driven decisions in healthcare?" "What are some potential long-term existential risks of relying on intelligent robotic systems in healthcare settings?" And "Is medicine moving forward to a future of technological determinism in which AI will dictate the evolution of healthcare practices and principles?"

Conclusion

How would the future appear from a theological care perspective, as seen through the lens of the neighbor-love system? While it is almost certain that AI robots will be part of the future in some ways, developing strategies to keep humans in the loop is necessary.[13] At the least, it is apparent that human responsibility in designing social robots is mandatory. The categories of privacy, security, control, transparency, and accountability are all some aspects that need caution. In addition, responsible design and use must be based on human-centered design that includes clear decision-making rules and appropriate sanctions, including in robots used in indirect care, such as assistive roles.[14] Theologians can make a distinctive contribution to the discussion by equipping a moral community to reflect on biblical values regarding care practices for those cared for and caregivers.[15]

Public Health: A Non-Linear Study from an International Perspective," *World Development* 174 (2024): article 106444.

13. Fosch-Villaronga et al., "Gathering Expert Opinions," 451.
14. Fosch-Villaronga et al., "Gathering Expert Opinions," 455.
15. Vallor, "Carebots and Caregivers," 267.

This dissertation makes a distinctive contribution to moral theology by evidencing the benefits of an ethical system informed by traditional, ecclesiological, and theological sources. The contribution to theological ethical knowledge is seen in the work's focus on the doctor-patient relationship. In contrast, few studies focus on the benefits or perils of the caregiver-cared-for bond.[16] The research also contributes substantially to knowledge by proposing a possible ethical system faithful to the gospel and the extended medical tradition, such as the neighbor-love covenantal system based on a theology of care. The proposed system encourages health providers to treat patients loyally as God's image bearers, to provide the best care that leads to flourishing even when a cure is not possible, and to offer hope for life after death through faith in Christ's redemptive and completed work on the cross.

---

16. Aurelia Sauerbrei et al., "The Impact of Artificial Intelligence on the Person-Centered, Doctor-Patient Relationship: Some Problems and Solutions," *BMC Medical Informatics and Decision Making* 23, no. 1 (2023): 12.

Bibliography

Adami, Christoph. "A Brief History of Artificial Intelligence Research." *Artificial Life* 27.2 (2021) 131–37.
Allen, Timothy Craig. "Regulating Artificial Intelligence for a Successful Pathology Future." *Archives of Pathology & Laboratory Medicine* 143.10 (2019) 1175–79.
Alp, Fethiye Yelkin, and Sebnem Cinar Yucel. "The Effect of Therapeutic Touch on the Comfort and Anxiety of Nursing Home Residents." *Journal of Religion and Health* 60.3 (2021) 2037–50.
Amann, Wolfgang, and Agata Stachowich-Stanusch, eds. *Artificial Intelligence and Its Impact on Business: Contemporary Perspectives in Corporate Social Performance and Policy.* Charlotte: Information Age Publishing, 2020.
Anderson, Tim L. "God Our Father as a Script of Intimacy for Those Suffering Shame." *Journal of Spiritual Formation and Care* 9.2 (2016) 247–69.
Arabnia, Hamid R., et al., eds. *Artificial Intelligence (ICAI' 18): The 2018 WorldComp International Conference Proceedings.* Las Vegas: CSREA, 2018.
Arnold, Bill T. *The Book of Deuteronomy Chapters 1–11.* The New International Commentary of the Old Testament. Grand Rapids: Eerdmans, 2022.
"Artificial Intelligence: An Evangelical Statement of Principles." ERLC, 2019. https://www.erlc.com/resource-library/statements/artificial-intelligence-an-evangelical-statement-of-principles/.
Atella, Vincenzo, et al. "The Future of the Elderly Population Health Status: Filling a Knowledge Gap." *Health Economics* 30.S1 (2021) 11–29. https://www.doi.org/10.1002/hec.4258.
Balboni, Michael J., and Tracy A. Balboni. *Hostility to Hospitality: Spirituality and Professional Socialization Within Medicine.* New York: Oxford University Press, 2019.
Banks, Marian R., et al. "Animal-Assisted Therapy and Loneliness in Nursing Homes: Use of Robotic Versus Living Dogs." *Journal of the American Medical Directors Association* 9.3 (Mar. 2008) 173–77.
Banks, Robert. "The Early Church as a Caring Community." *Evangelical Review of Theology* 7.2 (1983) 85–97.
Bargerhuff, Eric J. "Divine Discipline in Ecclesial Expression: An Analysis of God's 'Fatherly' Love as Embodied in the Church." PhD diss, Trinity Evangelical Divinity School, 2005.
Barnett, Paul. *The Second Epistle to the Corinthians.* The New International Commentary of the New Testament. Grand Rapids: Eerdmans, 1997.

Barth, Karl. *Church Dogmatics*. Edited by Geoffrey W. Bromiley and T. F. Torrance. Translated by A. T. Mackay, et al. Vol. III:4. New York: T&T Clark International, 2004.

———. *Church Dogmatics*. Edited by Geoffrey W. Bromiley and T. F. Torrance. Translated by H. Knight, et al. Vol. III:2. New York: T&T Clark International, 2004.

Bartholomew, Craig G. *Ecclesiastes*. Baker Commentary on the Old Testament Wisdom and Psalms. Grand Rapids: Baker Academic, 2009.

Beale, G. K. *Colossians and Philemon*. Baker Exegetical Commentary on the New Testament. Grand Rapids: Baker Academic, 2019.

Beauchamp, Tom L., and James F. Childress. *Principles of Biomedical Ethics*. 8th ed. New York: Oxford University Press, 2019.

Becker, Daniel. *Personhood: A Pragmatic Guide to Prolife Victory in the 21st Century and the Return to First Principles in Politics*. Alpharetta, GA: TKS, 2011.

Bentham, Jeremy. *An Introduction to the Principles of Morals and Legislation*. New York: Dover, 2007.

———. *Deontology; or, the Science of Morality: In Which the Harmony and Co-Incidence of Duty and Self-Interest, Virtue and Felicity, Prudence and Benevolence, Are Explained and Exemplified*. Edited by John Bowring. Vol. 1. London: Longman, 1834.

———. *Deontology; or, the Science of Morality: In Which the Harmony and Co-Incidence of Duty and Self-Interest, Virtue and Felicity, Prudence and Benevolence, Are Explained and Exemplified, and Applied to the Business of Life*. Edited by John Bowring, Vol. 2. London: Longman, Bees, Orme, Browne, Green, and Longman, 1834.

Bigney, Mark W. "Neither Mechanic nor High Priest." Master's thesis, McGill University, 2006.

Bishop, Jeffrey P. *The Anticipatory Corpse: Medicine, Power, and the Care of the Dying*. Notre Dame, IN: Notre Dame Press, 2011.

Bock, Darrell L. *A Theology of Luke and Acts*. The Biblical Theology of the New Testament. Grand Rapids: Zondervan, 2012.

———. *Luke*. The NIV Application Commentary. Grand Rapids: Zondervan, 1998.

Bogosian, Kyle. "Implementation of Moral Uncertainty in Intelligent Machines." *Minds and Machines* 27.4 (2017) 591–608.

Boorse, Christopher. "Health as a Theoretical Concept." *Philosophy of Science* 44.4 (1977) 542–73.

Booth, Anthony Robert. "Deontology in Ethics and Epistemology." *Metaphilosophy* 39.4/5 (2008) 530–45.

Bowen, Phillip. W. *Emotional Intelligence: Does It Really Matter?* Wilmington, DE: Vernon, 2019.

Boykin, Anne, Savina Schoenhofer, and Kathleen Valentine, eds. *Health Care System Transformation for Nursing and Health Care Leaders*. New York: Springer, 2014.

Bradley, James T. *Re-Creation Nature: Science, Technology, and Human Values in the Twenty-First Century*. Tuscaloosa: University of Alabama Press, 2019.

Brannigan, Michael C. *Caregiving, Carebots, and Contagion*. Revolutionary Bioethics. New York: Lexington Books, 2022.

Breed, Gert. "Living as a Diakonos of Christ and Pastoral Care to the Narcissistically Entitled Person." *In Die Skriflig* 55.1 (2021) 1–10.

Brown, Michael L., and Paul W. Ferris Jr. *Jeremiah, Lamentations*. Revised ed. The Expositor's Bible Commentary. Grand Rapids: Zondervan, 2010.
Bruce, Frederick Fyvie. *The Epistle to the Galatians*. The New International Greek Testament Commentary. Grand Rapids: Eerdmans, 1982.
Buber, Martin. *I And Thou*. 2nd ed. New York: Charles Scribner's Sons, 1958.
Burdett, Michael S. "Artificial Intelligence and Robotics: Contributions from the Science and Religion Forum." *Zygon* 55.2 (2020) 347–60.
Bykvist, Krister. *Utilitarianism: A Guide for the Perplexed*. Continuum Guides for the Perplexed. London: Continuum, 2010.
Cameron, Nigel. *The New Medicine: Life and Death After Hippocrates*. Wheaton, IL: Crossway, 1991.
Casto, R. Michael, and Steven A. Harsh. "Laying the Groundwork for a Christian Theology for Interprofessional Care." *Journal of Interprofessional Care* 12. 4 (1998) 389–97.
Chalaris, Michail. "In the Fourth Industrial Revolution Era, Security, Safety, and Health." *Journal of Engineering, Science and Technology Review* 16.2 (2023) 182–88.
Chamburuka, Philemon M., and Ishanesu S. Gusha. "An Exegesis of the Parable of the Good Samaritan (Lk 10:25–35) and Its Relevance to the Challenges Caused by COVID-19." *HTS Theological Studies* 76.1 (2020) 1–7.
Chant, Ken. *Healing in the Whole Bible: The Old Testament*. Ramona, CA: Vision, 2012.
Chen, Nan-Jou. "A Reflection on the Bioethical Dilemmas from the Perspective of a Human Being as a Relational Being and the Ethics of Caring: The Case of Genetic Screening." *Theologies and Cultures* 3.1 (2006) 51–63.
Cherney, Kenneth Jr. "Distinctively Human: An Anthropology of Genesis 1 and 2." *Wisconsin Lutheran Quarterly* 119.1 (2022) 6–27.
Cheshire, William P., Jr. "Virtual Physicians and Virtual Avatars." Deerfield, IL: Center for Bioethics and Human Dignity, 2017. https://www.youtube.com/watch?app=desktop&v=CJIrsHMPEZw.
Ciampa, Roy E. *New Dictionary of Biblical Theology*. S.v. "Adoption." Edited by T. Desmond Alexander and Brian S. Rosner. IVP Reference Collection. Downers Grove, IL: InterVarsity, 2000.
Clinebell, Howard. *Basic Types of Pastoral Care & Counseling*. Nashville: Abingdon, 1984.
Cockburn, Tom. "Care, Feminist Ethic Of." In *The SAGE Encyclopedia of Children and Childhood Studies*. Edited by Daniel Thomas Cook. London: SAGE Publications, 2020.
Coeckelbergh, Mark. *AI Ethics*. MIT Essential Knowledge. Cambridge: MIT Press, 2020.
———. "Health Care, Capabilities, and AI Assistive Technologies." *Ethical Theory and Moral Practice* 13.2 (2009) 181–90.
———. "How to Use Virtue Ethics for Thinking About the Moral Standing of Social Robots: A Relational Interpretation in Terms of Practices, Habits, and Performance." *International Journal of Social Robotics* 13 (2020) 31–40.
———. "Robot Rights? Towards a Social-Relational Justification of Moral Consideration." *Ethics and Information Technology* 12 (2012) 209–21.
———. "Should We Treat Teddy Bear 2.0 as a Kantian Dog? Four Arguments for the Indirect Moral Standing of Personal Social Robots, with Implications for Thinking About Animals and Humans." *Minds & Machines* 31.3 (2021) 337–60.

Cojocaru, Daniela, Cristina Gavrilovici, and Sorin Cace. "Christian and Secular Dimensions of the Doctor-Patient Relationship." *Journal for the Study of Religions and Ideologies* 12.34 (2013) 37–56.

Cole, R. Alan. *Exodus*. Tyndale Old Testament Commentaries. Downers Grove, IL: IVP Academic, 2008.

Compton, Michael T. "The Union of Religion and Health in Ancient Asklepieia." *Journal of Religion and Health* 37.4 (1998) 301–12.

Constantinescu, Mihaela, and Roger Crisp. "Can Robotic AI Systems Be Virtuous and Why Does This Matter?" *International Journal of Social Robotics* 14 (2022) 1547–57.

Cook, Brendan. *Pursuing Eudaimonia: Re-Appropriating the Greek Philosophical Foundations of the Christian Apophatic Tradition*. Newcastle: Cambridge Scholars Publishing, 2013.

Cortez, Jaime V. "The Moral Plausibility of Utilitarianism in Business Through the Lens of Christian." *Journal of Multidisciplinary Research* 15.2 (2023) 67–79.

Cranz, Isabel. "Advice for a Successful Doctor's Visit: King Asa Meets Ben Sira." *Catholic Biblical Quarterly* 80.2 (2018) 231–46.

Creamer, Deborah Beth. *Disability and Christian Theology: Embodied Limits and Constructive Possibilities*. Oxford: Oxford University Press, 2009.

Crowe, Brandon D. *The Lord Jesus Christ: The Biblical Doctrine of the Person and Work of Christ*. We Believe: Studies in Reformed Biblical Doctrine. Bellingham, WA: Lexham Academic, 2023.

Crysdale, Cynthia S. W. "Gilligan and the Ethics of Care: An Update." *Religious Studies Review* 20.1 (1994) 21–28.

Curlin, Farr A., and Christopher Tollefsen. "Medicine Against Suicide: Sustaining Solidarity with Those Diminished by Illness and Debility." *Christian Bioethics* 27.3 (2021) 250–63.

———. *The Way of Medicine: Ethics and the Healing Profession*. Notre Dame Studies in Medical Ethics and Bioethics. Notre Dame, IN: University of Notre Dame Press, 2021.

Das, J. P. "A Better Look at Intelligence." *Current Directions in Psychological Science* 11.1 (2002) 28–33.

Datteri, Edoardo. "Predicting the Long-Term Effects of Human-Robot Interaction: A Reflection on Responsibility in Medical Robotics." *Science and Engineering Ethics* 19.1 (2013) 139–60.

Davis, Christine S. "Hospitality Happens: Dialogic Ethics of Care." *Society* 56.2 (2019) 130–34.

Davis, John Jefferson. *Evangelical Ethics: Issues Facing the Church Today*. 4th ed. Phillipsburg, NJ: P&R, 2015.

De Lange, Frits. "The Heidelberg Catechism: Elements for a Theology of Care." *Acta Theologica* 20 (2014) 156–73.

De Vries, Raymond. "Making Medicine Care." *Society* 56.2 (2019) 135–40.

Delaney, James J. "The Doctor-Patient Relationship: Does Christianity Make a Difference?" *Christian Bioethics* 27.1 (2021) 1–13.

DeSilva, David A. *The Letter to the Galatians*. New International Commentary of the New Testament. Grand Rapids: Eerdmans, 2018.

Dinh, An, et al. "A Data-Driven Approach to Predicting Diabetes and Cardiovascular Disease with Machine Learning." *BMC Medical Informatics and Decision Making* 19.1 (2019) 211.

Dizon, Rose Angelique. "A New Way of Healing: Regulating Healthcare AI." *Ateneo Law Journal* 64.3 (2020) 1127–223.

Dollar, Harold Ellis. "A Cross-Cultural Theology of Healing." PhD diss., Fuller Theological Seminary, 1980.

Dosso, Jill A., et al. "User Perspectives on Emotionally Aligned Social Robots for Older Adults and Persons Living with Dementia." *Journal of Rehabilitation and Assistive Technologies Engineering* 9 (2022) 1–15. https://www.doi.org/10.1177/20556683221108364.

D'Souza, Sylvia, and Lucas D. Introna. "Recovering Aristotle's Practice-Based Ontology: Practical Wisdom as Embodied Ethical Intuition." *Journal of Business Ethics* 189.2 (2024) 287–300.

Dube, Zorodzai. "Reception of Jesus as Healer in Mark's Community." *HTS Theological Studies* 74.1 (2018) 1–5.

Dyer, John. *From the Garden to the City: The Redeeming and Corrupting Power of Technology*. Grand Rapids: Kregel, 2011.

Edwards, James R. *The Gospel According to Luke*. Pillar New Testament Commentary. Grand Rapids: Eerdmans, 2015.

Eibach, Ulrich. "Life History, Sin, and Disease." *Christian Bioethics: Non-Ecumenical Studies in Medical Morality* 12.2 (2006) 117–31.

Eiesland, Nancy L. *The Disabled God: Toward a Liberatory Theology of Disability*. Nashville: Abingdon, 1994.

Elder, Alexis M. "Robot Friends for Autistic Children: Monopoly Money or Counterfeit Currency?" In *Robot Ethics 2.0: From Autonomous Cars to Artificial Intelligence*, edited by Patrick Lin, Ryan Jenkins, and Keith Abney, 113–26. New York: Oxford University Press, 2017.

Elmore, Matthew. "The First Hospital and the Construction of Leprosy." *Dialog: A Journal of Theology* 61.2 (2022) 107–11.

Emanuel, Ezekiel J., and Linda L. Emanuel. "Four Models of the Physician-Patient Relationship." *Journal of the American Medical Association* 267.16 (1992) 2221–26.

Ernst, George W., and Allen Newell. "Some Issues of Representation in a General Problem Solver." In *Proceedings of the April 18–20, 1967, Spring Joint Computer Conference on - AFIPS '67 (Spring)*, 583. Atlantic City, NJ: ACM, 1967.

Etzioni, Amitai, and Oren Etzioni. "The Ethics of Robotic Caregivers." *Interaction Studies* 18.2 (2017) 174–90.

Evans, Abigail Rian. "Health, Healing, and Healers: A Theological and Philosophical Inquiry." PhD diss., Georgetown University, 1984.

Falkenheimer, Sharon Ann. "Equipping Healthcare Professionals to Care for the Whole Person." *Christian Journal for Global Health* 3.2 (2016) 129–33.

Feldman, Robin C., Ehrik Aldana, and Kara Stein. "Artificial Intelligence in the Health Care Space: How We Can Trust What We Cannot Know." *Stanford Law & Policy Review* 30.2 (2019) 399–420.

Felzmann, Heike. "Utilitarianism as an Approach to Ethical Decision Making in Health Care." In *Key Concepts and Issues in Nursing Ethics*, edited by P. Anne Scott, 29–41. Cham: Springer, 2017.

Ferngren, Gary B. *Medicine and Health Care in Early Christianity*. Baltimore: Johns Hopkins University Press, 2009.
Floridi, Luciano. "AI and Its New Winter: From Myths to Realities." *Philosophy & Technology* 33 (2020) 1–3.
Foreman, Mark Wesley, and Lindsay C. Leonard. *Christianity and Modern Medicine: Foundations for Bioethics*. Grand Rapids: Kregel Academic, 2022.
Formosa, Paul. "Robot Autonomy vs. Human Autonomy: Social Robots, Artificial Intelligence (AI), and the Nature of Autonomy." *Minds and Machines* 31.4 (2021) 595–616.
Fosch-Villaronga, Eduard. *Robots, Healthcare, and the Law: Regulating Automation in Personal Care*. London: Routledge, 2020.
Fosch-Villaronga, Eduard, Christoph Lutz, and Aurelia Tamò-Larrieux. "Gathering Expert Opinions for Social Robots' Ethical, Legal, and Societal Concerns: Findings from Four International Workshops." *International Journal of Social Robotics* 12.2 (2020) 441–58.
France, R. T. *Luke*. Teach the Text Commentary Series. Grand Rapids: Baker, 2013.
France, R. T., and George H. Guthrie. *Hebrews, James*. Revised ed. The Expositor's Bible Commentary. Grand Rapids: Zondervan, 2006.
Fredriksson, Lennart. "Models of Relating in a Caring Conversation: A Research Synthesis on Presence, Touch and Listening." *Journal of Advanced Nursing* 30.5 (1999) 1167–76.
Frennert, Susanne, Hedvig Aminoff, and Britt Östlund. "Technological Frames and Care Robots in Eldercare." *International Journal of Social Robotics* 13.2 (2021) 311–25.
Froomkin, Michael A., Ian Kerr, and Joelle Pineau. "When AIs Outperform Doctors: Confronting the Challenges of a Tort-Induced Over-Reliance on Machine Learning." *Arizona Law Review* 61.1 (2019) 33–100.
Frymorgen, Tomasz. "Sex Robot Sent for Repairs After Being Molested at Tech Fair." BBC, Sep. 29, 2017. https://www.bbc.co.uk/bbcthree/article/610ec648-b348-423a-bd3c-04dc701b2985.
Gaiser, Frederick J. *Healing in the Bible: Theological Insights for Christian Ministry*. Grand Rapids: Baker, 2010.
Gallagher, Ann. "Care Ethics and Nursing Practice." In *Key Concepts and Issues in Nursing*, edited by P. Anne Scott, 55–68. Cham: Springer, 2017.
Gardner, Howard. *Frames of Mind: The Theory of Multiple Intelligences*. New York: Basic, 2011.
Garland, David E. *1 Corinthians*. Baker Exegetical Commentary on the New Testament. Grand Rapids: Baker Academic, 2003.
Garland, David E. *2 Corinthians*. New American Commentary. Nashville: B&H, 1999.
Gasser, Georg. "The Dawn of Social Robots: Anthropological and Ethical Issues." *Minds and Machines* 31.3 (2021) 329–36.
Gilligan, Carol. *In a Different Voice: Psychological Theory and Women's Development*. Cambridge: Harvard University Press, 1982.
Goh, Michelle. "The Care of Ageing Persons: A Trinitarian Perspective." *Australasian Catholic Record* 94.3 (2017) 259–73.
Goldingay, John. "Theology and Healing." *Churchman* 92.1 (1978) 23–33.
Gordon, Brent M., ed. *Artificial Intelligence: Approaches, Tools, and Applications*. Scientific Revolutions. New York: Nova Science, 2011.

Gordon, John-Stewart. "Building Moral Robots: Ethical Pitfalls and Challenges." *Science and Engineering Ethics* 26 (2020) 141–57.

Gould, James B. "The Hope of Heavenly Healing of Disability Part 1 Theological Issues." *Journal of Disability & Religion* 20.4 (2016) 317–34.

Graves, Mark. "Theological Foundations for Moral Artificial Intelligence." *Journal of Moral Theology* 11 (2022) 182–211.

Green, J. B. *New Dictionary of Biblical Theology*. S.v. "Healing."Edited by Sinclair B. Ferguson and David F. Wright. IVP Reference Collection. Downers Grove, IL: InterVarsity, 2000.

Groothuis, Douglas R. "The Biblical View of Truth Challenges Postmodernist Truth Decay." *Themelios* 26.1 (2000) 11–33.

Grundmann, Christoffer H. "To Have Life, and Have It Abundantly! Health and Well-Being in Biblical Perspective." *Journal of Religion and Health* 53.2 (2014) 552–61.

Gurney, Jeffrey K. "Imputing Driverhood: Applying a Reasonable Driver Standard to Accidents Caused by Autonomous Vehicles." In *Robot Ethics 2.0: From Autonomous Cars to Artificial Intelligence*, edited by Patrick Lin, Ryan Jenkins, and Keith Abney, 51–65. New York: Oxford University Press, 2017.

Haenlein, Michael, and Andreas Kaplan. "A Brief History of Artificial Intelligence: On the Past, Present, and Future of Artificial Intelligence." *California Management Review* 61.4 (2019) 5–14.

Hamilton, Victor P. *The Book of Genesis Chapters 1–17*. New International Commentary of the Old Testament. Grand Rapids: Eerdmans, 1990.

Hamman, Jaco J. "Empowering Future Generations of Pastoral Caregivers and Theologians to Build a Just World." *Journal of Pastoral Theology* 32.2-3 (2022) 135–39.

Hammett, John S. "A Whole Bible Approach to Interpreting Creation in God's Image." *Southwestern Journal of Theology* 63.2 (2021) 29–47.

Hansson, Sven Ove. "John Stuart Mill and the Conflicts of Equality." *Journal of Ethics* 26.3 (2022) 433–53.

Hawhee, Debra. "Agonism and Aretê." *Philosophy & Rhetoric* 35.3 (2002) 185–207.

Heffernan, Teresa. "The Dangers of Mystifying Artificial Intelligence and Robotics." *Toronto Journal of Theology* 36.1 (2020) 93–95.

Heimbach, Daniel R. *Fundamental Christian Ethics*. Nashville: B&H Academic, 2022.

Held, Virginia. *The Ethics of Care*. New York: Oxford University Press, 2006.

Hickel, Jason. "The True Extent of Global Poverty and Hunger: Questioning the Good News Narrative of the Millennium Development Goals." *Third World Quarterly* 37.5 (2016) 749–67.

Hill, Andrew E. *1 & 2 Chronicles*. NIV Application Commentary. Grand Rapids: Zondervan, 2003.

Hill, Jessica, et al. "Investigating Dog Welfare When Interacting with Autistic Children Within Canine-Assisted Occupational Therapy Sessions: A Single Case Study." *Animals* 13.12 (2023) 1965.

Holman, Susan R. "Healing the Social Leper in Gregory of Nyssa's and Gregory of Nazianzus's 'Peri Philoptōchias.'" *Harvard Theological Review* 92.3 (1999) 283–309.

Hong, Hyehyun, and Jee Hyun Oh. "The Effects of Patient-Centered Communication: Exploring the Mediating Role of Trust in Healthcare Providers." *Health Communication* 35.4 (2020) 502–211.

Horden, Peregrine. "The Earliest Hospitals in Byzantium, Western Europe, and Islam." *Journal of Interdisciplinary History* 35.3 (2005) 361–89.
Howard, Ayanna, and Jason Borenstein. "The Ugly Truth About Ourselves and Our Robots Creations: The Problem of Bias and Social Inequity." *Science & Engineering Ethics* 24.5 (2018) 1521–36.
Hughes, Melanie Dobson. "The Holistic Way: John Wesley's Practical Piety as a Resource for Integrated Health Care." *Journal of Religion and Health* 47.2 (2008) 237–52.
Hurka, Thomas. *British Ethical Theorists from Sidgwick to Ewing*. Oxford History of Philosophy. Oxford: Oxford University Press, 2014.
Ide, Hiroo, et al. "The Ageing 'Care Crisis' in Japan: Is There a Role for Robotics-Based Solutions?" *International Journal of Care and Caring* 5.1 (2021) 165–71.
Innes, Keith. "Towards an Ecological Eschatology: Continuity and Discontinuity." *Evangelical Quarterly* 81.2 (2009) 126–44.
Irby, Georgia L. "Roman Military Medicine: The Nexus of Religion and Techne." In *The Roman Empire*, edited by Matthew Dillon and Christopher Matthew, 346–419. Yorkshire: Pen and Sword Military, 2022.
Israelowich, Ido. *Patients and Healers in the High Roman Empire*. Baltimore: Johns Hopkins University Press, 2015.
Jastram, Nathan. "The Image of God and Marriage." *Logia* 30.3 (2021) 41–44.
Jeanrond, Werner G. *A Theology of Love*. New York: T&T Clark, 2010.
Johnson, Andy. "Turning the World Upside Down in 1 Corinthians 15: Apocalyptic Epistemology, the Resurrected Body and the New Creation." *Evangelical Quarterly* 75.4 (2003) 291–309.
Johnson, David H. "The Image of God in Colossians." *Didaskalia* 3.2 (1992) 9–15.
Jonsen, Albert R. *A Short History of Medical Ethics*. New York: Oxford University Press, 2000.
Jourard, Sidney Marshall. *The Transparent Self*. Revised ed. New York: Von Nostrand Reinhold, 1971.
Jozuka, Emiko. "When Humans Bully Robots, There Will Be Consequences." Vice, Aug. 9, 2015. https://www.vice.com/en/article/ezv3ae/when-humans-bully-robots-there-will-be-consequences.
Kant, Immanuel. *Groundwork for the Metaphysics of Morals*. Translated by Allen W. Wood. New Haven: Yale University Press, 2002.
Kapic, Kelly M. *You're Only Human: How Our Limits Reflect God's Design and Why That's Good News*. Grand Rapids: Brazos, 2022.
Kaplan, Robert M. *More than Medicine: The Broken Promise of American Health*. Cambridge: Harvard University Press, 2019.
Karkkainen, Veli-Matti. "'The Christian as Christ to Our Neighbour': On Luther's Theology of Love." *International Journal of Systematic Theology* 6.2 (2004) 101–17.
Karlsson, Bengt, et al. "To See Each Other More Like Human Beings. . . From Both Sides. Patients and Therapists Going to a Study Course Together." *International Practice Development* 3.1 (2013).
Kearns, Alan J. "A Duty-Based Approach for Nursing Ethics & Practice." In *Key Concepts and Issues in Nursing Ethics*, edited by P. Anne Scott, 15–27. Cham: Springer International, 2017.
Keown, Gerald L., Pamela J. Scalise, and Thomas G. Smothers. *Jeremiah 26–52*. Word Biblical Commentary. Grand Rapids: Zondervan, 1995.

Kernaghan, Kenneth. "The Rights and Wrongs of Robotics: Ethics and Robots in Public Organizations." *Canadian Public Administration* 57.4 (2014) 485–506.
Kinghorn, Warren. "Why Health Care Needs Religion and Vice Versa: Religion Education and Theological Formation for Pre-Health Undergraduates." *Perspectives In Religious Studies* 48.2 (2021) 163–75.
Klink, Edward W., III. *John*. Zondervan Exegetical Commentary on the New Testament. Grand Rapids: Zondervan, 2016.
Klug, Eugene. "The Caring God." *Springfielder* 37.4 (1974) 224–29.
Koch, Philippa. "Experience and Soul in Eighteenth-Century Medicine." *Church History* 85.3 (2016) 552–86.
Koloroutis, Mary, and Michael Trout. *See Me as a Person: Creating Therapeutic Relationships with Patients and Their Families*. Minneapolis: Creative Health Care Management, 2012.
Kornu, Kimbell. "The Beauty of Healing: Covenant, Eschatology, and Jonathan Edwards' Theological Aesthetics Toward a Theology of Medicine." *Christian Bioethics* 20.1 (2014) 43–58.
Köstenberger, Andreas J. *A Theology of John's Gospel and Letters*. Biblical Theology of the New Testament. Grand Rapids: Zondervan, 2009.
Kurzweil, Ray. *The Age of Spiritual Machines: When Computers Exceed Human Intelligence*. New York: Penguin, 1999.
Kyrarini, Maria, et al. "A Survey of Robots in Healthcare." *Technologies* 9.8 (2021) 1–26.
Labrecque, Cory Andrew. "To Tend or to Subdue? Technology, Artificial Intelligence, and the Catholic Ecotheological Tradition." *Religions* 13.7 (2022) 1–10.
Landa, Apolos. "Shalom & Eirene: The Full Framework for Health Care." *Christian Journal for Global Health* 1.1 (2014) 57–59.
Lane, William L. *Hebrews 1–8*. Word Biblical Commentary. Grand Rapids: Zondervan, 1991.
Larsen, Timothy. *John Stuart Mill: A Secular Life*. Spiritual Lives. Oxford: Oxford University Press, 2018.
Lauritzen, Paul. "Covenant Keeper: William F. May & the Crisis of Bioethics." *Commonweal* 140.3 (2013) 10–15.
Lawrence, Louise J. *Sense and Stigma in the Gospels: Depictions of Sensory-Disabled Characters*. Oxford: Oxford University Press, 2013.
Lee, Chien-Chiang, and Zihao Yuan. "Impact of Energy Poverty on Public Health: A Non-Linear Study from an International Perspective." *World Development* 174 (2024) Article 106444.
Lee, Jieon, Daeho Lee, and Jae-gil Lee. "Can Robots Help Working Parents with Childcare? Optimizing Childcare Functions for Different Parenting Characteristics." *International Journal of Social Robotics* 14 (2022) 193–211.
Legath, Jenny Wiley. *Sanctified Sisters: A History of Protestant Deaconesses*. New York: New York University Press, 2019.
Liefeld, Walter L. *1 & 2 Timothy, Titus*. NIV Application Commentary. Grand Rapids: Zondervan, 1999.
Liu, Alex, Atefeh Farzindar, and Mingbo Gong, eds. *Transforming Healthcare with Big Data and AI*. New Methods in the Era of Big Data and AI. Charlotte: Information Age, 2020.
Looy, Heather. "Embodied and Embedded Morality: Divinity, Identity, and Disgust." *Zygon* 39.1 (2004) 219–35.

Lysaught, M. Therese, and Cory D. Mitchell. "Vicious Trauma: Race, Bodies and the Confounding of Virtue Ethics." *Journal of the Society of Christian Ethics* 42.1 (2022) 75–100.

Magdalino, Paul. *The Foundation of the Pantokrator Monastery in Its Urban Setting*. Edited by Sofia Kotzabassi. Berlin: De Gruyter, 2013.

Mandal, Jharna, Dinoop Korol Ponnambath, and Subhash Chandra Parija. "Utilitarian and Deontological Ethics in Medicine." *Tropical Parasitology* 6.1 (2016) 5–7.

Mangum, Douglas, ed. *A Dictionary of Biblical Languages with Semantic Domains: Hebrew*, s.v. "נֶפֶשׁ." Bellingham, WA: Lexham, 2014.

Manning, Christopher. "Artificial Intelligence Definitions." Stanford University: Human-Centered Aritificial Intelligence, 2020. https://hai-production.s3.amazonaws.com/files/2020–9/AI-Definitions-HAI.pdf.

Martin, Oren R. "How Do the Old and New Testaments Progress, Integrate, and Climax in Christ?" In *40 Questions about Biblical Theology*, 69–77. 40 Questions. Grand Rapids: Kregel Academic, 2020.

Martin, Ralph P. *2 Corinthians*. Word Biblical Commentary. Grand Rapids: Zondervan, 2014.

Mathews, Kenneth A. *Genesis 1–11:26*. New American Commentary. Nashville: B&H, 1996.

———. *Genesis 11:27–50:26*. New American Commentary. Nashville: B&H, 2005.

May, William F. *Testing the Medical Covenant: Active Euthanasia and Health Care Reform*. Eugene, OR: Wipf & Stock, 2003.

———. "Testing the Medical Covenant: Caring for Patients with Advanced Dementia." *Journal of Law, Medicine & Ethics* 40.1 (2012) 45–50.

———. *The Physician's Covenant: Images of the Healer in Medical Ethics*. 2nd ed. Louisville: Westminster John Knox, 2000.

Mayhue, Richard L. "The Gifts of Healing." *Master's Seminary Journal* 25.2 (2014) 17–28.

Mays, Kate Keener. "Humanizing Robots? The Influence of Appearance and Status on Social Perceptions of Robots." PhD diss., Boston University, 2021.

McCartney, Dan G. *James*. Baker Exegetical Commentary on the New Testament. Grand Rapids: Baker Academic, 2009.

McConville, J. Gordon. *Isaiah*. Baker Commentary on the Old Testament Prophetic Books. Grand Rapids: Baker Academic, 2023.

McDonald, Lynn. *Florence Nightingale: An Introduction to Her Life and Family*. Vol. 1. Ontario: Wilfrid Laurier University Press, 2001.

McFarland, Ian A. "God, the Father Almighty: A Theological Excursus." *International Journal of Systematic Theology* 18.3 (2016) 259–73.

McKnight, Scot. *The Letter to the Colossians*. New International Commentary on the New Testament. Grand Rapids: Eerdmans, 2018.

McLachlan, David. *Accessible Atonement: Disability, Theology, and the Cross of Christ*. Studies in Religion, Theology, and Disability. Waco, TX: Baylor University Press, 2021.

McLean, Haydn J. "Thinking Out Loud: Pondering the Providence of God." *Journal of Pastoral Care and Counseling* 62.3 (2008) 303–7.

Melick, Richard R. *Philippians, Colossians, Philemon*. New American Commentary. Nashville: B&H, 1991.

Messer, Neil. *Flourishing: Health, Disease, and Bioethics in Theological Perspective*. Grand Rapids: Eerdmans, 2013.
Metzger, Paul Louis. *More than Things: A Personalist Ethics for Throwaway Culture*. Downers Grove, IL: IVP Academic, 2023.
Mill, John Stuart. *Utilitarianism*. Luton: Andrews UK Limited, 2011.
Miller, Rebecca L. "The Power of Unlimited Care: An Examination of Nel Noddings's Feminist Care Ethics, Suzanne Collins's Hunger Games Trilogy and Anders Nygren's Theology of Agape." Master's thesis, Trinity International University, 2012.
Miller, Timothy S. "Byzantine Philanthropic Institutions and Modern Humanitarianism." *Review of Faith & International Affairs* 14.1 (2016) 18–25.
———. *The Birth of the Hospital in the Byzantine Empire*. Baltimore: Johns Hopkins University Press, 1997.
Mitchell, Ben C. "What It Means to Be Human." In *Created in the Image of God: Applications and Implications for Our Cultural Confusion*, edited by David S. Dockery and Lauren McAfee, 67–82. Nashville: Forefront Books, 2023.
———. "Medicine: Contract or Covenant. (Editorial)." *Ethics and Medicine* 36.1 (2020) 5–6.
Mohrmann, Margaret E. *Medicine as Ministry*. Cleveland: Pilgrim Press, 1995.
Moo, Douglas J. *Romans*. NIV Application Commentary. Grand Rapids: Zondervan, 2000.
Morril, Bruce T. "Christ the Healer: A Critical Investigation of Liturgical, Pastoral, and Biblical Sources." *Worship* 79.6 (2005) 482–504.
Morris, Leon. *Luke*. Tyndale New Testament Commentaries. Downers Grove, IL: IVP Academic, 2008.
Moss, Candida. "The Marks of the Nails: Scars, Wounds and the Resurrection of Jesus in John." *Early Christianity* 8.1 (2017) 48–68.
Mounce, Robert H. *Romans*. New American Commentary. Nashville: B&H, 1995.
Mulvihill, Jared. "The Defeat of Disability in the Victory of Christ: An Exegetical Theology of Healing in the Age to Come." PhD diss., Midwestern Baptist Theological Seminary, 2023.
Murphy, Robin. *Introduction to AI Robotics*. 2nd ed. Cambridge: MIT Press, 2019.
Mutie, Jeremiah. "Care for the Sick in Early Christianity: Lessons for the Current Covid-19 Stricken Church." *Vox Patrum* 78 (2021) 65–88.
Nallur, Vivek. "Landscape of Machine Implemented Ethics." *Science and Engineering Ethics* 26.5 (n.d.) 2381–99.
Nelson, Paul. "Fidelity to Covenant: Paul Ramsey Remembered." *Christian Century* 107.35 (1990) 1131–34.
Noddings, Nel. *Caring: A Relational Approach to Ethics & Moral Education*, 2nd ed. Berkeley: University of California Press, 2013.
Nolland, John. *Luke 1:1–9:30*. Word Biblical Commentary. Grand Rapids: Zondervan, 2000.
Nolte, Karen. "Deaconesses' Self-Understanding and Everyday Nursing Practice in the First Deaconess Community in Kaiserswerth, Germany." In *Deaconesses in Nursing Care: International Transfer of a Female Model Of Life and Work in the 19th and 20th Century*, edited by Susanne Kreutzer and Karen Nolte, 19–36. Stuttgart: Franz Steiner Verlag, 2016.

Nordenfelt, Lennart. "The Opposition Between Naturalistic and Holistic Theories of Health and Disease." In *Health, Illness and Disease: Philosophical Essays*, edited by Havi Carel and Rachel Cooper, 23–36. New York: Routledge, 2014.

Nutton, Vivian. "Rhodiapolis and Allianoi: Two Missing Links in the History of the Hospital?" *Early Christianity* 5.3 (2014) 371–89.

O'Brien, Graham. "A Theology of Care: Connecting the Present and the Eternal." *Churchman* 134.2 (2020) 143–56.

O'Connor, John D. "Are Virtue Ethics and Kantian Ethics Really So Very Different?" *New Blackfriars* 87.1009 (2006) 238–52.

Orme, Nicholas, and Margaret Webster. *The English Hospital: 1070–1570*. New Haven: Yale University Press, 1995.

Osborne, Grant R. *Revelation*. Baker Exegetical Commentary on the New Testament. Grand Rapids: Baker Academic, 2002.

Ostermann, Joachim. "Fraternity as Natural Being." *Religions* 13.9 (2022) 1–11.

Oswalt, John N. *The Book of Isaiah. Chapters 40–66*. New International Commentary on the Old Testament. Grand Rapids: Eerdmans, 1998.

Ott, Phillip W. "John Wesley, Eighteenth-Century Medicine, and Health Care for the Poor." *Methodist History* 60.2 (2022) 191–2011.

Pak, Joseph. "Self-Deception in Theology." *Themelios* 43.3 (2018) 405–16.

Patterson, Jennifer Marshall. "Human Beings Created in and for Relationship." In *Created in the Image of God: Applications and Implications for Our Cultural Confusion*, edited by David S. Dockery and Lauren McAfee, 84–101. Nashville: Forefront Books, 2023.

Peeters, Anco, and Pim Haselager. "Designing Virtuous Sex Robots." *International Journal of Social Robotics* 13 (2021) 55–66.

Pellegrino, Edmund D. "A Christian Response to Suffering in Dying Persons." *Sisters Today* 68.4 (1996) 259–62.

———. "The Commodification of Medical and Health Care: The Moral Consequences of a Paradigm Shift from a Professional to a Market Ethics." *Journal of Medicine and Philosophy* 24.3 (1999) 243–66.

Pellegrino, Edmund D., and David C. Thomasma. *For the Patient's Good: The Restoration of Beneficence in Health Care*. New York: Oxford University Press, 1988.

———. *Helping and Healing: Religious Commitment and Health Care*. Washington, DC: Georgetown University Press, 1997.

———. *The Christian Virtues in Medical Practice*. Edited by David G. Miller. Washington, DC: Georgetown University Press, 1996.

Percival, Thomas. *Medical Ethics: A Code of Institutes and Precepts Adapted to the Professional Conduct of Physicians and Surgeons*. 3rd ed. Edited by John Henry Parker. Oxford: I. Shrimpton, 1849.

Peterson, David G. *Hebrews*. Tyndale New Testament Commentaries. Downers Grove, IL: IVP Academic, 2015.

Peterson, Eugene H. "Teach Us to Care, and Not to Care." *Crux* 28.4 (1992) 2–9.

Poole, David L., and Alan K. Mackworth. *Artificial Intelligence: Foundations of Computational Agents*. Cambridge: Cambridge University Press, 2010.

Powell, Lisa. "Disability and Resurrection: Eschatological Bodies, Identity, and Continuity." *Journal of the Society of Christian Ethics* 41.1 (2021) 89–106.

Punith, Kumar, et al. "Artificial Intelligence in Healthcare: A Brief Review." *Suranaree Journal of Science & Technology* 29.2 (2022) 1–6.

Quarles, Charles L. *Matthew. Exegetical Guide to the Greek New Testament*. Nashville: B&H, 2017.

Quest, Daniel, et al. "Demystifying AI in Healthcare: Historical Perspectives and Current Considerations." *Physician Leadership Journal* 8.1 (2021) 59–66.

Rae, Scott B. *Moral Choices: An Introduction to Ethics*. 4th ed. Grand Rapids: Zondervan Academic, 2018.

Rakowski, Roman, Petr Polak, and Petra Kowalikova. "Ethical Aspects of the Impact of AI: The Status of Humans in the Era of Artificial Intelligence." *Society* 58.3 (2021) 196–203.

Ramsey, Paul. *Basic Christian Ethics*. Louisville: Westminster John Knox, 1950.

Reece, Steve. "Jesus as Healer: Etymologizing of Proper Names in Luke-Acts." *Zeitschrift Für Die Neutestamentliche Wissenschaft Und Die Kunde Der Älteren Kirche* 110.2 (2019) 186–201.

Reynolds, Thomas E. *Vulnerable Communion: A Theology of Disability and Hospitality*. Grand Rapids: Brazos, 2008.

Rogers, Carl R. *Client Centered Therapy: Its Current Practice, Implications and Theory*. Reprinted. London: Robinson, 2021.

Ronsberg, Lynn Renee. "Prescription for Health Care: The Church and Its Resources." PhD diss., The Union Institute, 1994.

Root, Terry. "Apathy or Passion? The New Testament View of God the Father at the Cross." *Evangelical Quarterly* 88.1 (2016) 3–21.

Rosenberg, Charles E. *The Care of Strangers: The Rise of America's Hospital System*. New York: Basic, 1987.

Ross, David W. *The Right and the Good*. Oxford: Oxford University Press, 2007.

Russell, Stuart, and Peter Norvig. *Artificial Intelligence: A Modern Approach*. 4th ed. London: Pearson, 2021.

Saleh Ibrahim, Yousif, et al. "Perception of the Impact of Artificial Intelligence in the Decision-Making Processes of Public Healthcare Professionals." *Journal of Environmental & Public Health* 2022 (2022) 1–8.

Salmela, Susanne. "The Human Being in Need of Nursing Care: Patient, Customer or Fellow Human Being?" *International Journal of Caring Sciences* 10.3 (2017) 1158–67.

Santoni de Sio, Filippo, and Aimee van Wynsberghe. "When Should We Use Care Robots? The Nature-of-Activities Approach." *Science & Engineering Ethics* 22.6 (2016) 1745–60.

Sather, Richard, III, et al. "Assistive Robots Designed for Eldery Care and Caregivers." *International Journal of Robotics and Control* 3.1 (2021) 1.

Sauerbrei, Aurelia, et al. "The Impact of Artificial Intelligence on the Person-Centered, Doctor-Patient Relationship: Some Problems and Solutions." *BMC Medical Informatics and Decision Making* 23.1 (2023) 73.

Scalberg, Daniel A., Paul Louis Metzger, and Gary B. Ferngren. "Health Care in the Early Church: An Interview with Gary Ferngren." *Cultural Encounters* 10.1 (2014) 63–67.

Schreiner, Thomas R. *1, 2 Peter, Jude*. New American Commentary. Nashville: B&H, 2003.

Schultz, Bart. *The Happiness Philosophers: The Lives and Works of the Great Utilitarians*. Princeton: Princeton University Press, 2017.

Schultz, Carl. *Evangelical Dictionary of Biblical Theology.* S.v. "Spirit." Edited by Walter A. Elwell. Grand Rapids: Baker, 1996.

Schuringa, Christoph. "Second Nature, Phronēsis, and Ethical Outlooks." *International Journal of Philosophical Studies* 30.1 (2022) 1–18.

Schuurman, Derek C. "Artificial Intelligence: Discerning a Christian Response." *Perspectives on Science and Christian Faith* 71.2 (2019) 75–82.

Schwab, Klaus. *The Fourth Industrial Revolution.* New York: Crown, 2016.

Sellman, Derek. "Virtue Ethics and Nursing Practice." In *Key Concepts and Issues in Nursing Ethics,* edited by P. Anne Scott, 43–54. Cham: Springer, 2017.

Senkbeil, Harold L. *The Care of Souls: Cultivating a Pastor's Heart.* Bellingham, WA: Lexham, 2019.

Sharkey, Amanda. "Can We Program or Train Robots to Be Good?" *Ethics and Information Technology* 22 (2020) 283–95.

Sharkey, Amanda, and Noel Sharkey. "We Need to Talk About Deception in Social Robotics!" *Ethics and Information Technology* 23.3 (2021) 309–16.

Sharkey, Noel, and Amanda Sharkey. "The Crying Shame of Robot Nannies: An Ethical Appraisal." *Interaction Studies* 11 (2010) 161–90.

———. "The Rights and Wrongs of Robot Care." In *Robot Ethics: The Ethical and Social Implications of Robotics,* edited by Patrick Lin, Keith Abney, and George A. Bekey, 267–82. Cambridge: MIT Press, 2012.

Shatzer, Jacob. "Fake and Future 'Humans': Artificial Intelligence, Transhumanism, and the Question of the Person." *Southwestern Journal of Theology* 63.2 (2021) 12–146.

———. "Theology and Technology: Mapping the Questions." *Ethics & Medicine: An International Journal of Bioethics* 31.2 (2015) 87–108.

Shea, Matthew. "Principlism's Balancing Act: Why the Principles of Biomedical Ethics Need a Theory of the Good." *Journal of Medicine and Philosophy: A Forum for Bioethics and Philosophy of Medicine* 45 (2020) 441–70.

Shelly, Judith Allen, Arlene B. Miller, and Kimberley H. Fenstermacher. *Called to Care: A Christian Vision for Nursing.* 3rd ed. Downers Grove, IL: InterVarsity, 2021.

Sidgwick, Henry. *The Methods of Ethics.* 7th ed. London: Macmillan, 1874.

Silitonga, Tumpal Samuel, and Ricky Pramono Hasibuan. "Humans, the Ad Imaginem: A Constructive Study in Building Human Relations with Other Created Beings." *Journal of Biblical Theology* 6.3 (2023) 73–90.

Singer, Peter. "Unsactifying Human Life." In *Applied Ethics: Critical Concepts in Philosophy.* Vol. 3. Edited by Ruth F. Chadwick and Doris Schroeder. New York: Routledge, 2002.

Sloane, Andrew. "Love in a Time of Ebola: Reflections on Theology of Medicine in Resource-Challenged Environments." *Christian Journal for Global Health* 3.1 (2016) 77–85.

———. *Vulnerability and Care: Christian Reflections on the Philosophy of Medicine.* T & T Clark Religion and the University Series 4. London: Bloomsbury T & T Clark, 2016.

Smith, Gary V. *Isaiah 40–66.* New American Commentary. Nashville: B&H, 2009.

Smith, Joshua K. "An Evangelical Critical Assessment of AI Driven Robotic Persons and the Risks of Dehumanization." PhD diss., Midwestern Baptist Theological Seminary, 2020.

———. *Robotic Persons.* Bloomington: WestBow, 2021.

Snodgrass, Klyne. *Ephesians*. NIV Application Commentary. Grand Rapids: Zondervan, 1996.
Sparrow, Robert. "Why Machines Cannot Be Moral." *AI & Society* 36 (2021) 685–93.
Sparrow, Robert, and Linda Sparrow. "In the Hands of Machines? The Future of Aged Care." *Minds & Machines* 16.2 (2006) 141–61.
Stahl, Devan. "A Christian Ontology of Genetic Disease and Disorder." *Journal of Disability & Religion* 19.2 (2015) 119–45.
Stahl, Rainer. "The Sixth Supplication of the Lord's Prayer: God, The Father, Does for US the Good." *Religion. Church. Society.* 9 (2020) 86–98.
Stein, Robert A. *Luke*. New American Commentary. Nashville: B&H, 1992.
Stein, Robert H. *Mark*. Baker Exegetical Commentary on the New Testament. Grand Rapids: Baker Academic, 2008.
Stokes, Felicia, and Amitabha Palmer. "Artificial Intelligence and Robotics in Nursing: Ethics of Caring as a Guide to Dividing Tasks Between AI and Humans." *Nursing Philosophy* 21.4 (2020) 1–9.
Strachan, Owen. *Reenchanting Humanity: A Theology of Mankind*. Fearn, Ross-shire: Mentor, 2019.
Sulmasy, Daniel P. *The Healer's Calling: A Spirituality for Physicians and Other Health Care Professionals*. New York: Paulist, 1997. Kindle.
Sumney, Jerry L. "The Role (or Lack Thereof) of Christ in the Eschaton in Paul and Revelation." *Perspectives In Religious Studies* 45.2 (2018) 139–51.
Swanson, James A. *Lexham Theological Wordbook*, s.v. "body." Faithlife: 2002.
Tan, Yeow Kee, et al. "Evaluation of the Pet Robot CuDDler Using Godspeed Questionnaire." In *Inclusive Society: Health and Wellbeing in the Community, and Care at Home*, edited by Jit Biswas, et al. *Lecture Notes in Computer Science* 7910:102–9. Berlin: Springer, 2013. https://www.doi.org/10.1007/978-3-642-39470-6_13.
Taylor, Mark. *1 Corinthians*. New American Commentary. Nashville: B&H, 2014.
Theodoropoulos, Helen Creticos. "Love of God and Love of Neighbor in the Mystical Theology of St. Bernard of Clairvaux and St. Symeon the New Theologian." PhD diss., University of Chicago, 1995.
Thomas, W. John. "Informed Consent, the Placebo Effect, and the Revenge of Thomas Percival." *Journal of Legal Medicine* 22.3 (2001) 313–48.
Thompson, J. A. *The Book of Jeremiah*. New International Commentary of the Old Testament. Grand Rapids: Eerdmans, 1980.
Tillich, Paul. *Systematic Theology*. Vol. 1. Chicago: University of Chicago Press, 1951.
Tobis, Slawomir, et al. "Robots in Eldercare: How Does a Real-World Interaction with the Machine Influence the Perceptions of Older People?" *Sensors* 22.5 (2022) 1717. https://www.doi.org/10.3390/s22051717.
Tollefsen, Christopher, and Farr A. Curlin. "Solidarity, Trust, and Christian Faith in the Doctor-Patient Relationship." *Christian Bioethics* 27.1 (2021) 14–29.
Topf, Daniel. "'Useless Class' or Uniquely Human? The Challenge of Artificial Intelligence." *Journal of Interdisciplinary Studies* 32.1–2 (2020) 17–38.
Tribe, Keith. "Henry Sidgwick, Moral Order, and Utilitarianism." *European Journal of the History of Economic Thought* 24.4 (2017) 907–30.
Tronto, Joan C. *Moral Boundaries: A Political Argument for an Ethic of Care*. New York: Routledge, 1994.

Turner, David. L. *Matthew. Baker Exegetical Commentary on the New Testament.* Grand Rapids: Baker Academic, 2008.
Tzafestas, Spyros G. *Roboethics: A Navigating Overview.* Intelligent Systems, Control and Automation: Science and Engineering 79. Cham: Springer International, 2016.
———. *Systems, Cybernetics, Control, and Automation: Ontological, Epistemological, Societal, and Ethical Issues.* River Publishers Series in Automation, Control, and Robotics. Gistrup: River, 2017.
Ujhelyi, Adrienn, Flora Almosdi, and Alexandra Fodor. "Would You Pass the Turing Test? Influencing Factors of the Turing Decision." *Psihologijske Teme/Psychological Topics* 31.1 (2022) 185–202.
Ungerer, André. "Homo Disruptus and the Future Church." *HTS Theological Studies* 75.4 (2019) 1–8.
Upton, Hugh. "Moral Theory and Theorizing in Health Care Ethics." *Ethical Theory and Moral Practice* 14.4 (2011) 431–43.
Uustal, Diann B. "The Ethic of Care: A Christian Perspective." *Journal of Christian Nursing* 20.4 (2003) 13–17.
Vallès-Peris, Núria, Oriol Barat-Auleda, and Miquel Domènech. "Robots in Healthcare? What Patients Say." *International Journal of Environmental Research and Public Health* 18.18 (2021) 1–18.
Vallor, Shannon. "Carebots and Caregivers: Sustaining the Ethical Ideal of Care in the Twenty-First Century." *Philosophy & Technology* 24.3 (2011) 251–68.
Van Wynsberghe, Aimee. "Designing Robots for Care: Care Centered Value-Sensitive Design." *Science & Engineering Ethics* 19, no. 2 (2013): 407–33.
———. "Social Robots and the Risks to Reciprocity." *AI & Society* 37.2 (2022) 479–85.
———., and Shuhong Li. "A Paradigm Shift for Robot Ethics: From HRI to Human-Robot-System Interaction (HRSI)." *Medicolegal & Bioethics* 9 (2019): 11–21.
Vanhoozer, Kevin, and Owen Strachan. "Introduction: Pastors, Theologians, and Other Public Figures." In *The Pastor as Public Theologian: Reclaiming a Lost Vision,* 13–63. Grand Rapids: Baker Academic, 2015.
Verghese, Abraham. "The Importance of Being." *Health Affairs* 35.10 (2016) 1924–27.
Verhey, Allen Dale. "The Good Samaritan and Scarce Medical Resources." *Christian Scholar's Review* 23.3 (1994) 360–73.
Viljoen, Francois P. "The Double Love Commandment." *In Die Skriflig* 49.1 (2015) 1–11.
Vogt, Gabriele, and Anne-Sophie König. "Robotic Devices and ICT in Long-Term Care in Japan: Their Potential and Limitations from a Workplace Perspective." *Contemporary Japan* 35.2 (2023) 270–90.
Wakabayashi, Ellie. "A Biomedical Ethical Analysis of Using Socially Assistive Robots with an Animal-Like Form with Elderly Individuals in Institutionalized Care." PhD diss., McGill University, 2021.
Wallach, Wendell. "From Robots to Techno Sapiens: Ethics, Law and Public Policy in the Development of Robotics and Neurotechnologies." *Law, Innovation and Technology* 3.2 (2011) 185–208.
Warner, C. Terry. *Bonds That Make Us Free: Healing Our Relationships, Coming to Ourselves.* Nashville: Shadow Mountain, 2001.
Warwick, Kevin. *Artificial Intelligence: The Basics.* London: Routledge, 2012.

Watson, Jean. *Nursing: The Philosophy and Science of Caring.* Revised ed. Boulder: University Press of Colorado, 2008.
Webb, Val. "Florence Nightingale: The Making of a Radical Theologian." *St. Mark's Review* 191 (2002) 13–19.
Weiser, Frederick S. "The Origins of Lutheran Deaconesses in America." *Lutheran Quarterly* 13.4 (1999) 423–34.
Werpehowski, William. "Christian Love and Covenant Faithfulness." *Journal of Religious Ethics* 19.2 (1991) 103–32.
Wesley, Cindy. "Medical Progress and the Physician-Patient Relationship." *ARC* 22 (1994) 91–101.
Wilhelm, Oliver, and Randall W. Engle, eds. *Handbook of Understanding and Measuring Intelligence.* London: Sage, 2005.
Williams, Nadya. "Pastoring Through a Pandemic: Cyprian and the Carthaginian Church in the Mid-Third Century." *Fides et Historia* 53.1 (2021) 1–14.
Wood, David. A., et al. "The ChatGPT Artificial Intelligence Chatbot: How Well Does It Answer Accounting Assessment Questions?" *Issues in Accounting Education* 38.4 (2023) 81–108.
Wright, James. "Inside Japan's Long Experiment in Automating Elder Care." *MIT Technology Review*, Jan. 9, 2023. https://www.technologyreview.com/2023/01/09/1065135/japan-automating-eldercare-robots/.
Yeewen, Huang. "Contemporary Challenges of the Physician-Patient Relationship." *Theologies and Cultures* 3.1 (2006) 64–81.
Yew Kok, Gary Chan. "Trust in and Ethical Design of Carebots: The Case for Ethics of Care." *International Journal of Social Robotics* 13 (2021) 629–45.
Yohannan, Thomas. "Holistic Pastoral Care Ministry in Dhading District: An Evaluation of the Holistic Pastoral Care Practice in the Village Churches in Dhading District of Nepal." DMin diss., Asbury Theological Seminary, 2022.
Yong, Amos. *Theology and Down Syndrome.* Waco, TX: Baylor University Press, 2007.
Zachman, Randall C. "Jesus Christ as the Image of God in Calvin's Theology." *Calvin Theological Journal* 25, no. 1 (1990): 45–62.
N.d., S.v. "A Dictionary of Biblical Languages with Semantic Domains: Hebrew."
N.d., S.v. "Lexham Theological Wordbook."
A Greek-English Lexicon of the New Testament and Other Early Christian Literature. 3rd ed., n.d., S.v. "Πνεῦμα."

www.ingramcontent.com/pod-product-compliance
Lightning Source LLC
Chambersburg PA
CBHW050559240426
43662CB00046BA/1569